Victory to the Mother

Victory to the Mother

The Hindu Goddess of Northwest India in Myth, Ritual, and Symbol

KATHLEEN M. ERNDL

New York Oxford Oxford University Press 1993

Oxford University Press

Oxford New York Toronto
Delhi Bombay Calcutta Madras Karachi
Kuala Lumpur Singapore Hong Kong Tokyo
Nairobi Dar es Salaam Cape Town
Melbourne Auckland Madrid

and associated companies in
Berlin Ibadan

Published by Oxford University Press, Inc.
198 Madison Avenue, New York, New York 10016-4314

Oxford is a registered trademark of Oxford University Press

Library of Congress Cataloging-in-Publication Data
Erndl, Kathleen M.
Victory to the Mother : the Hindu goddess of northwest India
in myth, ritual, and symbol / Kathleen M. Erndl.
p. cm. Includes bibliographical references and index.
ISBN 0-19-507014-3
ISBN 0-19-507015-1 (pbk.)
1. Goddesses, Hindu.
2. Punjab (India)—Religion,
3. Punjab (India)—Religious life and customs.
I. Title.
BL1216.4.P86E76 1993 294.5'2114—dc20
91-45548

9 8 7 6

Printed in the United States of America

Acknowledgments

Although it may seem so at times, scholarship is never a solitary endeavor. I owe thanks to many people, a few of whom I name here, for helping me complete this study. I wish to thank David M. Knipe, my doctoral adviser, who has been a source of encouragement, critical judgment, and moral support. I also wish to thank many others who have read all or part of the manuscript in various stages and have made valuable suggestions. They include Paul Courtright, Lindsey Harlan, Frances Wilson, V. Narayana Rao, Joseph Elder, and J. Mark Kenoyer. When I first decided to investigate the Goddess cult of northwest India, I received encouragement from Surinder Bhardwaj and Georgana Foster.

Research in India was funded through a Fulbright–Hays Doctoral Dissertation Award in 1982–83. In India I received help and hospitality from many people. I wish to thank the United States Educational Foundation–India staff for their friendly assistance, especially O. P. Bhardwaj, who took a special interest in my project. The Panjab University (Chandigarh) provided me with an affiliation. Shalina Mehta was my adviser as well as a confidante and friend. I also recieved assistance from B. N. Goswami, A. B. Mukherji, and the late Dr. Tiwari. Several graduate students from Panjab University helped me with fieldwork and/or transcribing tapes; among them were Maan Singh, Manjit, Vishalini, Anurag, and Gurbakhsh Singh. Nirankar Agarwal provided support and encouragement both in the United States and in India and accompanied me on several field trips. Amrit Bolaria made her home a refuge for me in Chandigarh, as did Mr. and Mrs. Sandhu. My landlady in Chandigarh, Jaswant Jeet, made my stay there a pleasant experience. Kathy and Joe Astroth and their sons, Joseph and Justin, provided me with an American community in Chandigarh. Most importantly, I wish to thank all the pilgrims, priests, and devotees of the

Goddess who welcomed me into their lives, put up with my presence, and answered my questions with patience and thoughtfulness.

The University of Wisconsin–Madison funded the writing of my dissertation in 1983–85. The National Endowment for the Humanities funded the revision and preparation of the book manuscript with a Summer Stripend in 1989. A Junior Sabbatical from Lewis and Clark College and an invitation from the California Institute of Integral Studies to teach a course on the Hindu Goddess on its Himalayan Study Tour allowed me to return to the Kangra Valley in October and November 1989 for a stint of follow-up research and photography.

Earlier versions of portions of this book have appeared in the *Journal of the American Academy of Religion* and in *Criminal Gods and Demon Devotees,* edited by Alf Hiltebeitel (Albany: State University of New York Press, 1989).

A few others played an important role, directly or indirectly, in the writing of this book, and I would like to mention them. Rita M. Gross, my first teacher of religious studies, inspired me to take up the study of Indian religions as a career. My students at Depauw University and Lewis and Clark College have been exposed to portions of the book in written and oral form; their thoughtful questions helped me clarify much that would otherwise be unintelligible to the nonspecialist reader. Kelly Clana has helped me maintain sanity and has provided support in countless ways during several years of writing and rewriting. Kali, Gabriel, and Ramona, my furry friends, have provided warmth and companionship during many lonely hours of writing. My parents, William Erndl and Edna Griffin, are responsible not only for my existence, but for instilling in me a love of learning and an insatiable curiosity.

Finally, I would like to thank the Goddess herself, without whose grace this book would never have been completed. *Jay mātā dī!*

Portland, Ore. K. M. E.
March 1992

Contents

Note on Transliteration

This study contains names and terms in the Sanskrit, Hindi, and Panjabi languages. I have tried to minimize confusion, but a certain amount of inconsistency is inevitable. I have used the Sanskrit form of a word in cases where it is more commonly used or in a Sanskritic context. For example, in a discussion of the Sanskrit text the *Devī Māhātmya,* I have referred to the buffalo demon as Mahiṣāsura, while in a discussion of the same myth in a vernacular pamphlet, I have used the Hindi–Panjabi form Mahiṣāsur. In many cases a word will take the same form in Hindi and Panjabi. Thus *jot,* the equivalent of the Sanskrit *jyoti* (flame), is used in both Hindi and Panjabi. Where there are differences, I have specified the language in the text. There is a considerable amount of switching back and forth between Hindi and Panjabi in ritual and narrative contexts. Thus the formulaic expression *jay mātā dī* (victory to the Mother) is grammatically Panjabi, while another formulaic expression, *bol sāce darbār kī jay* (say, victory to the true court), is grammatically Hindi.

I have used the conventional transliteration system, except for using the symbol ṛ for the "tongue-flap" consonant in Hindi and Panjabi as well as for the Sanskrit vowel. With a few exceptions, which I point out, I have pluralized words by adding the English *s*. For place-names (e.g., Chandigarh), names of languages (e.g., Hindi), caste names (e.g., Brahmin), and commonly used proper names (e.g., Indira Gandhi), I have used the more familiar Anglicized spellings.

Victory to the Mother

Introduction

In the middle of the night, in a suburban home, a loudspeaker blares: *jay mātā dī!* A motor rickshaw in Delhi sports the written slogan: *jay mātā dī!* Teenagers listen to cassette tapes of film tunes punctuated by cries of: *jay mātā dī!* Friends meeting on the street greet each other: *jay mātā dī!* Villagers traveling on foot to a mountain shrine chant in unison: *jay mātā dī!* A young woman with hair disheveled tosses her head about wildly, while onlookers cry out: *jay mātā dī!* In the bazaar one finds a poster of a beautiful multiarmed woman riding a lion above the caption: *jay mātā dī!*

This phrase, *jay mātā dī,* which in Panjabi means "victory to the Mother," is the rallying cry of the contemporary Mother Goddess cult of northwest India. The nature of this Goddess and her devotees' experience of her is the subject of this study.

Śerāṅvālī, the Lion Rider

The worship of Devī (the Goddess) is one of the most vigorous and visible of religious phenomena in northwest India today. Her cult is a regional variant of the pan-Hindu worship of the Great Goddess, known by such names as Durgā, Caṇḍī, and Ambā. In the greater Panjab region—which includes present-day Panjab, Haryana, Chandigarh, Delhi, and much of Himachal Pradesh[1]—she is most commonly called by the nickname Śerāṅvālī (Lion Rider) or simply Mātā (Mother). Her cult is one in which esoteric Tantric elements mingle with popular devotional (*bhakti*) worship. Although Śerāṅvālī has mythological and ritual associations with the great male deities Viṣṇu and Śiva, it is in her independent form that she is worshiped. That is, she is not seen as a consort deity like Lakṣmī or Pārvatī, each of whose significance depends on her relationship with a male deity. A deity who is both transcendent and immanent, her functions range from generalized ones such as the creation, preservation, and destruction of the universe to more specific ones such as curing diseases and helping people in distress. She is the embodiment of *śakti,* the dynamic power of the universe.

Although many goddesses with various names are worshiped as aspects of Devī or Śerāṅvālī, devotees use two names, Vaiṣṇo and Kālī, to distinguish between the two complementary sides of her nature, gentle and fierce. Both are independent deities; neither is the consort of a male deity. The designation Vaiṣṇo refers to both a specific local goddess and a more generalized aspect of the Goddess. As a specific local goddess, Vaiṣṇo Devī is one of Seven Sisters worshiped as an aspect of Śerāṅvālī at her shrine in District Jammu in the form of three stone outcroppings (*piṇḍīs*) that represent the three members of the Śākta trinity: Mahālakṣmī, Mahāsarasvatī, and Mahākālī. When she is shown anthropomorphically, her iconography is similar to that of Durgā or Ambā. In popular bazaar lithographs she is portrayed as having eight arms and as being seated on a lion or tiger. She holds in her hands a discus, club, and conch (emblems of Viṣṇu) and a trident, sword, and bow and arrow (emblems of Śiva). She holds a lotus in one of the remaining hands and displays the "fear-not" gesture (*abhaya mudrā*) in the other. Dressed in a red sari and bedecked with jewelry, she is beautiful, fair-skinned, strong, and capable. While she appears gentle and friendly, she is no weakling; her loose, flowing hair signifies that she is under the control of no one.[2] She is flanked by her two servants or bodyguards. On the right is the monkey god Laṅgur Vīr, another name for Hanumān, who in other contexts is associated with the Rāma incarnation of Viṣṇu. On the left is Bhairo, who in other contexts appears as a fierce form of Śiva, but here is Bāl (child) Bhairo, white in color with four arms holding a severed head, drum, chowrie, and sword and accompanied by a dog. This iconographic depiction of Vaiṣṇo Devī has become standard for most of the other goddesses in the Panjab Hills who are manifested in their temples in aniconic form. It could be called the generic Śerāṅvālī poster iconography.

The concept of Vaiṣṇo is not restricted to the manifestation at the Vaiṣṇo Devī temple but is an aspect that applies to Śerāṅvālī generally. The name Vaiṣṇo itself comes from *vaiṣṇava,* meaning literally pertaining to or a follower of the god Viṣṇu. In this case it is more appropriate to translate it as "in the style or manner of Viṣṇu and his followers," for in the northwest of India, *vaiṣṇav* or *vaiṣṇo* commonly means vegetarian. Restaurants and food stands in the Panjab that style themselves "*vaiṣṇav bhojanālay*" or "*vaiṣṇav ḍhābā*" serve vegetarian food but invariably boast a picture of Vaiṣṇo Devī, not of Viṣṇu, on their signboards. Similarly, Panjabi Hindus who call themselves Vaiṣṇav are not necessarily stating their sectarian affiliation to Viṣṇu. More likely, they are vegetarians and worshipers of the Goddess in her vegetarian form (Vaiṣṇo *rūp*). Vaiṣṇo is the vegetarian aspect of the Goddess who is auspicious, powerful, and sometimes fierce and punitive, but who accepts no animal sacrifice.[3]

Kālī, on the other hand, is unabashedly carnivorous. Pictured with black or blue skin, pendulous breasts, and a lolling tongue, she sports a garland of skulls and stands either alone or on the corpse of Śiva, surrounded by jackals. She haunts cremation grounds and frightens the weak of heart. While both the Vaiṣṇo and Kālī aspects kill demons, Kālī takes particular delight in drinking their blood. In the Panjab she has the nickname Kalkattevālī, an allusion to her famous shrine in Calcutta, West Bengal, where hundreds of goats are sacrificed every day. Kālī is a more specialized form of the Goddess than is Vaiṣṇo, whose functions are more generalized. In the Sanskrit text *Devī Māhātmya,* Kālī emerges from the forehead of the lion-riding Devī specifically to lap up the blood of the demons. This task she performs gleefully, and she is later reabsorbed into the body of the Goddess. She is the "henchwoman" who performs a bloody but necessary service. It is in deference to this bloodthirsty aspect of the Goddess that animals are sacrificed, for when pleased, Kālī is a gracious boon giver. One may worship the Goddess in either or both aspects, but modern-day practice has tended to stress the Vaiṣṇo—that is, vegetarian—form of worship even for Kālī. Animal sacrifice is gradually disappearing and is no longer practiced at the larger temples known as the Seven Sisters. But the darker side is always acknowledged, and an attempt is made to provide suitable substitutes for blood offerings.

While the dual nature of the Goddess as Vaiṣṇo and Kālī is explicitly recognized by devotees in the cult, there is another seeming duality, that of virgin and mother, which has struck outside observers. Anthropologist Paul Hershman has pointed out that Panjabis view the Goddess as both a virgin and a mother but not as a wife.[4] When she appears before devotees in visions or dreams, it is often as a beautiful maiden (*kanyā*). On certain ritual occasions, young virgin girls are worshiped as manifestations of the Goddess. Virginity (or chastity) in both males and females is associated with the purity and power born of asceticism. As one informant stated, any girl below the age of seven is the "direct form" (*sākṣāt rūp*) of the Goddess; after that age anyone who controls one's body and senses is also the form of the Goddess. The Goddess is also a mother, not in the literal sense of being the biological mother of children but in the sense of being the source of fertility and nourishment, the grantor of all wishes. Thus the idea of the Goddess as virgin and mother is not the contradiction it first appears, since she is not a virgin–mother in the sense that Mary of Christianity is. Even most properly married consort goddesses do not experience motherhood in the usual biological sense. Lakṣmī, the wife of Viṣṇu, has no children, and Pārvatī, the wife of Śiva, has only children who are, as A. K. Ramanujan, puts it "extrauterine miracles."[5] Both the virgin and the mother are symbols of power and auspiciousness; the Goddess shares in both these symbols.

Context of This Study

When I began this study, I was motivated by interest in two overlapping areas, the symbolization of female divinity and the dynamics of modern popular Hinduism. In recent studies of religion and culture, symbolization of the feminine has captured much of the limelight.[6] Within Western religions, which traditionally have been male-dominated, both women's roles and the use of female imagery in religious literature and ritual have attracted new attention. Efforts in this direction have ranged from the creation of women's rituals in Judaism, to the use of female god language in Protestant church services, to the reinterpretation and revaloration of feminine symbolism in feminist theology, to the reconstruction and revival of ancient "matriarchal" goddess cults.[7] The revival of female symbolism in the West is strongly connected with and heavily informed by the ideology of political feminist movements.

By contrast, the worship of female deities in contemporary Hinduism is by and large not explicitly connected with feminist movements per se. While some Indian women's groups, such as the press Kali for Women, have appropriated Goddess symbolism, they are drawing on traditions that are current in mainstream Hindu culture, not revalorizing forgotten symbols from an ancient past. The statement "God is a woman" simply would not have the shock value for Hindus that it would for Christians, Jews, or Muslims. I suspect that the reason for this is that Hindu conceptions of both the divine and femaleness are radically different from those in the West. The divine feminine has long been at the center of Hindu religious symbolism. The Hindu Great Goddess in her various forms is particularly worthy of attention because she has survived the ravages of time and has emerged triumphant in the modern age. The ancient goddesses of the Western world were long ago replaced by male gods, with the possible exception of the popular Marian cults, or by a monotheistic God conceived of in masculine terms, while the Hindu Goddess has become more and more popular throughout the ages, coexisting with male gods and in many cases making them superfluous. Her cults throughout India continue to grow in numbers and importance. Hindu Goddess worship is a highly developed complex of myth, ritual, and theology, with many regional variants. In this study I attempt to contribute to a greater understanding of Hindu female divinity in general by exploring the religious expressions connected with the Goddess Śerāṅvālī current in northwest India.

Scholarship on Hindu goddesses has burgeoned in recent years, particularly in the fields of history of religions and anthropology.[8] Two main factors, I believe, account for this blossoming of scholarly interest. First, this new emphasis on goddesses is part of a general movement in academia to accord recognition to previously ignored or denigrated aspects of culture, particularly the roles and contributions of women and the symbolization of the feminine. Recognizing that no scholarship is value-neutral, scholars of religion, following the lead of their colleagues in other disciplines, have begun to question the notion that the study of male religious experience and masculine symbolism is adequate for understanding the totality of human religious experience.

Second, and I believe closely related to the first, there has been within Indology a move toward understanding Hinduism in its full religious expression. Building on the studies of earlier generations of scholars who regarded Sanskrit texts, philosophical schools such as Vedānta, and the renunciant tradition as normative, the present generation of scholars has expanded its understanding of Hinduism to include theistic, popular, folk, non-Sanskritic, and regional traditions. At the most abstract, philosophical level, the ultimate reality in Hinduism is understood as neither male nor female but the neuter *brahman,* the absolute devoid of all qualities and beyond all distinctions. But in practice, Hinduism is a theistic religion with a high degree of anthropomorphism. Although the sacred is beyond all qualities and distinctions, it is also present in various manifestations. God appears as male in the case of such gods as Viṣṇu and Śiva or female in the case of such goddesses as Durgā, Ambā, Caṇḍī, and Kālī. The sacred also reveals itself in human beings, in animals, and in such natural objects as mountains, rivers, stones, trees, and plants. These "embodied" forms of divinity are finally receiving the attention they deserve.[9] These new studies serve as a corrective to the stereotype of Hinduism as abstract, otherworldly, and life-denying.

Settings and Interpretations

In this study I have chosen to focus on the regional cult of Śerāṅvālī rather than the religious practices of a village, caste, or other unit. By "cult" I mean a cluster of religious expressions centered on a particular deity or group of deities, usually connected with religious sites, myths, and rituals. Anthropologist Ursula Sharma characterizes a cult—as distinguished from a church or sect—as

> a complex of religious activity directed towards a common object of reverence (be it a deity, saint, animal, spirit, natural feature, or indeed a living human being). That is, members of a cult are united by the fact that they all worship the same object, rather than by the fact that they all hold the same views or dogmas (although obviously some common ideas must be assumed). You "belong" to a cult only as long as you care to practice it, and membership is seldom exclusive; it is generally possible to participate in more than one at a time and most Hindus do so, although they may have their preferences and favorites.[10]

This study centers itself in the "universe" of the Goddess and her devotees, a universe that is constantly fluctuating. However, the reader should not get the impression that she is the only deity worshiped. Panjabi Hindus, like Hindus in most other parts of India, are by and large nonsectarian. They worship an assortment of deities, heroes, and saints, including the all-India Śiva, Rādhā-Kṛṣṇa, and Rāma; more local figures such as Bābā Bālak Nāth and Guggā Pīr; and the Sikh gurus. The eclectic and nonsectarian quality of the popular religion extends beyond Hinduism to embrace Sikhism (and in prepartition India included folk Islam as well). Many Sikhs are enthusiastic participants in the Goddess cult, in spite of the fact that Sikh religious leaders are at pains to distinguish Sikhism from Hinduism and that present political tensions have driven the wedge even further.

Worshipers of Śerāṅvālī include people of all castes. In fact, I was repeatedly assured that even a Muslim could enter her temples, since she grants her *darśan* (sacred vision) equally to all. On the whole, Panjabi Hindu culture is not as strictly hierarchical as in other areas of India. This may be due to the fact that the Panjab has survived waves of immigration and invasion for many centuries and thus has been exposed to many different customs and ideologies. Flexibility and adaptability have been the hallmark of Panjabi culture. While caste remains an important source of group identity, caste restrictions are not nearly as rigid in the Panjab as in other areas of India, and the Brahmins as a caste are not as powerful. As Prakash Tandon, a Panjabi of the merchant Khattri caste wrote in his autobiography, "That they [Brahmins] could be leaders of society, in a position of privilege, I only discovered when I went to live outside the Punjab. With us the Brahmins were an underprivileged class and exercised little or no influence on the community."[11] Thus while the Goddess cult among Panjabis is known for being open to all castes, even untouchables, part of that openness may be due to the relative laxity of the caste system in Panjabi culture generally.

Who is the Goddess? What is the allure of the Goddess? Why do people worship her? What makes her different from other deities? How do devotees interact with the Goddess? What characterizes their relationship with her? These are the questions I carry throughout this study. Let us start here with a sample of brief responses that devotees gave me:

> Devī is worshiped because she manifests herself in front of one, because of her power. She is the accumulation of the powers of all the gods. She protects all the gods. (female, age forty-four, Brahmin)

> Devī is worshiped because she is *śakti*, and by worshiping her one gets happiness and peace. She has the heart of a mother; because she is like a

mother, she gives more than the other gods. (female, age twenty-one, Khattri)

Devī is worshiped because she fulfills all wishes. All the other gods worship Devī, so she is the most powerful. (female, age fifty, Khattri)

Devī is the creator and protector of this world. She makes our destinies. *Mokṣa* [liberation] can be obtained through the worship of Devī, the Mother. Whatever you ask for, you will get. (male, age fifty, Brahmin)

Devī is worshiped out of faith; she fulfills all desires. People worship all the gods, but they have more faith in Devī because of family interest; she fulfills wishes. (female, age twenty-four, Agrawal)

People worship Devī because she has *śakti*. She is a lady, so she has more *śakti*. All the gods worship Devī, so that means she is more powerful. (male, age eighteen, Rajput)

Dhyānū Bhagat offered his head to Devī and got it back; therefore people worship her. People worship out of faith. She is different from other deities because she gave Dhyānū Bhagat back his head, and because she fulfills all wishes. (male, age eighteen, Rajput)

She fulfilled all wishes in "The Story of Queen Tārā," so she fulfills wishes for everyone. She gives everything. (female, age thirty-five, Agrawal)

Whatever god you worship, if it is with good intentions and with prayer and practice, it is a vehicle for attaining *paramātma* [the supreme soul]. God is one with many names, but a person should have one object of devotion, as a vehicle for the practice. Devī is special; she shows herself in dreams. (male, age thirty, Kayasth)

The Mother listens to our requests immediately. Besides this, when I do the recitation of the Mother [*Devī Māhātmya*], I remain all right. Otherwise, I am usually involved in this or that fighting, etc. The Mother is a great power, and I believe in it. (male, age twenty-three, Khattri)

In the following chapters I attempt to unpack these statements, to explore the various theological, mythological, and ritual meanings embedded in them. For the moment I will simply highlight two recurrent themes. One concerns the concept of *śakti*, the female power that pervades the universe, and how it manifests itself in various forms. What is the nature of this power? Is the Goddess one or many? How do these different forms relate to each other? While the devotees quoted above emphasize the benevolent aspects of the Goddess's personality, some scholars have suggested that the Goddess is split into benevolent and malevolent poles, and that these appear as married and unmarried goddesses, respectively.[12] How does this theory relate to the Goddess cult in northwest India? The second is the importance of *bhakti* (devotion) in the Goddess cult and how it relates to "this world" (*samsāra*) and release from the world (*mokṣa*). How is the concern for material welfare, so prominent in the Goddess cult, reconciled with the spiritual goal of transcending these desires?

I have characterized the focus of this study as the universe of the Goddess and her devotees, but where do I, the researcher, fit into that "universe"? Why did I choose to study this topic, and why have I gone about it in the way that I have? These are questions I have asked myself many times and that other Americans have also asked me. Surprisingly enough, I was seldom asked such questions in India by devotees I encountered at Goddess temples and rituals. Certainly, they were curious about me, wanting to know how far I had had to travel, how much money I made, whether or not I was married, whether there is Goddess worship in the United States. But they seemed to take my presence for granted, saying that one can enter into the powerful presence of the Goddess only in response to her "call." I have discussed some of the intellectual currents that led me to this topic, but I also consider the "call of the Goddess" an appropriate metaphor for the pull she has exerted on me over the years.

I first became aware of the Panjab Hills Goddess cult in April 1978, while on the way back to Delhi from a trip to Kashmir. An Indian friend of mine, enrolled in a yoga training course in Katra, invited me to stop there and make the pilgrimage to nearby Vaiṣṇo Devī. I jumped at the chance, for I had long been interested in Hindu goddesses but had mainly read of them as village deities and was unaware of a larger cultic orientation toward the Goddess outside of Bengal and certain areas of the south. I was amazed to discover a regional cult of such magnitude and popularity that was so little known in scholarly literature on Hinduism. I further discovered, upon conversing with pilgrims and reading some of the available pamphlet literature, that there were other goddesses connected with Vaiṣṇo Devī, her "sisters," and that all of them were somehow identified with the pan-Indian Durgā. A few weeks later I visited one of these sisters, Jvālā Mukhī, and was enchanted by the sacred vision of her "flame tongue" emerging from the rock. After returning to the United States later that year, I spent the next several years studying the sacred texts of the Goddess, doing background research and planning my return. During the year September 1982 to September 1983, I conducted an intensive field study of the cult, returning for a brief follow-up visit to several of the temples in the fall of 1989.

As I wanted to get an overall sense of the cult, I made extensive visits to the major Goddess temples in the area, the Seven Sisters: namely Vaiṣṇo Devī, Jvālā Mukhī, Kāṅgṛevālī Devī, Cintpūrṇī, Nainā Devī, Mansā Devī, and Cāmuṇḍā Devī. During the main period of my study, I chose to live in the city of Chandigarh and use it as a home base, making trips to the various Goddess temples from there. This turned out to be a fortunate choice for several reasons. First of all, Chandigarh is a major transportation center, and all of the temples were reasonably accessible from there. Secondly, Chandigarh itself is a lively center of religious activity and provided many opportunities for research. I was able to interview numerous devotees in Chandigarh and to attend *jagrātās* (all-night performances to worship the Goddess) and other functions there. I also participated in an organized group pilgrimage, briefly described in chapter 3, which originated from Chandigarh. Mansā Devī, one of the Seven Sisters of the cult, is located only about eight miles from Chandigarh on a regular bus route, so I was able to visit that temple frequently. I should also mention that Chandigarh is a particularly auspicious place to study the Goddess, since it means "fort of Caṇḍī," being so named because of a small Caṇḍī temple in the vicinity.

The city of Chandigarh, having been recently founded as the capital of two states, Haryana and Panjab, houses a vibrant mix of urban and village life. Although the city is planned (probably more so than any other city in India) and laid out on a grid, there are still villages to be found within the city limits, and venturing a mile or two in any direction lands one squarely in the countryside. The population of the city, like that of the Panjab, is about half Hindu and half Sikh. The languages spoken in Chandigarh are Hindi (or rather the colloquial Hindi–Urdu sometimes called Hindustani) and Panjabi, with most residents demonstrating proficiency in both and

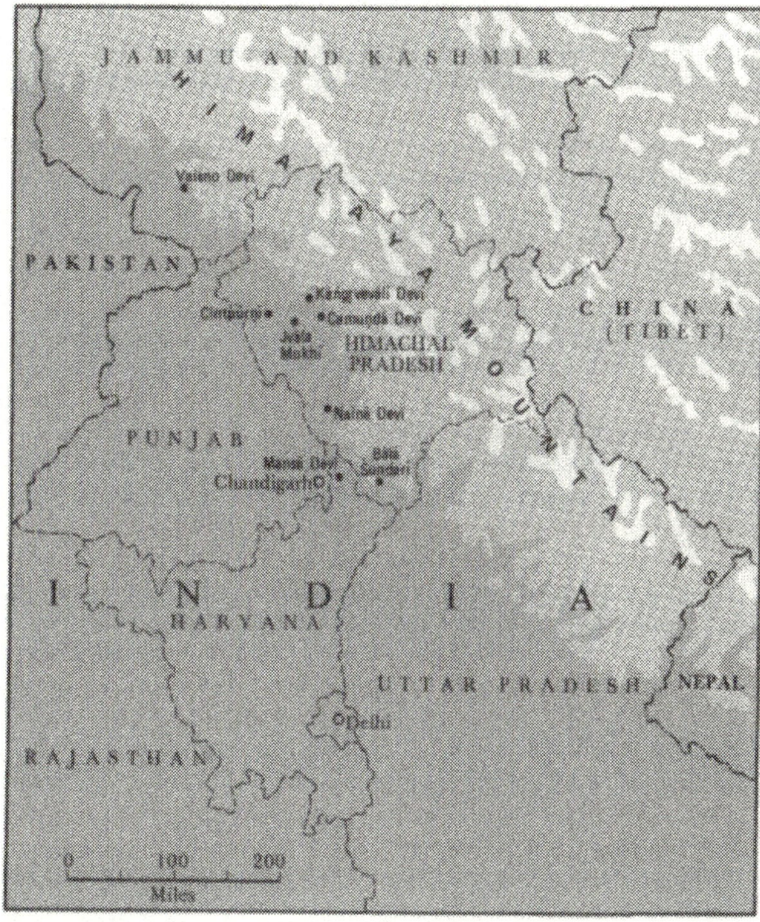

Map of the study area, with the approximate locations of the temples mentioned in this book. (Adapted from Ursula Sharma, *Women, Work, and Property in North-West India* [London: Tavistock, 1980] x)

frequently switching back and forth. On the whole, language posed few problems, as I communicated mainly in Hindi, which all my informants understood, and I could understand Panjabi.

At the pilgrimage places, since there are so many people speaking different dialects of Hindi and Panjabi, a kind of lingua franca based on Hindustani is in common use. The language used in songs and stories and at performances such as *jagrātās* was usually a mixture of

Hindi and Panjabi. The popular pamphlets that were such an important source for this study are written in standard Hindi or in a mixture of Hindi and Panjabi, the latter being found particularly in song lyrics. They are written primarily in Devanagari script, although occasionally I came across one in Gurmukhi script. I was able to collect such pamphlets at pilgrimage places and at bazaars in Chandigarh and Delhi.

My research methods were eclectic, encompassing interviews, participant observation, and analysis of oral and written texts. I did not have a regular research assistant throughout my stay; several different Indian friends and graduate students accompanied me on field trips. Although I usually had specific questions in mind, my interviews with informants were wide-ranging, informal, and often impromptu. In most cases devotees, priests, and other religious practitioners were more than willing to discuss their religious beliefs and experiences, and often told me more than I would have thought to ask had I used a questionnaire. I also engaged in participant observation at pilgrimage places and at religious performances. This proved to be the most valuable source of information, as well as the most enjoyable part of my research, since devotees welcomed my participation and the atmosphere was always lively and invigorating. Fieldwork was not something separated from the rest of my life. I must admit that much of the most interesting and valuable material I gathered came to me not through any systematic planning on my part but through happenstance. A routine trip to the bank, a conversation with my research assistant's mother, a neighbor dropping in on my landlady, a remark overheard on the bus—all yielded unexpected treasures. Once while on a train in Kerala, in the deep south of India, I happened to sit next to an elderly Panjabi man who, noticing that I was reading a popular pamphlet about the Goddess, regaled me for hours with stories of his pilgrimages to Vaiṣṇo Devī and of the miracles he had witnessed there.

My training as a scholar has been in the history and phenomenology of religions, and this training has largely guided my theoretical approach to the materials in this study. That is, while I have taken note of relevant sociological and psychological factors, I treat the Goddess cult primarily as a *religious* phenomenon. I have taken seriously the dictum that one must attempt to understand religious phenomena, as Mircea Eliade has written, "*on their own plane of reference*."[13] From the beginning I was determined to view the Goddess as a phenomenon in her own right, as an actor who interacts with her devotees, not as a thinly disguised expression of something else such as the social structure or a psychological process. I wanted to view the Goddess from the perspective of the lived experience of her devotees. This is far easier said than done, and at various points in my fieldwork I wondered if it was not at best naive and at worst arrogant to believe such a thing was possible. However, I have had several experiences in my encounter with Goddess worship, epiphanies one might even call them, which, while not mitigating these misgivings, have broadened my perspective. I will tell two stories here that I believe illustrate some of what I have experienced in fieldwork and in trying to interpret that experience to a scholarly audience.

The first took place in the Panjabi town of Mohali, a suburb of Chandigarh, in the winter of 1983. I was sitting on the floor in the home of a lower-middle-class family with about fifty festively dressed people—women, men, and children. It was about 2:00 A.M. We were attending a Devī *jagrātā,* an all-night ritual performance held to worship the Goddess with devotional songs and stories of her exploits. The performers, joined by the congregation, were singing a *bheṇṭ,* a devotional song, to the lively beat of a drum. The Goddess was present that night, in the form of a flame (*jot*) that had been lit, consecrated, surrounded by offerings of fruit and flowers, and placed on a platform in front of the room. She was also present in the form of a sixteen-year-old girl called the "Little Mother" seated on a platform next to the flame. The Goddess had entered her body and was "playing" within her. Her long, black hair flew out from her face as though charged with electricity as her head spun around in rhythmic circles. From time to time people from the congregation would go up and make offerings to her. I was listening to the music, watching the "Little Mother," joining in the singing from time to time, checking my tape recorder, holding onto my camera. My stomach ached from consuming countless cups of sweet, milky tea. I was tired and, frankly, a little bored. I had seen all this before and found myself wishing that I had chosen to research something that took place at a reasonable hour. Then for some reason, I glanced at the woman sitting next to me, a late-middle-aged, plump, well-dressed matronly-looking woman. I had not spoken with her, but earlier we had nodded to each other in greeting. Nothing out of the ordinary. Suddenly, the woman's head began to move from side to side, her eyes glazed over, and she began to shake. Standing up, she began to dance frenetically, her tightly bound hair loosening and then fanning out from her face. I was frozen with fear and could not move. The next thing I remember is the other people moving away from her and pulling me along with them. Later, I do not remember how much later, she calmed down and sat quietly, her eyes unfocused. I remember wondering if this could happen to me.

The second story takes place in Madison, Wisconsin, at the Conference on South Asia in November 1983, where having just returned from the field, I presented a scholarly paper on the Devī *jagrātā* as a ritual performance. The setting for this presentation was, of course, very different from the setting in India I have just described. A small portion of my presentation dealt with the phenomenon I glossed as "Goddess possession," yet it was this part that evoked the most comment in the question-and-answer period. Afterward, in the elevator, a senior colleague asked me if I had ever believed that it really was the Goddess possessing those women. I answered, simply, "Yes."

I tell these stories now not as a confession of faith, for though I acknowledge the presence of the Goddess and the meaning she has in the lives of her devotees, that does not make me a Hindu. Rather, I believe these stories are interesting because of the epistemological and hermeneutical questions they raise. After thinking about the matter some more, I would say that the reality of the Goddess is not a matter of belief or disbelief but rather an experience, a way of seeing, a way of knowing. I have had a glimpse into that way of knowing, although of course my perspective is not privileged in any way. Although I am certainly not an "insider," neither am I a "detached observer."

In this study I do not attempt to develop any kind of universal theory of religion or of Goddess worship. I have used many different interpretive tools in my attempt to understand the complex phenomenon of Goddess worship, avoiding exclusive adherence to models of explanation such as structuralism and psychoanalysis that remove the phenomenon from its cultic and cultural context. These models have been used with varying results, for example, in the cross-cultural study of myth. In this study I summarize numerous myths concerning the Goddess. I realize that many of these myths have important themes that could be applied cross-culturally. However, I have resisted the temptation to delve into interpretations too far afield of the lived experience of the cult. Although such approaches may be useful for eliciting deep structures and speculating on universal truths, I have decided to stick to the more modest goal of contributing to the understanding of particular religious expressions in a particular historical time and geographical place. I invite readers of this study to take the interpretations I offer as a starting place and to make wider connections on their own.

I

Divine Materialism

Myth and Theology of Goddess Worship

O Goddess, remover of affliction, be gracious, be gracious, O Mother of the entire world.
Be gracious, O Queen of the universe, protect the universe. You, O Goddess, are the Queen of all that moves and does not move.

You alone are the support of the world, because you exist in the form of the earth.
By you who exist in the form of the waters, the whole world is filled, O inviolable warrior.

O you who dwell in the form of intelligence in the hearts of all beings,
O giver of heaven and liberation, O Goddess, O Nārāyaṇī, praise be to you.

O power of creation, preservation, and destruction, O eternal one,
O basis of all qualities of matter, O one who is filled with qualities of matter, O Nārāyaṇī, praise be to you.

O one whose hands and feet are everywhere, whose eyes, head, and mouth are everywhere,
O one whose ears and nose are everywhere, O Nārāyaṇī, praise be to you.

O one whose form is everything, O Queen of all, O one endowed with all powers,

Protect us from all fears, O Goddess, O Durgā, O Goddess, praise be to you.

When satisfied, you ward off all diseases; but when angry you destroy all that is desired.
Those who take refuge in you do not become afflicted; yea, those who take refuge in you become a refuge.

Be gracious to those who have bowed before you, O Goddess, O remover of the misfortune of the universe.
O you who are worthy of praise by the dwellers of the three worlds, be a boon giver to the worlds.[1]

What is special about Goddess worship in the Hindu tradition? What makes it different from other forms of Hindu devotionalism? What is unique about Goddess traditions in northwest India? How do they relate to pan-Indian and other regional Goddess traditions? Is the Śerāṅvālī of the Panjab Hills the same as the demon-slaying Durgā of the Sanskrit Purāṇas? Is she the same as, say, the lion-riding Ambā of Gujarat or the bountiful Annapūrṇā of Varanasi? In this chapter I begin to weave together a context in which to explore these questions, drawing on historical, philosophical, and literary studies of the pan-Indian Goddess tradition. My survey here is necessarily brief and highly selective, aiming to provide a background for approaching the more localized ethnographic material in subsequent chapters.

Goddesses and the Goddess

Worship of the divine feminine is one of the most ancient religious expressions in India. It has become a truism among scholars of Hinduism that worship of goddesses has its basis in the Indus Valley civilization (2500–1500 B.C.E) or another indigenous Indian culture (Austric or Dravidian) rather than in the Vedic or Brahmanic tradition which was imported into the subcontinent during the second millennium B.C.E. by waves of Aryan immigrants. The general argument, stated with various degrees of refinement, is that the pre-Aryans, being concerned mainly with agriculture, worshiped female (and to a lesser extent male) earth deities who represented fertility, regeneration, and the processes of life and death. The Aryans, on the other hand, being nomadic cattle herders and warriors, worshiped primarily male sky deities. When the Aryans settled in India, the argument continues, they took up agriculture and gradually assimilated the indigenous culture(s); thus, the various philosophical movements and cults that came to be called Hinduism are a synthesis of Aryan and non-Aryan elements.[2]

The worship of goddesses in particular is integrated rather late into the elite Sanskritic tradition. With a few notable exceptions such as the Vāgāṃbhṛṇī Sūkta (*Ṛg Veda* 10.125),[3] a hymn to the goddess of speech, Vāk, Vedic imagery is overwhelmingly masculine. Such goddesses as figure in the Vedic hymns do so in a very minor way. While there is little evidence to suggest the Vedic origins of a Goddess cult, there are foreshadowings of the concept of *śakti* in the Vedas and even more definite indications of the concept in the Upaniṣads.[4] The period of the epics, the *Mahābhārata* and the *Rāmāyaṇa* (ca. 400 B.C.E.–400 C.E.), is one of transition in the integration of goddesses into the Hindu pantheon. Goddesses figure strongly in mythology, but not as major deities. The worship of the Goddess as a supreme being has not yet been legitimized and absorbed into the Sanskritic tradition. Usually goddesses are portrayed as wives of the gods, but there is little emphasis on their soteriological, cosmogonic, or ontological significance.

It is during the period of the Purāṇas (400 C.E. onward) that goddesses as individual deities and the concept of the Goddess become prominent in Sanskrit literature. Goddesses who are paired with gods as their consorts are portrayed as instrumental in their partners' activities or even dominant over them.[5] Furthermore, there is a growing tendency to conceive of an independent cosmic Goddess, Devī or Great Goddess, Mahādevī who contains within her all goddesses and is the Supreme Being. By the period between 400 and 800 C.E. a full-blown cult of such a Mother Goddess had arisen in Aryan India. In succeeding centuries the movement spread, both influencing and absorbing various cultic, mythic, and symbolic elements of tribal and local deities. According to Vasudeva S. Agrawala, the following strands compose Goddess worship: (1) the Vedic tradition, with its notions of Vāk and Trayī Vidyā (triple knowledge); (2) the philosophical traditions of Saṃkhyā and Vedānta, with their concepts of Prakṛti; (3) Purāṇic mythology in which Lakṣmī, Sarasvatī, and Durgā are conceived as the three *śaktis* of Viṣṇu, Brahmā, and Śiva respectively, and of the

Purāṇic cult of the seven Mātṛkās; and (4) prevailing local and tribal cults.[6] This Goddess embodies not only all feminine qualities, but masculine qualities as well. As David Kinsley points out, in taking over the roles of creator, preserver, and destroyer from Brahmā, Viṣṇu, and Śiva, respectively, she makes the male gods superfluous.[7] The earliest Sanskrit text presenting this picture of the Goddess, and still the most important text in the Śākta tradition, is the *Devī Māhātmya* (sixth century C.E.), a part of the *Mārkaṇḍeya Purāṇa,* which will be discussed in the next section.

Thus from the period of the Purāṇas onward, it becomes possible to speak of Śāktism as a cultic and sectarian orientation in the elite Sanskritic tradition. Since Śāktism is sometimes considered to be synonymous with Tantrism or to be an offshoot of Śaivism, I will hazard a few brief definitions here, keeping in mind that Śāktism has many forms, both regional and with respect to philosophical elaboration, and that it overlaps in many areas with other tendencies in Hinduism. André Padoux characterizes Tantrism as "a practical way to attain supernatural powers and liberation in this life through the use of specific and complex techniques and based on a particular ideology, that of a cosmic reintegration by means of which the adept is established in a position of power, freed from worldly fetters, while remaining in this world and dominating it by a union with (or proximity to) a godhead who is the supreme power itself."[8] Teun Goudriaan lists at least eighteen features, the combination of which, rather than any single one, distinguish Tantrism from non-Tantric Hinduism. These features include the use of verbal formulas (*mantras*), mystical diagrams (*yantra* and *maṇḍala*), visualization of images, coded language, the intentional reversal of accepted social norms, and the importance of initiation by a guru. Goudriaan states that Śāktism and Tantrism are not the same, that Tantric elements are found in all Indian religions but are most prevalent in Śāktism. He defines Śāktism as the worship of *śakti,* "the universal and all-embracing dynamis which manifests itself in the human consciousness as a female deity," adding that an inactive male partner is inseparably connected with her and that she functions as his power of action and movement.[9] N. N. Bhattacharyya distinguishes between "dependent" Śāktism, the cult of the female principle under the garb of Vaiṣṇavism, Śaivism, Buddhism, or Jainism, and an "independent" Śāktism, the cult of the female deity as Supreme Being in her own right.[10] Pushpendra Kumar simply states that "Śāktism is the worship of Śakti or the female principle, the primary factor in the creation and reproduction of the universe."[11]

Śāktism is not an offshoot of Śaivism, although in later times and in certain regions such as Bengal the cult of Śakti has been closely associated with that of Śiva. In earlier Śākta texts such as the *Devī Māhātmya,* the Goddess is associated more with Viṣṇu, as in her epithets Nārāyaṇī and Viṣṇumāyā, than with Śiva, who is mentioned only once in the role of messenger. The same text shows that the Goddess can be represented as the personified *śakti* or creative power of male gods without being represented as a consort.[12] Furthermore, the Goddess can produce her own *śaktis;* she does not need a male counterpart. The Goddess as virgin or independent is more predominant within Śāktism than the Goddess as divine consort, although the glorification of Rādhā or Lakṣmī within Vaiṣṇavism certainly reflects Śākta ideas. Thus, I would define Śāktism as the worship of *śakti,* the primordial power underlying the universe, personified as a female deity who is the Supreme Being, the totality of all existence. As such, it stresses the dynamic quality of the deity as both deluding and saving power. Śāktism has a more esoteric Tantric side, as well as the more exoteric form found in popular cults throughout India.

The *Devī Māhātmya*

The *Devī Māhātmya* represents a major focal point in the process of Sanskritization of indigenous religious forms. This Sanskritization process can be seen on two levels. On one hand, the *Devī Māhātmya* is an example, the prime example, of indigenous goddess cults "Sanskritized." In this text the Goddess's exploits appear in a Vedic context; the gods of the Vedic pantheon have been displaced and deprived of their portions of the sacrifice. She restores the cosmic order that has been threatened. Furthermore, there is a high degree of Vedic resonance, with epithets such as Svāhā and Svadhā, associated with the oblations of the fire sacrifice, juxtaposed with the more frequent epithets Ambikā and Caṇḍikā, revealing the motherly and destructive aspects of the Goddess, respectively. On the other hand, the *Devī Māhātmya* itself later becomes a vehicle of Sanskritization in which local goddesses become identified with the Goddess who is extolled in it.

As mentioned previously, the *Devī Māhātmya* is both the oldest and the most popular text in the Śākta tradition. As Thomas Coburn demonstrates in his comprehensive study of the text, it is the first time a well-integrated theology and mythology of the Goddess as Supreme Being is presented in the Sanskrit language, "crystallizing" earlier images of goddesses and the Goddess.[13] It plays an important part in both esoteric and exoteric practices all over India and is also greatly appreciated by non-Śāktas. Although it is part of a Purāṇa, it has a textual integrity of its own and is probably somewhat later than the rest of the *Mārkaṇḍeya Purāṇa*. In the contemporary Panjab Hills Goddess cult, as in other regional Goddess cults, the text is important from two points of view. The first, not surprisingly, is its content. The theology of the Goddess and myths connected with her in the *Devī Māhātmya* have become strongly associated with Serāṅvālī and her geographical manifestations. The second is its ritual significance. The words of the text are considered to be a potent collection of *mantras* that have power far beyond their verbal content. Both of these aspects will be discussed here.

The structure of the *Devī Māhātmya* is simple and elegant, a frame story enclosing three episodes illustrating the greatness of the Goddess. The text constitutes chapters 81–93 of the *Mārkaṇḍeya Purāṇa* and is introduced by the sage Mārkaṇḍeya saying that it is the story of the birth of Sāvarṇi Manu.[14] The frame story begins with a king named Suratha who has been deprived of his sovereignty and a merchant Samādhi who has been cheated out of his riches. They meet in the forest and go to the hermitage of the Ṛṣi Medhas, who tells them that all the world is deluded by Mahāmāyā (the Great Illusion), who is also responsible for the creation of the world and for granting liberation. In answer to their questions, the Ṛṣi narrates the deeds of this Great Goddess, saying that although she is eternal, she manifests herself in various ways.

The first episode begins before the creation when the world is covered by water, and the sleeping Viṣṇu is floating on the serpent Śeṣa. Brahmā is seated on a lotus emerging from Viṣṇu's navel. He sees two demons, Madhu and Kaiṭabha, who have been born from the dirt of Viṣṇu's ears. The two demons start to attack Brahmā, so he sings a hymn to the Goddess as Yoganidrā (Sleep of Yoga) asking her to vacate Viṣṇu's body so that he can awaken and slay the demons. It is clear that the Goddess here is the personification of sleep; she is also called Tāmasī, the dark, sluggish force. In the hymn Brahmā calls her the creator, preserver, and destroyer of the universe, as well as Prakṛti (Primordial Matter-energy). He calls her both Great Goddess (Mahādevī) and Great Demon (Mahāsurī). After being praised by Brahmā, she emerges from Viṣṇu's body, and he slays the demons after a five-thousand-year battle.

By the time of the *Devī Māhātmya*'s composition, the myth of Viṣṇu's killing Madhu and Kaiṭabha was well known; Madhusūdana (Killer of Madhu) is a common epithet of Viṣṇu in the *Mahābhārata*.[15] The *Devī Māhātmya* version is similar to the *Mahābhārata* version with the very important difference that Viṣṇu's capacity to act is shown to be derivative of the Goddess, to be contingent upon the withdrawal of Yoganidrā from his body. The epithet linking the Goddess to the Madhu-Kaiṭabha myth is Mahāmāyā, the Great Illusion, for she deludes the two demons into thinking that they can overpower and outwit the divine. In the same way, she deludes human beings, for whose benefit the story is told, and it is through her that they must seek a way out of this delusion. Thus, the story is both a cosmic creation myth and one that has relevance for the salvation of human beings.

The second episode of the *Devī Māhātmya* centers around the Goddess's killing of Mahiṣāsura, the buffalo demon. Here the dynamic of the text moves from the cosmic orientation of the first episode to the more mundane activity of preserving order in the created universe. The demon Mahiṣa has usurped the power of the gods so that they no longer receive their proper shares of the sacrifice, and they are unable to kill him themselves. They approach Viṣṇu and Śiva for help, and all the gods together, through their anger, emit a great brilliance (*tejas*), which fuses together "like a flaming mountain whose flames pervaded the entire sky" (2.11). This heap of brilliance becomes a beautiful woman, each part of her body formed from the brilliance of a particular god. Each god then gives her a weapon, ornament, or other emblem: Śiva gives her a trident, Kṛṣṇa a discus, the Himālaya a lion as her vehicle, and so on. The Goddess, her eyes burning with anger, then proceeds to demolish Mahiṣa's armies while her lion devours the dead bodies. Finally, she faces Mahiṣa himself, who in the course of the battle takes on successively the forms of a buffalo, a lion, a man holding a sword, an elephant, and again a buffalo. Pausing to guzzle wine and filling the sky with her eerie laughter, the Goddess places her foot on the buffalo demon's neck and pierces it with her trident. As the demon tries to emerge from the buffalo's mouth, the Goddess cuts off his head with a flourish. The gods praise her lavishly in a lengthy hymn, extolling her as the supreme protector and boon giver; she has saved the world from ruin and has even been gracious to the defeated demons, who go to heaven by being purified by her weapons. The gods ask her to return whenever they remember her. She agrees and then disappears.

The image of the Goddess as a warrior seated on a lion, her most sustained image in the *Devī Māhātmya,* is difficult to trace in earlier Sanskrit literature, although it was probably common in folk traditions. That it is also connected with royal traditions is evident from the almost identical description of the creation of a king from the collective powers of the gods found in the *Laws of Manu.*[16] It is not surprising that the Goddess would be portrayed according to a kingly model, for she is the supreme ruler and protector. Her paramountcy is obvious in that she is able to accomplish what the male deities could not.

The killing of the buffalo demon is the myth most commonly associated with the Goddess in post–*Devī Māhātmya* times, but unlike the Madhu–Kaiṭabha theme, there are few references to it in pre–*Devī Māhātmya* literature. In the *Mahābhārata* (3.221) it is Skanda, not the Goddess, who kills Mahisāsura after recognizing Śiva as his father.[17] It could be argued that the story of Devī killing Mahiṣāsura is an adapted form of the Skanda myth. The motif of a goddess slaying a buffalo, however, is of considerable antiquity, and iconographic evidence has been found that predates literary sources.[18]

The third episode moves even closer toward the terrestrial plane, as it takes place in the Himālaya, which is the "borderland" between the realm of humans and the realm of the gods. It is the longest of the three episodes, containing several episodes within it, and from a narrative point of view is the most complicated. It is also the most syncretic in that it introduces numerous individual goddesses, such as Kālī and Cāmuṇḍā, who are integrated into the total picture of the Goddess.

The story resumes after an indeterminate length of time when once again the gods are in trouble because the three worlds and the shares of the sacrifice have been snatched from them by demons, this time by the brothers Śumbha and Niśumbha. Remembering the Goddess's promise to return when needed, the gods go to the

Himālaya to invoke her as the "extremely gentle and extremely fierce" (5.11) Goddess Viṣṇumāyā who exists in all beings in the form of such multifarious qualities as consciousness, intelligence, sleep, hunger, shadow, *śakti,* desire, patience, production, modesty, faith, beauty, Lakṣmī, conduct, remembrance, mercy, satisfaction, mother, and mistake (5.13–32). As the gods were engaged in their praise, Pārvatī approached that spot to bathe in the Ganges. She asked the gods who they were praising. Then the beautiful Ambikā (also called Śivā or Kauśikī) emerged from Pārvatī's bodily sheath, saying that it was she whom the gods were invoking. Here the text states that Ambikā was created from Pārvatī's bodily sheath (*kośa*); therefore she is known as Kauśikī. When she emerged, Pārvatī became black and is therefore known as Kālikā. At this point Pārvatī–Kālikā plays no further part, and Ambikā–Kausikī takes over the action. Then Caṇḍa and Muṇḍa, the servants of Śumbha and Niśumbha, see the beautiful Ambikā and describe her to their masters. Śumbha sends these two to Ambikā with a message that she should choose either him or his brother to be her husband. The Goddess refuses, saying that she had long ago made a vow that she would marry only one who defeated her in battle. Hearing this, Śumbha and Niśumbha send out their general Dhūmralocana (Smokey-eyed) to capture her alive, but she slays him. Caṇḍa and Muṇḍa and their armies attack, and a bloody battle ensues. From her forehead, the Goddess produces a *śakti,* the goddess Kālī, who kills Caṇḍa and Muṇḍa, thus gaining the appellation Cāmuṇḍā.[19] As the battle continues, *śaktis* emerge from the bodies of seven male gods (who presumably have been nonparticipant observers up to this point). These are not consorts but the feminine essence of each god. They are the famous "Seven Mothers" (*saptamātṛkā*) of Hindu myth and iconography, designated in this text as Brahmāṇī (from Brahmā), Māheśvarī (from Śiva), Kaumārī (from Skanda), Vaiṣṇavī (from Viṣṇu), Vārāhī (from Viṣṇu's boar incarnation), Nārasiṃhī (from Viṣṇu's man–lion incarnation), and Aindrī (from Indra). In addition to these seven, the Goddess herself emits a *śakti* called Śivadūtī because she enlists Śiva as a messenger to challenge the demons to further battle. In a dramatic scene, the demon Raktabīja (Blood-drop) appears on the battlefield. This demon's claim to fame is that every drop of his blood that falls on the ground gives rise to another demon. Kālī saves the situation by drinking all his blood. With the help of the Seven Mothers, the Goddess kills

Niśumbha and the whole army, leaving Śumbha standing alone. When Śumbha taunts her that she is receiving help from so many other women, she says to him, "I am one. Where in this world is there another besides me? Look, O evil one, as these manifestations of mine enter back into me" (10.3). Then all the *śaktis* disappear into the body of the Goddess, and she alone defeats Śumbha.

The third episode concludes with the gods singing a lengthy hymn to the Goddess, the famous Nārāyaṇī Stuti, part of which appears at the beginning of this chapter, which summarizes the theological conception of the Goddess in the *Devī Māhātmya*. The Goddess then appears before them, in a manner reminiscent of the *Bhagavad Gītā,* saying that whenever evil threatens the world, she will reappear in the form of various incarnations (*avatāras*).

The names Śumbha and Niśumbha (and their variants Kumbha and Nikumbha) and other demons in the final episode are found in the *Mahābhārata* and *Rāmāyaṇa,* where they appear as minor demonic figures. The entire episode is a very complex myth, and the sorting out of the various goddesses and demons in it could be the subject of an entire study. One point I wish to mention here, however, is the intriguing connection of the Goddess in this episode with the legend of Kṛṣṇa Gopāla, pointing to the complex intertextuality of which the *Devī Māhātmya* is a part. During the narration of the episode itself, there is no mention of any possible connection, but in a later chapter when Devī is recounting her future *avatāras* she says, "When the 28th Yuga has arrived in the Vaisvata Manu period, two other great Asuras named Śumbha and Niśumbha will be born. Then born from the womb of Yaśodā in the house of the cow-herd king Nanda, dwelling on the Vindhya mountain, I shall destroy these two Asuras" (11.38–39). The *Harivaṃśa,* a roughly contemporaneous text, recounts that Viṣṇu went to the underworld and requested the aid of the goddess Nidrā (Sleep) to be born to Yaśodā. She would be switched with Kṛṣṇa, the eighth child of Devakī. Later, she would go to the Vindhya mountains and kill the demons Śumbha and Niśumbha.[20]

Thus, the *Devī Māhātmya* has integrated diverse myths in its portrayal of the Goddess. The Madhu–Kaiṭabha myth connects her with Viṣṇu/Nārāyaṇa, the Mahiṣāsura myth with Skanda, and the Śumbha–Niśumbha myth with Kṛṣṇa. Śiva, although he is closely identified with the Goddess in later mythology, as we will see in the story of the *śakti pīṭhas,* in this text has a very low profile. In the first episode he is completely absent. In the second episode he figures only as one of the many gods who help to produce Devī. In the third episode Pārvatī, who in other contexts is the wife of Śiva, appears, but after Kauśikī (Ambikā–Caṇḍikā) emerges from her body, she plays no further part in the action. Furthermore, Pārvatī seems not to have been brought in because of her association with Śiva (since he is not described as her husband) but because of her association with the Himālaya. Śiva appears one other time in a role unflattering to him, when he is dispatched as a messenger to Śumbha and Niśumbha by Devī's *śakti,* Śivadūtī.

Although in the *Devī Māhātmya* the Goddess is more closely associated with Viṣṇu than with Śiva, the major purpose of the text is not to associate her with any particular male god but to show her as the ultimate reality who is both immanent and transcendent, who is the grantor of both material pleasures and liberation. The *Devī Māhātmya* scrupulously avoids portraying any of the goddesses as consorts of the male gods. Even the Seven Mothers emanate from the god's bodies as their own power of activity, not as their consorts. Furthermore, the notion of *śakti* is not limited to the female manifestation of a male god. The Goddess is able to produce her own *śaktis* such as Kālī and Śivadūtī. Likewise, even though the Seven Mothers have emerged from the bodies of the male gods, when they are recalled to their origin, they go back into the body of the Goddess herself. Thus as Coburn has pointed out, the *Devī Māhātmya* does not put forth the conception well known to later Śākta and Tantric texts that *śakti* is feminine and its possessor (*śaktimān*) is masculine, for the Goddess who is the embodiment of *śakti* is also herself the possessor of *śakti.* This point is important to remember in the context of the Panjab Hills Goddess cult, whose theology tends more toward the vision of a holistic Śakti than toward the male–female Śiva–Śakti polarity.

Besides being included as part of a Purāṇa and having importance from a mythological and theological point of view, the *Devī Māhātmya* has an independent liturgical life of its own. As well as being a written document, its importance in subsequent times has been in the form of oral transmission through ritual recitation. The ritual significance of the text is pointed out in the twelfth chapter of the text itself when the Goddess says that those who recite or listen to her *Māhātmya* with devotion on the eighth, fourteenth, or ninth days of the lunar fortnight, at the time of offering an animal sacrifice, during a fire sacrifice, or during the autumn worship (the

Navarātra), will have all their afflictions removed and all their wishes fulfilled. In the thirteenth and final chapter, the king Suratha and the merchant Samādhi, having heard all the exploits of the Goddess, set out to attain her *darśan.* Seated on a riverbank, they chant her praises as the gods had done and make an earthen image of her, worshiping it with flowers, incense, fire, sprinkled water, and blood from their own bodies. After three years the Goddess appears and grants them boons. The king would regain his kingdom and be reborn in the future as Sāvarṇi Manu, the universal ruler. The merchant is granted the knowledge that would cut the bonds of attachment and lead to liberation.

In the ritual setting, the text is usually called *Durgā-saptaśatī, Durgā-pāṭha,* or *Caṇḍī-pāṭha.* The word *saptaśatī* (seven hundred) refers to the number of verses (*ślokas*), fitting it into the pattern of a text such as the *Bhāgavad Gītā,* which also has seven hundred verses. The text actually contains somewhat fewer than six hundred verses, the remainder being made up by counting stage directions and splitting some of the verses for numbering purposes. It has intrinsic potency as a collection of *mantras* and is recited as a way of pleasing the Goddess. It is also meant to be understood for its meaning; in editions published for ritual use, a translation is provided in the vernacular. P. V. Kane points out that the *Durgā-saptaśatī* is in some ways treated as a Vedic hymn, being lifted from its *smṛti* context as part of a Purāṇa and functioning as *śruti* in the ritual context.[21] In editions intended for recitation, each important division in the text is preceded by a *viniyoga* verse that specifies the Ṛṣi (seer), deity, meter, and the purpose of its recitation, just as is the case for Vedic hymns. In addition, numerous Tantric features accompany the recitation of the text. These include the Goddess's nine-syllable *mantra* (Oṃ Aiṃ Hrīṃ Klīṃ Cāmuṇḍāyai Vicce), *nyāsa* (blessing each part of the body) and special protective recitations such as the *kavaca* (armor), *argala* (bolt for fastening), and *kīlaka* (pin, the inner syllable of a *mantra*). A different *dhyānam* or verse describing the iconography of a manifestation of the Goddess is recited before each chapter. The *Devī Māhātmya* can be recited by oneself or by a Brahmin recitant (*pāṭhaka* or *vācaka*) hired for the occasion. Usually it is done on all nine days of the Navarātra, followed by a fire sacrifice (*havan*) on the tenth day, or on a selected day during that time. It can also be recited at any other time, particularly in fulfillment of a vow.[22] Ritual editions of the text contain directions for its recitation as well as for the more elaborate and time-consuming *śatacaṇḍī* and *lakṣacaṇḍī*, hundred- and thousand-fold recitations.

The *Devī Māhātmya* takes on further ritual and theological significance by its division into three episodes (*caritas*), each governed by one of the three cosmic forms of the Devī associated with one of the three *guṇas* (qualities). Thus, the first episode is that of Mahākālī, who is black and has the nature of *tamas* (lethargy, inertia). The second is that of Mahālakṣmī, who is red and has the nature of *rajas* (activity, passion). The third is that of Mahāsarasvatī, who is white and has the nature of *sattva* (purity). Mahālakṣmī, however, is also the original form, the first cause who is endowed with all three *guṇas*. This scheme has been elaborated in the *Rahasya Traya* (Threefold Mystery), a short text of unknown date that is recited after the *Devī Māhātmya* and considered an integral part of the text by Hindu commentators. The *Rahasya Traya* serves as an esoteric interpretation of the *Devī Māhātmya*, putting the Goddess into a cosmogonic and ritual–soteriological framework. The dynamic of the text follows the same pattern as that of the *Devī Māhātmya*, being divided into three parts. The *Pradhānika Rahasya* (Prime Mystery), like the first episode of the *Devī Māhātmya*, is a creation myth in which the cosmogonic importance of the Goddess is stressed. It describes Mahālakṣmī's creation of Mahākālī and Mahāsarasvatī and their subsequent creation of male and female deities who created the world. The *Vaikṛtika Rahasya* (Mystery of Manifestations), like the second episode of the *Devī Māhātmya*, brings the discussion closer to the human sphere with a description of the iconographic forms of the three cosmic manifestations (Mahālakṣmī, Mahākālī, and Mahāsarasvatī), their activities, and the methods of worshiping them. The *Mūrti Rahasya* (Mystery of Forms), like the third episode of the *Devī Māhātmya*, is even closer to the mundane level, being a discussion of the earthly, immanent incarnations of the Goddess. References to this tripartate structure appear again and again in the Panjab Hills Goddess cult, for example in the three rock images at the Vaiṣṇo Devī shrine and in the organizational schemes of the popular pilgrimage pamphlets.

Embodiment of Divinity: Theological Concepts

At this point it will be useful to discuss some key concepts associated with Śākta theology, that is, the theology of the Goddess as supreme being. That is not to say that all devotees will necessarily subscribe to such views or be able to articulate them, but rather that they are imbedded in the texts, stories, and songs connected with the Goddess. By separating these concepts out and discussing them here in this rather abstract fashion, I seek not only to provide a bit of background but to highlight concepts that will crop up repeatedly, often in very condensed form, in the mass of ethnographic material I present in the following chapters.

Implicit in this Goddess theology is a kind of monism in which matter and spirit are not differentiated but are a continuity subsumed within *śakti,* the dynamic feminine creative principle. Whereas the Śaiva and Vaiṣṇava theologies associated with the male deities Śiva and Viṣṇu both recognize *śakti,* to be the active aspect of the Divine, the complement to the inactive aspect, Śākta theology understands *śakti,* identified with the Great Goddess, to be the ultimate reality itself and the totality of all being. Wendell Beane has rightly stated that *śakti* is the "irreducible (*sui generis*) ground for understanding both the non-Sanskritic, popular, exoteric and the Sanskritic, philosophical, esoteric" aspects of the worship of the Divine Feminine.[23]

Although Śākta theology has much in common with the formal philosophical systems of dualistic Sāṃkhya and monistic Advaita Vedānta, it differs from them in its relentless exaltation of the material world. It is more thoroughly "world-affirming" than either of them. The Goddess is often identified with Prakṛti, the matter–energy that is the basis of all creation. In the Sāṃkhya system and the Yoga school based on it, Prakṛti has a somewhat negative connotation; it is seen as the web of matter in which the spirit, Puruṣa, is entrapped. Liberation in Sāṃkhya–Yoga terms is the isolation (*kaivalya*) of Puruṣa (literally, the male) from Prakṛti. This formulation is similar to the Greek (and subsequently Christian) identification of the male with spirit and the female with matter, with the devaluation of the latter. Śāktism turns this concept of Prakṛti on its head, giving it not only ontological and cosmogonic status but soteriological status by identifying it with the Great Goddess, who pervades the phenomenal world and saves all beings.[24] As Prakṛti, the Goddess contains within herself the three *guṇas,* personified as her three major manifestations: Mahālakṣmī, Mahākālī, and Mahāsarasvatī. From the Śākta point of view, Puruṣa and Prakṛti are ultimately the same, or rather Prakṛti contains within her Puruṣa.

Similarly, the Goddess is identified with *māyā,* one of her major epithets being Mahāmāyā. This term is most closely associated with the Advaita Vedānta school, where it refers to the illusion or ignorance that prevents one from seeing things the way they really are. According to the Advaitins, *brahman,* the nonmaterial absolute, is the only real entity; it is only by overcoming *māyā* (which has no reality in any case) that one can attain liberation. The Śākta idea of *māyā,* as in the first episode of the *Devī Māhātmya,* retains some of the negative connotation. But as the power of the Goddess that animates the world, *māyā* is a necessary part of existence and thus is considered her blessing.

In some contexts the Goddess is also equated with *brahman.* This is not surprising, as *brahman* from the time of the *Upaniṣads* on has been the most commonly accepted term in Hinduism for the ultimate reality.[25] *Brahman* has been described in two ways, *nirguṇa* (beyond all qualities) and *saguṇa* (having qualities). As *nirguṇa,* it is the basis of all existence yet defies all description; as *saguṇa* it manifests in the form of various deities. Some texts, despite their elaborate descriptions of the Goddess's feminine *saguṇa* manifestations, state that ultimately she is beyond the distinction of male and female.[26] Śāktism and Advaita are both monistic. The difference between them is that Advaita sees only *brahman* as real; the material world is ultimately unreal. Śāktism, on the other hand, recognizes the world as real and says that it is ultimately identical to *brahman.*

The general thrust, then, of Goddess theology is to affirm the reality, power, and life force that pervade the material world. Matter itself, while always changing, is sacred and is not different from spirit. The Goddess is the totality of all existence. Thus, as a reflection of how things really are, she takes on both gentle (*saumya*) and fierce (*raudra*) forms. Creation and destruction, life and death, are two sides of reality. The Goddess encompasses both.

Divinization of Matter: The *Śakti Pīṭhas*

The idea of the Goddess as dynamic force inherent in matter is given further expression in the myth and ritual of the *śakti pīṭhas* (places of power). The image of the earth itself and, more particularly, the land of India as a goddess is ancient and pervasive in the Hindu tradition. Similarly, the idea that certain geographical features such as mountains, rivers, lakes, and caves are a manifestation of the sacred is one of great antiquity. These geographical hierophanies have become objects of worship in themselves. While they are often associated with a particular deity or saint, it is the place itself that is sacred. In Hinduism there developed an elaborate system of pilgrimage to *tīrthas,* literally river fords, places where one can "cross over" from the human realm to the divine realm.

At some point the worship of the Goddess became associated with a formal system of *pīṭhas* (seats, abodes), places that enshrine parts of her body. The earliest reference to *pīṭhas* is in the *Hevajra Tantra* (seventh century), which lists four: (1) Jālandhara (in the Panjab Hills), (2) Oḍiyāna (or Uḍḍiyāna in the Swat Valley), (3) Pūrṇagiri (location unknown), and (4) Kāmarūpa (in Assam). A system of four *pīṭhas* is common to both Hindu and Buddhist Tantric texts and may have some connection with legends that the Buddha's body was divided at his death and enshrined in *stūpas.*[27]

The mythical source for the *pīṭha* scheme is the story of Satī and the destruction of Dakṣa's fire sacrifice, a story found in germ form in the Brāhmaṇas and in more elaborate form in most of the Purāṇas in numerous variations. The most extensive work on *śakti pīṭhas* has been done by D. C. Sircar, who has painstakingly traced the development of this myth. The following is extracted from his classic account:

> The earliest form of the legend of *Dakṣa-yajña-nāśa* is probably to be traced in the *Mahābhārata* (XII, chapters 282–83; cf. *Brahma Purāṇa,* ch. 39) and a slightly modified form is found in many of the Purāṇas (*Matsya,* ch. 12; *Padma, Sṛṣṭkhaṇḍa,* ch. 5; *Kūrma* I, ch. 15; *Brahmāṇḍa,* ch. 31, etc.) as well as in the *Kumārasambhava* (I, 21) of Kālidāsa who flourished in the fourth and fifth centuries. . . . According to this modified from of the legend, the mother-goddess, who was the wife of Śiva, was in the form of Satī one of the daughters of Dakṣa Prajāpati. Dakṣa was celebrating a great sacrifice for which neither Satī nor Śiva was invited. Satī, however, went to her father's sacrifice uninvited, but was greatly insulted by Dakṣa. As a result of this ill-treatment, Satī is said to have died by *yoga* or of a broken heart, or, as Kālidāsa says, she put herself into the fire and perished. . . . When the news of Satī's death reached her husband, Śiva is said to have become furious and hastened to the scene with his numerous attendants. The sacrifice of Prajāpati Dakṣa was completely destroyed. Śiva, according to some of the sources, decapitated Dakṣa who was afterward restored to life and thenceforward acknowledged the superiority of Śiva to all the gods.[28]

It is clear that these versions of the story are told from a sectarian point of view in order to establish the superiority of Śiva. Later versions, however, take on a distinctly Śākta slant as the narrative centers on Satī rather than Śiva. Sircar continues:

> In still later times, probably about the earlier part of the medieval period, a new legend was engrafted to the old story simply for the sake of explaining the origin of the Pīṭhas. According to certain later Purāṇas and Tantras (*Devī Bhāgavata,* VII, ch. 30; *Kālikā Purāṇa,* ch. 18, etc.), Śiva became inconsolable at the death of his beloved wife Satī, and, after the destruction of Dakṣa's sacrifice, he wandered over the earth in a mad dance with Satī's dead body on his shoulder (or, head). The gods now became anxious to free Śiva from his infatuation and made a conspiracy to deprive him of his wife's dead body. Thereupon Brahman, Viṣṇu and Śani entered the dead body by *yoga* and disposed of it gradually and bit by bit. The places where pieces of Satī's dead body fell are said to have become Pīṭhas, i.e., holy seats or resorts of the mother-goddess, in all of which she is represented to be constantly living in some form together with a Bhairava, i.e., a form of her husband Śiva. According to a modified version of this story, it was Viṣṇu who, while following Śiva cut Satī's dead body on Śiva's shoulder or head piece by piece by his arrows or his discus.

According to various schemes there are 4, 7, 8, 42, 51, or 108 of these *pīṭhas,* lists reflecting the local loyalties and perhaps literary license of the writer. The scheme has also passed into local and regional oral traditions, with Goddess shrines all over India being counted among the *śakti pīṭhas* whether or not there is any textual basis for doing so. It is clear that the myth serves to both enhance the importance of Satī over Śiva (as is graphically portrayed by his placing her on his head) and to integrate various local goddess shrines into the body of the Goddess. The myth also is an example of universalization by division.[29] It is an inversion of the *Devī Māhātmya* myth in which the Goddess is put together limb by limb through the efforts of the gods. Here she is dismembered piece by piece and distributed throughout the landscape. The places where her limbs fell, however, are alive with her presence and thus infused with *śakti.*

Dismemberment is an extremely archaic motif in the history of religions, being found in Southeast Asia, Oceania, North and South America, and the ancient Middle East. Mircea Eliade writes that the *pīṭha* system in India is an example of the coalescence among the Great Goddess and fertility cults and popular *yoga,* for the *pīṭhas* were places of pilgrimage for Śāktas and Tantrics. He adds that most of them were aniconic altars that had acquired rank as holy places by virtue of the fact that ascetics and *yogīs* had meditated and obtained special powers (*siddhis*) there.[30] Sircar speculates that the earliest *pīṭhas* were associated with the phallus (*liṅga*) of a male god, and the female organs (*yoni*) and breasts of a goddess. Hills and mountains were regarded as self-born *liṅgas,* tanks and pools as *yonis,* and a pair of hills as breasts. Water coming out of the springs in these hills would be regarded as the goddess's milk. These male and female hierophanies, he theorizes, were worshiped by the pre-Aryans.[31] Whatever their origins, it is clear that the *pīṭhas* express a worldview in which the earth is considered sacred and the deity embodies herself in earthly form.

Sources vary as to which part of Satī fell where, although the *yoni* is invariably placed at Kāmarūpa in Assam.[32] Popular pamphlet literature and oral tradition of the Panjab Hills Goddess cult adopt the *pīṭha* scheme, the general consensus being that Satī's tongue fell at Jvālā Mukhī, breast at Kāṅgṛevālī Devī, eyes at Nainā Devī, arms at Vaiṣṇo Devī, feet at Cintpūrṇī, and forehead at Mansā Devī. Only the first two of these are attested to in the Sanskrit Purāṇic and Tantric literature. According to the *Pīṭhanirṇaya,* the Tantric text that represents the culmination of the *pīṭha* tradition, Jvālā Mukhī is the place where the tongue (*jihvā*) fell and where the Goddess resides under the name of Siddhidā (giver of powers) or Ambikā (mother) accompanied by the Bhairava Unmatta. According to the same text, Jālandhara (identified with modern-day Kangra and Kāṅgṛevālī Devī) is where the breast (*stana*) fell and where the Goddess resides under the names of Tripuramālinī or Tripuranāsinī (destroyer of the three worlds) accompanied by the Bhairava Bhīṣaṇa or Īsāna. Nowadays Kāṅgṛevālī Devī is known by the name Vajresvarī. Jālandhara Pīṭha is said to have been the center of the Kapālika cult and of Vajrayāna.[33] All of these names suggest strong Tantric connections.

Besides these, other *pīṭhas* are located in the northwest, such as Bhīmastāna (in Peshawar) and Hing Lāj (in Baluchistan). Numerous other place-names suggest the popularity of Goddess worship in the northwest. A historian of the Sikh religion has written:

> Very few people pause to consider . . . the significance of such toponyms in this region as, for instance, Ambala which is derived from Ambā, one of the many names of Durgā, Chandigarh which is named after Caṇḍī, Panchkula (a growing village between Kalka and Chandigarh), a technical term of unmistakable Tāntric significance, Kalka which is a vulgarization of Kālikā, Simla which is Syāmalā Devī in its anglicized version. A careful look at the postal directories of the Punjab, Hariyana, and Himachal would yield a long list of such toponyms from which one may draw one's own conclusion. Besides, throughout these regions one still finds countless numbers of small, lowly shrines with all but shapeless of crude form [*sic*] placed on their altars, which worshippers, lowly village folks, describe as Manasā, Caṇḍī, Kālī, Naynā, Durgā, etc.[34]

Research indicates that the Panjab Hills, with their connection to Jālandhara Pīṭha,[35] and indeed the whole northwest of India were in the medieval period a hotbed of Tantric activity. In this connection, Sircar writes:

> The greatest center of Tāntricism seems to have originally been in north-western India. Before the Medieval period, the Tāntric school of the north-east rose to eminence and became a great rival to the north-western school. With the gradual decline of Tāntric culture in the north-west as a result of foreign occupation, Bengal seems to have come to the forefront as the abode of great leaders of Tāntric thought.[36]

The foreign occupation that Sircar speaks of was the Muslim rule that was established most strongly in the northwest, beginning in the eleventh century. Goddess worship on both the popular and esoteric levels has been exposed to numerous religious movements over the centuries, including Islam, sectarian Vaiṣṇavism, Sikhism, Christianity, and most recently the Ārya Samāj. In spite of the northwest's decline as an esoteric Tantric center, traces of which still remain, the Śākta tradition infused with popular *bhakti* devotionalism continues to be a vital religious force. It is to this popular cult that we now turn our attention.

2

Speaking of the Goddess

Stories of the Seven Sisters

In this chapter I turn the discussion from the broad outlines of pan-Indian Śākta myth and theology to the local stories of the Goddess's manifestations in the greater Panjab area. Here we will meet Śerāṅvālī, the lion rider, in her various forms. I have adopted the scheme of the Seven Sisters as an organizing principle, for it is a very common way in the northwest, as in other regions of India, of speaking of collectivities of goddesses. Why the number seven? The most likely explanation is that it is connected with the Saptamātrikās (Seven Little Mothers) of Purāṇic fame, but I think it also has to do with seven as a number of completion and wholeness, which also suggests multiplicity. There are many goddesses, far more than seven, who are all connected with each other and who are all ultimately manifestations of the one Great Goddess. Seven is an auspicious number to use when speaking of them collectively. That may account for the difficulty some devotees have in naming all seven and for the variation in lists. Devotees are generally aware that there are Seven Sisters but will often vary the list to include a favorite goddess or simply to round it out with the name of a goddess with which they are familiar. As an informant once told me, "Everyone knows that there are Seven Sisters, but who will be able to name them?" The seven I have chosen to discuss here are those most often listed in the popular pilgrimage pamphlets of the region and those with which I am most familiar. They are Vaiṣṇo Devī, Jvālā Mukhī, Kāṅgṛevālī Devī, Cintpūrṇī, Nainā Devī,

Mansā Devī, and Cāmuṇḍā Devī, each of which is the name of both a physical place where a temple is located and a goddess with a unique story and personality.[1] I will discuss each temple separately, paying special attention to the founding myth or legend but also including details concerning the unique features of each temple.

Vaiṣṇo Devī

While not as ancient as some of the other Goddess temples, Vaiṣṇo Devī in recent years has become the most popular in the regional cult and has even achieved some national recognition. She is often considered the eldest of the Seven Sisters. The shrine lies on the outer hills bounding the valley of Kashmir and the plains of Jammu. It is situated on the side of a mountain called Trikuṭ because of its three conical peaks. At the foot of the mountain is the thriving pilgrimage town of Katra, District Jammu, which serves as a bazaar, lodging place, and base camp for pilgrims going to Vaiṣṇo Devī. The area is dominated by the Dogra caste, famous for its martial abilities and its devotion to the Goddess. No one knows how old the shrine is, but Guru Nānak (1469–1539), founder of the Sikhs, and Nām Dev (1270–1350), the Maharashtrian saint, are said to have visited there.[2] Frederic Drew, who was employed by Maharaja Ranbir Singh in the 1860s, wrote of Vaiṣṇo Devī,

> In the beginning of the hot weather [Navarātras of Caitra, the month of March/April], one everyday sees passing through Jammoo numbers of people from the plains, mostly of about the rank of shopkeepers, on their way to this place, with their wives and families, the women mounted astride a pony and supporting a child or two.[3]

The Vaiṣṇo Devī shrine has traditionally received patronage from the maharajas of Jammu and Kashmir, and for over 150 years was administered by the Dharmarth Trust founded by Ranbir Singh's father, Maharaja Gulab Singh, in about 1830 for the maintenance of various shrines. The present trustee of the Dharmarth Trust is his descendant Dr. Karan Singh. In 1986 the governor of Jammu and Kashmir handed over control of the shrine to an independent statutory board in response to public outcry at mismanagement of funds by the *bārīdārs* (turn takers), hereditary priests of the shrine.[4]

Although popular pamphlets fit Vaiṣṇo Devī into the *śakti pīṭha* scheme by attesting it to be the place where Satī's arms fell, the arms play no further part in the myth or cult of the shrine. A more common way of integrating her with the other goddesses of the area is to call her the eldest of the Seven Sisters. Vaiṣṇo Devī is particularly well known for ritual purity, the name Vaiṣṇo, as discussed already, denoting her vegetarian status. The deity is worshiped here in the form of three *piṇḍīs* (stone outcroppings), which represent the three cosmic forms of *śakti*—Mahākālī, Mahālākṣmī (the middle *piṇḍī,* who is also called Vaiṣṇo Devī), and Mahāsarasvatī. These three forms of the Goddess are the same as those figuring in the *Rahasya Traya,* the companion text to the *Devī Māhātmya* discussed in chapter 1. Vaiṣṇo Devī is said to be the only shrine in India where the three cosmic *śaktis* are naturally manifested. It is also significant that the middle *piṇḍī,* Mahālakṣmī, is most closely identified with Vaiṣṇo Devī, since Mahālakṣmī not only governs the episode of the *Devī Māhātmya* in which the demon Mahiṣa is slayed but is also said to be the original manifestation of *śakti.*

The three *piṇḍīs* are enshrined at the end of a ninety-foot tunnel through which pilgrims must crawl in order to receive *darśan.* In 1976 the Dharmarth Trust built an opening at the end of the tunnel, making the flow of pilgrims easier to control and allowing as many as 5,600 per day to visit the shrine.[5] The popularity of Vaiṣṇo Devī has grown tremendously in recent years. According to an article in the *Times of India,* in 1977, 900,000 people visited the shrine; ten years before that only 50,000 did so.[6] One reason is that Vaiṣṇo Devī has become more accessible since the opening of a railhead from Pathankot to Jammu in 1972. Several of my informants also mentioned that prior to partition in 1947, mainly people from West Panjab (now in Pakistan) made pilgrimages to the shrine, but that after partition the West Panjabis who settled in East Panjab, Delhi, Uttari Pradesh, and other places influenced the local people to make the pilgrimage as well. Vaiṣṇo Devī appeals to people of all castes and walks of life, from the Delhi rickshaw driver who sports a decal with the slogan *jay mātā dī* to the rising urban middle-class professional to the high-ranking government official.[7] Vaiṣṇo Devī has captured the imagination of the popular media as well. For example, the Hindi film *Āṣā* (ca. 1979) featured a segment in which the hero and heroine make a pilgrimage to Vaiṣṇo Devī, to the accompaniment of playback singer Narendra Chanchal singing in Hindi "You Called Me, O Serāṅvālī" (*tū ne mujhe bulāyā,* Serāṅvālīye).

Oral and written sources for the myths of Vaiṣṇo Devī are reasonably homogenous. The written sources consist of popular bazaar pamphlets in colloquial Hindi, which pilgrims buy and read as part of the pilgrimage experience. Most of these popular pamphlets start out by telling the story of the Great Goddess as it appears in the second and third episodes of the Sanskrit text *Devī Māhātmya,* that is, of her creation through the combined powers of the gods and her killing of the demons Mahiṣāsura, Śumbha, and Niśumbha. The inclusion of these mythic episodes clearly identifies Vaiṣṇo Devī as an aspect of the pan-Indian Great Goddess.

The story more immediately relevant to the cult of Vaiṣṇo Devī concerns her birth and establishment in the sacred geography of Trikuṭ mountain. The first episode of this story, detailing her birth and apotheosis, takes place in the Treṭā Yuga, connecting Vaiṣṇo Devī with Viṣṇu and the *Rāmāyaṇa.* The second episode, detailing the founding and discovery of the shrine, occurs in the present Kali Yuga, connecting Vaiṣṇo Devī with Bhairo and the Nāth sect of yogis.

The following is an abridgment of the story taken from a popular pamphlet in Hindi:[8]

> From time to time Mahāśakti takes on different forms to destroy evildoers and protect devotees. At different times this Mahāśakti who was born of the accumulated brilliance (*tej*) of the gods has taken on the forms of Mahākālī, Mahālakṣmī, and Mahāsarasvatī, the symbols of *raj, tam,* and *sāttvik* qualities.[9]
>
> In the Treṭā Yuga, when Rāvaṇ and the other demons worked their evil, the three Mahāśaktis, in order to protect the *dharm,* pooled their powers and produced a *śakti* in the form of a beautiful divine maiden (*kanyā*). They sent her to take birth in South India as the daughter of one Ratnasāgar. She was given the name Trikuṭā. Later she became known as Vaiṣṇavī or Vaiṣṇo, because she had been produced as a part (*aṃś*) of Viṣṇu.[10]
>
> At a very young age, the goddess Trikuṭā had already distinguished herself with supernatural (*alaukik*) powers and was attracting holy men and devotees from far away who came seeking her *darśan.* After some time, Trikuṭā, with her father's permission, went to the oceanside to perform austerities while meditating on Lord Rām and waiting for him. After Sītā had been abducted by Rāvaṇ, Rām passed her way with his army of monkeys and saw the divine maiden seated in a deep trance

(*samādhi*). She told him that she was performing austerities in order to obtain him as her husband. Rām replied that he had made a vow to remain faithful to only one wife, Sītā, in this incarnation. But Trikuṭā would not change her mind. Finally, Rām promised that he would return later and marry her if she would recognize him. While returning to Ayodhya from Lanka, Rām appeared before her in the guise of an old man, but she did not recognize him. Rām consoled her by promising that in the Kali Yug when he would incarnate as Kalkī, she would be his consort. In the meantime, she should go to a cave on Trikuṭ mountain in North India where the three Mahāśaktis live and perform austerities there. Sending Hanumān and the other monkeys to be her sentries, he told her that she would become famous as Vaiṣṇo Devī.

In this way, it is believed that the Goddess became established in her cave. With the passing of the ages, the Mother showed her divine play (*līlā*) and other stories arose. In the Kali Yug the following story has become well known:

About seven hundred years ago, in Hansali village near Katra there lived a Brahmin named Śrīdhar who was a great devotee of the Mother. One day he was performing a *kanyā pūjā* [worship of small girls as manifestations of the Goddess] in order to obtain a son. When Śrīdhar began to feed the girls, Vaiṣṇo Devī in the form of a divine maiden appeared among them. She ordered him to host a grand feast for his village and the surrounding area the following day. He knew that she must be some kind of *śakti* so he went from village to village inviting people to the feast. On the road he met a group of mendicants led by Gorakhnāth and invited them as well. Gorakhnāth issued a challenge that Śrīdhar would never be able to satisfy him, his disciple Bhaironāth, and his 360 other disciples, as even Indra himself had been unable to satisfy them.

The next day when the guests began to arrive, Śrīdhar was worried that he would not be able to feed them all, but they all managed to fit into his tiny hut and the divine maiden began to serve everyone food. When she started to serve Bhaironāth, he objected to the vegetarian fare, demanding to be served meat and wine. The maiden replied that this is a Brahmin's house and that one should accept whatever is offered in a *vaiṣṇava* feast. Bhairo became angry and tried to grab her, but she was able to read the evil desires in his mind and disappeared.

Bhairo set out in search of her, stopping at stations along the way [each of which is now a feature of the pilgrimage route]. The first place was Darśanī Darvāzā where one catches the first glimpse of Trikut mountain. Farther along the route, the Goddess struck a rock with her arrow [*bān*] in order to produce water for her thirsty companion Laṅgur Vīr [a form of Hanumān]. This stream is now known as the Bān Gaṅgā. At a place farther up the mountain, the Goddess looked back to see if Bhairo was still following her. Because her footprints are still there, the place is called Caraṇ Pādukā. After some time, she came upon a small cave and climbed inside. Just as a child remains in its mother's womb for nine months, so did the maiden remain in the cave for nine months performing austerities. Bhairo also arrived there and inquired from a nearby mendicant if he had seen a maiden. The mendicant said, "The one whom you consider to be an ordinary woman is actually the Mahāśakti and Ādikumārī [primeval virgin]." But Bhairo ignored him and entered the cave. The Mother used her trident to make an opening and emerge from the other end of the cave. This cave is now called Garbh-jūn [Sanskrit: Garbha-yoni], and the place is called Ādikumārī.

Bhairo continued to follow her even though she kept telling him to go back. Mahāmāyā [Great Illusion] was capable of doing whatever she wanted, but Bhairo's desire was also true! Finally, the Goddess entered a beautiful cave on Trikuṭ mountain, posting Laṅgur Vīr at the door as a guard. Bhairo attacked and almost killed him. At that point, Śakti took on the form of Caṇḍī [a fierce form of the Goddess] and cut off his head. The head fell into the valley below, while the body remained at the entrance to the cave where it can be seen today as a large boulder. As his head was severed, Bhairo yelled out, "O Ādi Śakti [Primeval Energy], O Generous Mother, I am not sorry to meet death, because it is at the hands of the Mother who created the world. O Māteśvarī [Mother-Lord], forgive me. I was not familiar with this form of yours. Ma, if you don't forgive me, then the coming age will view me as a sinner and castigate my name. A mother can never be a bad mother."[11] Hearing these words again and again, the gracious Mother gave him the boon that after worshiping her people would also worship him and that he would also attain *mokṣa* [liberation]. If people worshiped at his shrine, their wishes would be fulfilled. A temple was built where Bhairo's head fell, and pilgrims stop there today on their way back from Vaiṣṇo Devī's temple.

In another version of the story,[12] a multiform of Bhaironāth appears as Bhairo Bali or Bhairav Bali, an evil king who tortured followers of the Vaiṣṇava tradition. The episode occurs also in the Kali Yuga but before and in addition to the episode with

Bhaironāth. The king Bhairo Bali controlled a kingdom from the Satluj to the Jhelum rivers in the Panjab. One day Vaiṣṇo Devī held a feast. Bhairo Bali saw her and wanted to marry her, but she refused, so he chased her up the mountain. On the way the Goddess liberated many places from the rule of the evil king and established goddesses there. In this version the story continues in the same way summarized above, repeating the section on Bhaironāth.

After Vaiṣṇo Devī's beheading of Bhaironāth, the story continues:

> Meanwhile, the devotee Śrīdhar who had hosted the feast was so upset when the divine maiden disappeared that he stopped eating and drinking. To show him her grace, the Mother appeared before him in a dream and showed him her cave dwelling, taking him through the whole pilgrimage route. Upon awaking, Śrīdhar searched for the cave he had seen in his dream. He eventually found it and received there a face-to-face vision [*sākṣāt darśan*] of the Mother. She gave him a boon of four sons and instructed him to continue worshiping her. Thus, Śrīdhar is credited with the propagation of Vaiṣṇo Devī worship, and the present-day temple priests trace their descent from him.

It is very tempting to read this charter myth historically as a chronicle of the tension between Vaiṣṇava and Śākta or Tantric values. From this point of view, the references to Rām and Śrīdhar represent a later Vaiṣṇava strand in which vegetarianism and chastity are predominant themes, while the references to Bhairo represent a Śākta or Tantric strand in which blood sacrifice, sexual union, and the theme of the Goddess slaying the buffalo demon are dominant. It is a well-known fact that Śāktism predates Vaiṣṇavism as the dominant cult of the Panjab Hills. Art historian Karuna Goswamy places the beginnings of Vaiṣṇavism in the Panjab Hills between 1625 and 1660 through the efforts of missionaries from the plains.[13] She cites Vaiṣṇo Devī as an exception to the rule that the Goddess is worshiped in the hills in her fierce sacrifice-accepting form, saying that she represents a fusion of Vaiṣṇava and Śākta beliefs.[14] Similarly, Madhu Wangu demonstrates how in nineteenth-century Kashmir, the Dogri maharajas of Jammu grafted the worship of their Vaiṣṇava deity Rāma onto an indigenous goddess cult.[15]

However, it is impossible to separate Vaiṣṇavism and Śāktism absolutely. All Hindu myths are syncretic, and as we have seen in chapter 1, the earliest texts about the Goddess, such as the *Devī Māhātmya,* connect her more closely with Viṣṇu than they do with Śiva. Furthermore, on a structural level, the two conflicting sets of values are reconciled through the theology of *bhakti,* a theme I explore more thoroughly in chapter 7. Bhairo receives *mokṣa,* while Śrīdhar is granted *darśan* and the boon of sons,[16] just as in the *Devī Māhātmya* the merchant receives *mokṣa* and the king is made the next universal ruler.

Jvālā Mukhī

This shrine, whose name means "Flame mouth," is built into a cave where flames emerge mysteriously from the earth.[17] According to some sources there are seven flames, analogous to the Seven Sisters; according to others there are nine flames, analogous to the Nine Goddesses or Nine Durgās.[18] These flames (*jvālā*), the object of worship, are said to be the tongue of Satī, which fell here after her dismemberment.[19] Also known as Jalpā or Jvālājī, Jvālā Mukhī, in the village of Darang, Tahsil Dera Gopipur, District Kangra, is the most famous of the temples in this study and the most clearly attested to in Sanskrit sources. According to S. M. Bhardwaj, the site is mentioned in the *Mahābhārata* as Vadava, presided over by the "deity of seven flames."[20] Along with her sister Kāṅgṛevālī Devī or Vajreśvarī, with whom she is sometimes confused, she is associated with the celebrated Jālandhara Pīṭha of the Tantric texts. Bharati points out the Buddhist significance of the shrine, describing Jvālā Mukhī as

> one of the four great *pīṭhas* in Buddhist and Hindu tantrism; the tantric significance of the site is lost to most Hindus, and the Panjabi *khattri* caste has the heads of their sons shaved at the place. . . . The site is connected with Jalandharipa, one of Milarepa's spiritual preceptors, and he figures importantly in the accounts of the 84 siddhas in Tibetan hagiological literature. The Tibetan[s] worship this goddess as "me lee zhal mo." The shrine is visited by Tibetan pilgrims from Lahul, Panjab [now Himachal Pradesh], an ethnically and linguistically Tibetan area about 150 miles due north of Jalandhara.[21]

Abul Fazul in the *'Ain-i-Akbarī* (sixteenth century) refers to Jvālā Mukhī as follows:

> Torch-like flames issue from the ground in some places, and others resemble the blaze of lamps. There is a concourse of pilgrims and various things are cast into the flames with the expectation of obtaining temporal blessings. Over them a domed temple has been erected and an astonishing crowd assembles therein. The vulgar impute to miraculous agency what is simply a mine of brimstone.[22]

I know of two stories concerning the origin of the shrine. The first is as follows:

> Satī's tongue fell on the earth in a mountainous spot where only cowherds used to graze their cattle. The Goddess wanted to show herself, so she attached her tongue to a cow's breast and drank the milk. The cowherd was astonished that the cow's milk had run dry, so he followed her the next day. He saw a young girl come out of the bushes, drink the cow's milk, and disappear in a flash of light. The cowherd told the whole story to his master, King Bhūmi Candra. The king somehow found out that Satī's tongue had fallen in the vicinity, but he was unable to locate the exact spot, so he built a small temple in Nagarkot [Kangra]. Some years later a cowherd told him that he had seen a flame burning in the mountains some distance from the temple. The king went to that place, received *darśan* of the flame, and performed *pūjā*. He built a temple there and brought in from Śākdvīp Brahmins of the Bhojak [Bhojkī] caste to act as *pujārīs*. These Brahmins were known as Paṇḍit Śrīdhar and Paṇḍit Kamlāpati; their descendants still officiate at the temple today. Later, the five Pāṇḍavas came to this temple and renovated it.[23]

This story not only connects Jvālā Mukhī to the myth of Satī and the *śakti pīṭhas,* but also establishes the rights of the Bhojkīs, even since the time preceding the Pāṇḍavas.

The other story regarding the origin of the shrine is as follows:

> At this place Śrī Satī's tongue had fallen, so here Devī is known by the name Jvālājī, and in Calcutta some evil-minded people began to slaughter male buffaloes and goats to offer to Kālī Mātā. So the Mother of the World left there and began to live in the mountains. Here also evil-minded people began to slaughter animals and offer them to her, but they did not think that Mātājī had killed a buffalo to feed to Mahiṣāsur, instead they began to give meat offerings to Mātājī herself.[24] Therefore Mātājī became angry and took on the form of a flame. This flame which is the true form of God dispels all darkness. Mātājī came to the place now

known as Jvālā Mukhī. The seven flames, which are the *darśan* of the Seven Sisters, burn without oil through the power of Durgā. Devotees come here from far away to get Mātājī's *darśan*.[25]

This story seems to have the sole purpose of condemning animal sacrifice, a touchy subject at all the Goddess temples, as will be discussed in chapter 3. It shows a recognition of the fact that animal sacrifice is a traditional practice but asserts that the Goddess herself does not like it.

The most well-known story connected with Jvālā Mukhī is that of Dhyānū Bhagat, a legendary devotee of the sixteenth century, a summary of which I present here:

There once was a devotee of the Goddess named Dhyānū Bhagat who lived at the same time as the Mughal Emperor Akbar. Once he was leading a group of pilgrims to the temple of Jvālā Mukhī where the Goddess appears in the form of a flame. As the group was passing through Delhi, Akbar summoned Dhyānū to the court, demanding to know who this goddess was and why he worshiped her. Dhyānū replied that she is the all-powerful Goddess who grants wishes to her devotees.

In order to test Dhyānū, Akbar ordered the head of his horse to be cut off and told Dhyānū to have his goddess join the horse's head back to its body.

Dhyānū went to Jvālā Mukhī where he prayed day and night to the Goddess, but he got no answer. Finally, in desperation, he cut off his own head and offered it to the Goddess. At that point, the Goddess appeared before him in full splendor, seated on her lion. She joined his head back to his body and also joined the horse's head back to its body. Then she offered him a boon. He asked that in the future, devotees not be required to go to such extreme lengths to prove their devotion. So, she granted him the boon that from then on, she would accept the offering of a coconut to be equal to that of a head. That is why people today offer coconuts to the Goddess.[26]

Dhyānū is revered as a kind of folk hero, his name appearing as the *bhanitā*, or signature line, in numerous devotional songs. The scene of his presenting his severed head to the Goddess has become a standard icon in the popular posters of the cult. According to some versions of the story, Dhyānū visited Jvālā Mukhī but actually cut off his head at Kāṅgṛevālī Devī.[27]

Some versions of the story state that after this miracle, Akbar tried in vain to extinguish the flames by various means such as placing heavy metal plates over them or diverting a canal through the cave. Finally, the story goes, upon the advice of his Brahmins, he offered to the Goddess a solid gold umbrella, having carried it to the temple on his own shoulders. The Goddess, however, was displeased with his pride, and broke the umbrella, turning it into a metal of indeterminate composition. This umbrella is on display today in a room adjacent to the temple courtyard. The motif of a Muslim ruler offering an umbrella at Jvālā Mukhī predates Akbar by at least two centuries. Shams-i-Shiraj 'Afif in the fourteenth century wrote, "Some of the infidels have reported that Sultan Firuz went specifically to see this idol and held a golden umbrella over its head. . . . Other infidels said that Sultan Muhammad Shah bin Tughlak held an umbrella over the same idol; but this is also a lie."[28]

In spite of the antiquity of the site, the present temple is relatively recent, constructed in what is called the "Sikh style." Its imposing gilded roof was donated in 1813 by Maharaja Ranjit Singh (r. 1810–17), the Sikh ruler of the Panjab, in order to mark his victory over the Afghans. In honor of this, a handwritten manuscript of the *Guru Granth Sāhib* is kept at the temple.

There are a number of subsidiary shrines adjacent to and up the mountain from the main shrine. The most interesting of these is one called Gorakh Ḍibbī, a pit of cold boiling water that is under the control of the Gorakhnāth *sādhus*. A Jvālā Mukhī priest told me the following story about it:

> Mātājī was boiling some water to cook *khicaṛī* [rice and lentils]. Gorakhnāth was performing austerities nearby, so Mā appeared before him and invited him to eat her food. He replied, "How can I eat your food when I eat only *sāttvik* food and your form is *tamas?*" While Mā was looking the other way, he put ash [*bhasm*] in the water, so that it would boil but not produce heat. As a result, Mā continues to stay among the mortals trying to boil water.

Another priest gave a different version of the story:

> Mā was making some *khicaṛī* for Gorakhnāth and put the water on to boil. Gorakhnāth went off to get some rice but never came back. Waiting for him, Jvālā Māī keeps the water boiling. The water is boiling, but the water is cold. When Gorakhnāth returns, the water will get warm. Until

> then it will remain as it is. That is because Gorakhnāth is an *avatār* of Śaṅkar (Śiva) and Jvālā Māī is an *avatār* of Pārvatī. From Mā's *śakti* the water boils; from Nāthjī's *śakti* it stays cold.

This shrine is one of the more popular attractions at Jvālā Mukhī, since a priest will guide pilgrims through and perform a "miracle." First he will sprinkle water on the pilgrims in order to demonstrate that, although bubbling, the water is cold to the touch. Then he will hold a lighted incense stick to another water hole in the same pit, whereupon the water will appear to burst into flames. The Gorakhnāth Ḍibbī shrine is attended by *sādhus* of the Gorakhnāth order who, according to the Jvālā Mukhī priests, receive all the offerings made there.

Other subsidiary shrines include Vīr Kuṇḍ, where childless women bathe to get children and those afflicted by evil spirits are cured; Rādhā-Kṛṣṇa temple, Śiv-Śakti Lāl Sivālay; Kālī-Bhairav temple, Siddh Nāgārjun, who has remained there in a deep meditative trance waiting for his friend Gorakhnāth to return; a new Santoṣī Mā shrine, Ambikeśvar, who is said to be the Bhairava associated with this *śakti pīṭha;* Sītā-Rām temple, Kapisthal, which has images of Bhairo and Hanumān and where Tantric *sādhus* live; Tārā Devī temple; and Aṣṭabhujī Devī, which is about a mile downhill from Jvālā Mukhī near the cremation ground and has a bathing tank that is said to cure leukoderma. The village boasts several pilgrims' hostels (*dharmsālās*) and a modern hotel run by the Himachal Pradesh Tourist Board.

Kāṅgṛevālī Devī

This goddess, also called Vajreśvarī or Brajeśvarī, is enshrined in the town of Kangra (Nagarkot). The site is most probably the Jālandhara Pīṭha of Tantric fame. The temple that stands now was built over the remains of an older one that was destroyed in the earthquake of 1905. The older temple was said to have been built by Raja Sansar Cand I of Kangra in 1440, and a gilded roof like the one at Jvālā Mukhī was donated by Maharaja Ranjit Singh in the early nineteenth century. The site itself is much older, with inscriptions dating back at least to 950 C.E.[29] According to tradition, the temple was plundered on three occasions by Muslim invaders—by Mahmud of Ghazni in 1009, by Feroz Tughluk in 1360, and by Sher

Shah Suri in 1540.[30] A reference to it occurs in Abul Fazl's *'Ain-i-Akbari* (ca. 1590):

> Nagarkot is a city situated on a hill; its fort is called Kangarh. Near the town is the shrine of Mahāmāyā. . . . Pilgrims from distant parts visit it and obtain their desires. Strange it is that in order that their prayers be favorably heard, they cut out their tongues; with some it grows again on the spot; with others after one or two days. Although the medical faculty allow the possibility of growth in the tongue, yet in so short a space of time it is sufficiently amazing. In the Hindu mythology, Mahāmāyā is said to be the wife of Mahādeva, and the learned of this creed represent by this name the energizing power of the deity. It is said that on beholding the disrespect shown to herself and her husband Śiva she cut herself into pieces, and her body fell in four places: her head and some of her limbs in the northern mountains of Kashmir near Kāmrāj and these relics are called Śaradā; other parts fell near Bijapur in the Deccan and are known as Tuljā (Turjā) Bhavānī. Such portions as reached the eastern quarter near Kāmarūpa are called Kāmākhyā, and the remnant that kept its place is celebrated as Jālandharī which is this particular spot.[31]

This spot is the *śakti pīṭha* where, according to several Sanskirt texts as well as the local Bhojkī priests, the breast of Satī fell. It is clear that the site has ancient Tantric connections, possibly Buddhist as well as Hindu. The name Vajreśvarī, "Queen of the Thunderbolt," certainly suggests a former identity as a Vajrayāna Buddhist deity. However, as art historian B. N. Goswamy pointed out to me when I asked him about it, the name may actually be Vrajeśvarī or Brajeśvarī, "Queen of Vraja" (the place of Kṛṣṇa's childhood), which has no Buddhist overtones but instead would suggest the connection between the Goddess and the cult of Kṛṣṇa.[32] Also, there is a small temple to Tārā on the grounds, which survived the 1905 earthquake. Tārā is of course better known as a Buddhist than a Hindu goddess, but this evidence is not conclusive, since she is also counted as one of the ten Mahāvidyās who are often represented in Hindu Goddess temples. Other evidence connecting the site with Buddhism is a pillar, also a survivor of the 1905 earthquake, standing in the middle of the courtyard, which has a relief sculpture on one side of what can only be Gautama Buddha because of the characteristic "earth-touching pose" (*bhūmisparśa mudrā*). Again, this evidence is not conclusive, since the Buddha is often counted by Hindus as an incarnation of Viṣṇu and is included with groups of deities. Carved on the other faces of the same pillar are Durgā, Śiva, and Gaṇeśa. If the temple itself ever was a Buddhist cult center, the association has long been lost; however, the general area of Kangra is still sacred to Tibetan Buddhists, who occasionally visit from nearby Dharmsala.

The Goddess is worshiped here in the form of a *piṇḍī* enshrined in a square building in the middle of a large marble courtyard. Next to her *piṇḍī* is another *piṇḍī* that represents Śiva or the Bhairava of the *pīṭha*. The role of Śiva in the cult, however, is downplayed. His *piṇḍī* is bathed and decorated in the morning and evening along with Vajreśvarī, but he does not receive a separate *bhog* (food offering).[33] Instead, the *bhog* is divided into three parts for Mahālakṣmī, Mahākālī, and Mahāsarasvatī. In front of the main shrine is an "oath stone," a slab of rock upon which suspected criminals were once questioned and where people still take oaths today. A number of subsidiary shrines and images are adjacent to the shrine, including Dhyānū Bhagat, whom the Kangra Bhojkīs claim as their own, Hanumān, Santoṣī Mā, and the ten Mahāvidyās. A Sanskrit college is located on the temple grounds.

Kāṅgṛevālī Devī is the only temple in this study located in a town rather than a small village or remote jungle area. The historical fort, a few miles away, was the original center of the town, but now the town has grown up around the temple in what used to be the suburb of Bhavan. Kangra, formerly the district headquarters, is now a bustling commercial and educational center.

Another feature of Kāṅgṛevālī Devī that sets it apart from the other Goddess temples is the remarkable number of pilgrims who come from Uttar Pradesh,[34] especially during the spring Navarātra, dressed in yellow clothing. These pilgrims, from a variety of castes, consider Kāṅgṛevālī Devī to be their *kul-devī* (family goddess) and have their sons' *muṇḍan* (first head shaving) performed there. According to the priests of the shrine, Dhyānū Bhagat had come to this temple wearing yellow clothing, and because he was a resident of Agra, Uttar Pradesh, people from Uttar Pradesh come today wearing yellow clothes.

Cintpūrṇī

The temple of Cintpūrṇī is located on a hill in a village of the same name about halfway between Kangra and Hoshiarpur in District

Una, Himachal Pradesh. The deity is a single *piṇḍī* enshrined in a palanquin of white marble within a stone building. On the domed roof of the temple are engraved stone images of Hanumān and Bhairo. This is the *śakti pīṭha* where, according to the local scheme—though not to any Sanskrit source—the feet of Satī fell. It forms a triangle with Jvālā Mukhī and Kāṅgṛevālī Devī and is considered by some to be a part of Jālandhara Pīṭha. The three shrines are closely connected, with Cintpūrṇī considered to be the youngest sister. If pilgrims are visiting all three on the same trip, they will make it a point to visit Cintpūrṇī last, since it is forbidden to take *prasād* from her temple to her elder sisters'. The reason for this is that in North Indian Hindu families, it is considered improper for an elder sister to accept a gift from her younger sister. An elder may give to a younger in the family, but not the other way around.[35]

The name written on the gateway to the temple is Chinnamastikā; according to the temple priests it is the original name of Cintpūrṇī. Chinnamastikā or Chinnamastā is a Tantric goddess counted among the ten Mahāvidyās. She is usually pictured holding her severed head on a platter as if making an offering. Three streams of blood spurt from her neck; one flows into her own mouth, the other two into the mouths of flanking *yoginīs*. She stands atop a copulating couple stretched out on a lotus. Often the backdrop is a cremation ground. This fierce and gruesome goddess is, according to David Kinsley, almost always associated with esoteric Tantric practices and is not popularly worshiped by most Hindus.[36] It is possible that the site was once a center of Tantric practice; now, however, the practices are exoteric. It is worth noting in this connection that several of the priests took pains to emphasize to me that *pūjās* they conduct during their daily attendance upon the *piṇḍī* are, in their words "completely ordinary" (*sādhāraṇ*), Vaiṣṇav (i.e., vegetarian), not of the left-hand path (*vām mārg*). Having said this, however, they would immediately launch into tales of having witnessed devotees cutting off their tongues to offer to the Goddess and later getting them restored.

The name Cintpūrṇī is explained as "she who fulfills all one's wishes"; she is also known as Cintharaṇī, "who takes away all one's worries." She is particularly known for taking away mental anxieties and giving one "peace of mind." I quote the following account of the shrine's founding, which agrees with versions told by the priests, from the Panjab census report.

It is said that Mai Das, a Brahmin priest of village Rapoh Muchilian, Tahsil Una, District Hoshiarpur, was on his way to village Pirthipur in that very Tahsil to see his parents-in-law. Chintpurni [the village] fell in his way and when he reached there, he heard devotional songs from the peak of the hillock. Attracted by the tunes, he climbed up the hillock and witnessed a beautiful girl of about twelve to fourteen years sitting with a lion by her side and surrounded by a number of gods humming devotional songs in her praise. He could not face the celestial light radiating from the girl and was horrified. The girl, however, came to his rescue and disclosing that she was Goddess Durga and that she was pleased with him, she asked him to shed his fear. Addressing him further she said she would like to stay at the site of her appearance in the form of a *Pindi* [stone], and asked Mai Das that he and, after his death, his progeny should do *puja* [worship] of the *Pindi,* twice a day, regarding it as her own image. She further blessed that anyone who visited this place and worshiped the *Pindi* with sincere devotion would be emancipated from all worldly anxieties and worries and that hence she [the Goddess there] would be known as "Chintan Purni Devi" [Goddess relieving one of all worries].

Mai Das was aged eighty and with folded hands, he told the Goddess that he was issueless and that the place, besides being without habitation, had no trace of water.[37] The Goddess blessed Mai Das that he would have a son, and further directed him to a place about 2 furlongs away where underneath a slab of stone, $1^1/_4$ *hath* [hand unit] long, he would find water. Mai Das undertook to worship the Goddess and she disappeared only to appear again as a *Pindi*. Mai Das also discovered water under a slab at the spot indicated by the Goddess. He brought that slab and kept it near the *Pindi*. The slab still lies at the temple. He gave a bath to the *Pindi* and did its *puja* as he had been directed to do by the Goddess. However, next day he left the place and set out for the house of his in-laws. On the way he became blind. He met a passerby to whom he narrated the whole story repenting [*sic*] as to how he had become blind after leaving the place and thereby breaking his pledge of continuing *puja* of the *Pindi*. The passerby brought back Mai Das to the *Pindi*. Mai Das apologized to the Goddess and he regained his eyesight. He then constructed a small *chhappar* [straw hut] there and became the first inhabitant of the place. The habitation grew, as a larger and larger number of devotees were attracted to pay homage to the goddess. The village was shown in the earlier Revenue records as "Chhapro" on account of its association with the *chhappar* of Mai Das, but later on it has become known as Chintpurni, after the name of the Goddess.[38]

This story illustrates the dark side of the Goddess's grace; when Māī Dās neglected to carry out his duty, she struck him blind as punishment. The priests of this temple, who now number 100 to 150 households, all claim to be descendants of Māī Dās in the paternal line, and thus are all of the same *gotra* (exogamous kinship group), which has four divisions (*ṭolā*). This is unusual, since closely related priests of the same *gotra* are normally not allowed to perform *pūjā* to a deity during the period of pollution after a birth or death. For example, at Jvālā Mukhī, a priest explained to me that there are several *gotras* represented so that the problem of birth and death pollution does not arise. Presumably, new *gotras* are introduced by men marrying daughters of priests and becoming priests themselves. At Cintpūrṇī, on the other hand, the priests claim that the Goddess gave only the descendants of Māī Dās the authority to perform her *pūjā,* so that the only provision made during times of birth and death pollution is that a priest from one of the other three *ṭolās* must perform the *pūjā*. The priests of Cintpūrṇī consider themselves to be orthodox Brahmins and do not intermarry with the Bhojkī Brahmins.

Māī Dās's *samādhi* (tomb) lies downhill from the main temple near a bathing tank. It is a favorite spot for traveling *sādhus* and is presided over by a Mahātma. Every year for ten days during May a Sahasra Caṇḍī Yajña (*havan,* or fire sacrifice, in which the *Devī Māhātmya* is recited one thousand times) is conducted here.

Although Cintpūrṇī attracts a large crowd during the spring and autumn Navarātras, its main festival is Śravaṇ Aṣṭamī, during the first ten days of the lunar month of July–August. When I visited the shrine at that time in 1983, there was a special attraction, an all-night songfest (*jagrātā*) performed by the famous Narendra Chanchal.

Nainā Devī

Nainā Devī temple is located on the top of a mountain peak at a height of about 3,500 feet in District Bilaspur, Himachal Pradesh, nine miles uphill from the Sikh holy place Anandpur Sahib. It is surrounded by the Sutlej River on three sides. According to the local *śakti pīṭha* scheme, the eye of Satī fell here; hence the name Nainā (Sanskrit: *nayanā*). There are several layers of myth connected with the shrine. The site is also called Mahiṣpīṭh and is connected with the following story:

> There is a neighborhood in Anandpur Sahib called Makhowal [Mākhovāl]. Its original name was Mahiṣālay. It was the capital of Mahiṣāsur who had been given a boon by Brahmā that he would not be killed by any man but by a maiden. Mahiṣāsur made all the gods his slaves and made life so difficult for them that they finally put all their energies together and produced a *śakti* [a divine maiden]. She made her home at the top of the mountain called Mahiṣpīṭh. Mahiṣāsur heard about her and wanted to marry her, but she refused. He attempted to conquer her in battle, but she killed all his armies and finally Mahiṣāsur himself. She plucked out both his eyes and gave his skull to Brahmā. The skull was placed near the temple where it exists today as a pit called Brahmā Kāpālī Kuṇḍ. The eyes fell about a mile from the temple and are still present in the form of two tanks. When the Goddess took out Mahiṣāsur's eyes, the gods threw flowers from heaven and exclaimed, "*jay naine, jay naine,*" [victory to the eyes] so the place received the name Nainā Devī.[39]

Still another legend explains the name and origin of the shrine:

> There once was a Gujar or Ahir [Cowherd] named Nainā who used to look after the cattle of the village. One day he was surprised to see one of the cows standing underneath a pipal tree dripping milk on the ground. He removed the leaves on the ground and found underneath a stone *piṇḍī* with eyes engraved on it. That night Mā appeared to him in dream saying that the *piṇḍī* he had seen was her own form and that he should build a small temple there. He did so. Later Raja Bir Cand of Bilaspur [eighth century] built a larger temple there, which he named after the Ahir.[40]

The Gujars living in the area today claim to be descendants of Nainā and to have some rights over the temple. The Bhojkī priests of the temple, however, say that the cowherd story is not true and that the true story is the one concerning Mahiṣāsur. They claim also that although many believe that Satī's eye fell here, that is not the true story either. Some pamphleteers combine the Satī story with the cowherd story, saying that Nainā had discovered the eye, which had fallen there long before.[41]

The main shrine has three *piṇḍī,* all with strikingly large gold metal eyes. One is Gaṇeś, one is the original *svayambhu* (self-born) *piṇḍī* of Nainā Devī, and the third is a larger one, which the priests said was established by the five Pāṇḍavas. Inside the temple compound are several subsidiary shrines: Śrī Śvet Vatukjī (a form of Bhairo), Lakṣmī-Nārāyaṇ, Śankar Āśutoṣ Bhairav, Śrī Ek Pad

Kṛṣṇ Vaṭukjī (another form of Bhairo), Mahāvīr (Hanumān), and Gaṇes.

Because of its proximity to Anandpur Sahib, the place where guru Gobind Singh, the tenth guru of the Sikhs, established the Khalsa in 1699, a large number of Sikh pilgrims visit Nainā Devī. Hindus and some Sikhs also claim that Guru Gobind Singh was an ardent devotee of Nainā Devī. In the temple courtyard a large *havan* pit is kept burning day and night, where legends say that he offered 1¼ lakh (125,000) maunds of *havan* material. After this, the legend continues, Nainā Devī appeared to him in her eight-armed form, showed him her third eye, and gave him a sword that would ensure his victory.[42]

Stories of present-day miracles also abound. During one of my visits to Nainā Devī, a severe electrical storm struck, keeping me awake half the night as I tried to sleep in the government rest house, just down the mountain from the temple. The next morning, several priests and devotees at the temple, saying, "You should have been up here last night," described to me how Jvālā Mukhī had come the night before in the form of lightning to visit her sister, Nainā Devī, and had accepted offerings from their hands. They said that she appears this way two or three times a year and that devotees who are fortunate enough to witness this visit can make an offering of sweets to Jvālā Mukhī. The flame will come down from the sky and eat the sweets from the devotee's hand.

Like Cintpūrṇī, Nainā Devī has the largest crowds during the Śravaṇ Aṣṭamī festival in July and August when over three hundred thousand pilgrims visit the shrine over a ten-day period.[43]

Mansā Devī

Mansā Devī is located in District Kalka, Haryana, one mile from the old fort village of Mani Majra and eight miles from the city of Chandigarh. It has the most localized appeal of the temples in this study, being frequented mainly by residents of Chandigarh and of the surrounding districts in Panjab state. It is counted in the regional scheme as the *śakti pīṭha* where the forehead or mind of Satī fell. There are two explanations of the name Mansā. According to one it is connected with the mind (*man or manas*) of Satī. According to the other, since the Goddess fulfills all one's wishes (*mansā*), she is called Mansā Devī.

Concerning the founding of the temple, the following story is current:

> During the time of the Emperor Akbar, the area around Mani Majra was administered by Rajput landlords [*jāgīrdārs*] who collected taxes from the farmers in the form of grain. One time the crop was very sparse, and they were unable to pay the taxes. Akbar had the *jāgīrdārs* arrested. Hearing about this, the poet Garīb Dās supplicated the Goddess with *pūjā* and *havan*. She appeared before him in a vision and agreed to his request. The *jāgīrdārs* were released and the taxes forgiven for that year. In appreciation to the Goddess, they joined together and built a temple, which became famous as Mansā Devī.[44]

An engraving on the temple gateway states that it was built in 1868 (Vikramī era = A.D. 1811) by Raja Gopal Singh of Mani Majra. The priests of the temple say that the raja had a dream directing him to a certain spot. He went there and saw a stone that burst into flame. In that spot was a *piṇḍī*, the fallen mind (*man*) of Satī, which is still there today. The raja enshrined this *piṇḍī* and later installed an anthropomorphic image as well. This is the main temple, which most pilgrims consider to be the authentic one. It is presided over by a family of Sarasvat Brahmins, three brothers and their paternal aunt who take turns performing the rituals, taking the offerings, and seeing to the upkeep of the temple.

Adjacent to this temple are two other Mansā Devī temples. One was built by the Maharaja Karansingh of Patiala in 1861 to commemorate his success in battle against the Gurkhas. Oral accounts add that the maharaja built this temple after the Goddess appeared to him in a dream. This is not a *śakti pīṭha* but a *sukhnā* temple, one that is built in fulfillment of a vow to thank a deity. This temple has no connection with the main Mansā Devī temple and is under separate administration. The official *pujārī* is an elderly Sarasvat Brahmin woman who inherited the office from her late husband, whose ancestors were appointed by the maharaja of Patiala. She hires other *pujārīs* to help her give out *prasād* and watch over the temple. There are also numerous miniature shrines of the *sukhnā* variety built by individual devotees in villages adjacent to the Mansā Devī temple. During the Navarātras, the people who built them come to make offerings in them and do repairs. The main temple is not responsible for their upkeep.

A short distance downhill from the main Mansā Devī temple and forming a triangle with the Patiala temple is a third Mansā Devī temple that claims to be the original or ancient (*prācīn*) temple. It was an old, abandoned temple when about 1970 the present *pujārī* received a message from the Goddess that this was her original temple. Prior to that he had lived in the village Bejwara (now Sectors 22 and 35 in Chandigarh) and served in the military. He started sitting there every day and has achieved some local notoriety. He claims to have documents proving the age of the temple and has installed a loudspeaker system over which he plays recorded devotional songs punctuated by requests for pilgrims to visit the ancient temple.[45] Pilgrims have in fact begun to visit this temple, perhaps more out of curiosity than for any other reason, and the *pujārī* is able to make a meager living from their offerings.

Near the entrance to the main temple and next to a tank is a shrine called the Bābā Mansā Nāth Zindā Samādhi. It is the tomb of a Gorakhnāthī *sādhu*, who was a devotee of Mansā Devī and the guru of Raja Gopal Singh (or of his ancestor Bhagvan Singh). According to legend, he sat in *samādhi* and allowed himself to be buried alive by stones. He is said to be still alive under the stones and will fulfill people's wishes. When people get their wishes fulfilled, they offer him meat and wine. Currently a Gorakhnāthī *sādhu* watches over the *samādhi* and receives the offerings made there, although the site itself and the tank are owned by the main Mansā Devī temple.

There is also a well-known temple by the name of Mansā Devī in the all-India pilgrimage city of Hardwar, and a goddess of the same name is popularly worshiped in Bengal as the protector of snakes and wife of the sage Jaratkāru.[46] The priests of the main Mansā Devī temple had a vague idea that Mansā Devī was somehow connected with snakes but did not know any further details. When I asked them about it, they called over another Brahmin, an astrologer who rents a room from them but is otherwise unconnected to the temple. The astrologer knew of the story from the *Devī Bhāgavata Purāṇa* and said that it is the same Mansā Devī. The woman *pujārī* of the Patiala temple was a bit more knowledgeable about Mansā Devī's connection with snakes, saying that once someone had cursed all the snakes to be sacrificed and held a *yajña,* but Mansā Devī saved them.[47] She also knew the *dhyāna mantra* of Mansā Devī (*Devī Bhāgavata Purāṇa* 9.48.2–3), which she had learned from her guru, a *paṇḍit* who had lived in the area for forty years. In general, however, the stories of Mansā Devī as goddess of snakes do not seem to have much prominence in the local cult and do not appear in any of the popular pamphlets.

The largest number of pilgrims visit Mansā Devī during the spring Navarātras when a *melā* is held. Besides the religious activities, there are more secular attractions than at the *melās* of other Devī temples. During the Navarātras in the spring of 1983, there were besides the usual stalls selling books, toys, food, and handicrafts, a traveling zoo, house of mirrors, Ferris wheels, and other carnival attractions.

Cāmuṇḍā Devī

Cāmuṇḍā Devī is located in Jadrangal village in District Kangra on the right bank of the Bān Gaṅga, a tributary of the Beas River. She is usually counted among the Seven Sisters and Nine Goddesses, but her shrine is not considered to be a *śakti pīṭha*. There is a Śiva *liṅga* under a boulder nearby, so the shrine is also called Cāmuṇḍā Nandikeśvar (Lord of Nandika, the bull vehicle of Śiva). This is identified locally as the very spot where in the third episode of the *Devī Māhātmya* Kālī, the *śakti* of Devī, killed Caṇḍa and Muṇḍa, the two generals of the demons Śumbha and Niśumbha, and thereby received the name Cāmuṇḍā.[48]

According to one of the temple priests, the temple was originally built in a deserted spot high in the mountains by the Katoch rulers of Kangra. It was reestablished in its present spot in the following way:

> About four hundred years ago, during the reign of Raja Candra Bhan, the people petitioned him to move the temple to a more accessible and less dangerous spot. So, he had a Brahmin priest perform worship to the Goddess in the correct manner. The Goddess appeared to the priest in a dream, saying that she was pleased with the worship and that he should build a temple. He asked what kind of image should be installed, and she replied that if he dug in a certain spot an ancient image would be there. The king had a temple built, and when the time came to install the image, he sent his men out to dig for it. They found it buried in the earth, but no matter how hard they tried they were not able to lift it. It would not budge. The priest who had had the dream was very upset. That night the Goddess appeared before him again in a dream, saying that it would not move because they had considered it to be an ordinary stone. She

> instructed him to get up during the Brahma *muhūrt* [after 3:00 A.M.], bathe in the river, wear a cotton cloth [*dhotī*], and only then go to get the image. He did as he was told and went to the place where the image lay in the ground. He was able to lift it with no effort at all and brought it to the temple. The people were all amazed that the priest was able to carry what a hundred men had been unable to lift from the ground. The priest said that it was not he who brought the image there, but the power of the Goddess. This is the image that is worshiped in the temple today.

This image is flanked by images of Hanumān and Bhairo. Scenes from the *Devī Māhātmya* are painted on the walls along with the ten Mahāvidyās, the seven Mātrikās, and eight other goddesses. A *satsaṅg* (congregation) hall with mural paintings from the *Mahābhārata* and *Rāmāyaṇa* is adjacent. A new bathing area on the riverbank has been built and named Sanjay Ghat in commemoration of Indira Gandhi's visit to Cāmuṇḍā Devī in 1980. In the late 1980s a large plaster Hanumān and other images were installed in the Sanjay Ghat area through donations from the Mohan Meakin Brewery, giving it the appearance of a theme park. Several hundred yards from the temple is a small shrine to Mansā Devī and another small temple in which images of Vaiṣṇo Devī, Gaṇeś, and Hanumān have recently been installed by an industrialist family from Jullunder. A short distance from the temple is a cremation ground, which is appropriate since Cāmuṇḍā as a form of Kālī is associated with death.

According to the temple priest and to a popular pamphlet,[49] animal sacrifice was once offered here but has been discontinued because of its offensiveness to some devotees. A sign is now posted forbidding the use of meat and liquor and card playing in the temple precincts.

A pilgrims' hostel (*dharmsālā*) has been recently built by the temple committee. The temple priest explained that unlike Jvālā Mukhī and Cintpūrṇī, which are run as family businesses, Cāmuṇḍā Devī is managed by a committee of which anyone can be a member. The temple priests do not receive any share of the offerings but rather are paid a salary.

The Power of the Place

There is no limit to the number of pilgrimage places or to the number of Goddess manifestations. New places are always cropping up, and even "standard" lists such as the Seven Sisters are fluid. This fluidity is possible because of the theology of unity discussed in chapter 1, the belief that "they are all *śakti*." Yet each place, each goddess, has its own uniqueness, its own history and individual personality. Kālī in one place is both the same and different from Kālī in another place. Jvālā Mukhī is both the same and different from Vaiṣṇo Devī. E. Alan Morinis, writing in the same vein, has observed that the tendency within Hinduism is

> to represent its deities as both converging into supreme deities and splintering these into a myriad of lesser deities. The paradox in thought which makes this even more complex is the belief that even at the most lowly, form-bound level, the goddess is simultaneously her cosmic, formless self, and that in that cosmic, characterless aspect, she is still Durgā, Kālī, Tārā, Ūmā and the rest. [50]

This paradox defies distinctions between monotheism and polytheism, spirituality and materialism, "great" and "little" traditions. This phenomenon, which David Shulman calls "the phenomenon of localization"[51] and Kees Bolle calls "the symbolism of being there,"[52] allows for a rich variety within a unified tradition. In fact, the deity and the place become identified with each other. It is difficult to say which is named after the other. For example, Vaiṣṇo Devī and Jvālā Mukhī both refer to physical places with geographical features as well as to the goddesses who live there. The individual goddess *is* the place and the place *is* the goddess. In order to experience the Goddess as place, to get the feel of "being there," devotees journey into the mountains, receiving the sacred vision (*darśan*) of the Goddess in her concrete local forms. Chapter 3 provides a glimpse into this pilgrimage process.

3

The Call of the Goddess

The Dynamics of Pilgrimage

You called me, Śerāṅvālī
Here I am, here I am, Śerāṅvālī.
O Flame Mother, Mountain Mother, Gracious Mother.

The whole world is but a wayfarer
Whose destination is your door.
High mountains, long roads
Couldn't keep me away, Śerāṅvālī.

In an empty mind, a flame has ignited
On your path, friends have joined.
How can I open my mouth and ask you,
Without asking, I get everything, Śerāṅvālī

Who's a king; who's a beggar?
All your worshipers are equal.
Giving *darśan* to all,
You draw them to your breast, Śerāṅvālī.[1]

We'll come every year, Ma, we'll come to you
Bringing coconuts, offerings, umbrellas,
Lighting your flame during *ārtī,*
Offering a red flag, Ma, we'll come to you.

Mothers are like a cooling shade.
Sons have lapses; mothers never do.
Look after us, Ma, we'll come to you.

With children you shower us with happiness,
Rid us of desire, hunger, and thirst.
Bringing our family, Ma, we'll come to you.

Give happiness, peace, intelligence, Ma.
Give the children milk, Ma.
Fulfill our request, Ma, we'll come to you.

Send children to us,
Teach them good works, auspicious works.
May the eighty-four snares vanish, Ma, we'll come to you.[2]

While worshipers of the Goddess often express the sentiment that she is present everywhere and that one could worship her within oneself, at home, or in a local temple, her pilgrimage places are *śakti pīṭhas* (seats of power), which exert a tremendous pull on her devotees. Those who visit her sacred places do so, they say, in response to her "call." As one pilgrim (female, Brahmin, age about forty-four) told me,

> The reason why I have come on this pilgrimage is that there was a *kīrtan* [devotional songfest] in my neighborhood, and the Mother became manifest [through possession] in someone and told me to come to Vaiṣṇo Devī. The Mother called me. I wished for my health to improve, and by the Mother's grace I was able to climb the fourteen kilometers.

Pilgrimage to places sacred to the Goddess is one of the most vigorous and visible aspects of the cult—indeed, one could call it the focal point. Discussions I had with devotees of the Goddess about her powers and attributes inevitably centered around the physical places where she manifests herself and the motivation the devotee feels to visit those places. Most of the devotional songs make reference to one or more of these "personalities" of the Goddess. In this chapter I describe the ritual elements, what pilgrims do while on pilgrimage. I also hope to give a taste of what the experience of pilgrimage is like for those who undertake a sacred journey. While I make reference to individual shrines as examples, my emphasis will be on the features common to Goddess pilgrimages in general.

In the Footsteps of the Goddess

All the myths and legends of the Goddess discussed in chapter 2 concern events that can be located in time and space. Even those that took place in mythic time or what Eliade has called *in illo tempore* can be visually and physically reexperienced in the here and now by the pilgrim on his or her sacred journey. The story of the "flame tongue" at Jvālā Mukhī, for example, is not just a picturesque fable for pilgrims, for the flame can still be seen and experienced as a manifestation of the Goddess. Similarly, pilgrims who worship Vaiṣṇo Devī at Trikuṭ mountain today trace the steps the Goddess took in her flight from Bhaironāth, including the literal crawl through the womb cave at Ādikumārī. Thus, they are reexperiencing Bhairo's pursuit of Vaiṣṇo Devī. Since the stations of the pilgrimage are more clearly delineated at Vaiṣṇo Devī than at any of the other Goddess temples, I will describe them here.

Arriving in Katra, usually by bus, pilgrims register for a *yātrā* (pilgrimage) pass that will be checked later on in an attempt at crowd control. If they have arrived late in the day, they may wish to spend the night at one of the pilgrims' hostels or hotels. In the bazaar they may purchase the items to offer at the main shrine, usually a packet including a coconut, sweets, *sindūr* (red powder), incense, *maulī* (red string), and a red flag wrapped in a red *cunnī* (scarf). Since no leather is allowed on the mountain, pilgrims may rent canvas shoes for the hike as well as other items such as umbrellas, flashlights, and cameras. Most pilgrims will choose to make the nine-mile climb on foot, either by the steep path with many stairs or by the longer but more gradual bridal path, while the very ill or elderly may rent a donkey. Several years ago, a helicopter pad was built near the top of the mountain to accommodate the busy schedules of visiting dignitaries. The pilgrimage route is lined at intervals with small temples and images, tea stalls, and young girls (*kanyās*) who collect offerings of small coins from pilgrims.

The atmosphere is exhuberant. Colorfully dressed pilgrims of all ages sing devotional songs as they walk the steep path. When the going gets rough, they will shout to each other: *jay mātā dī* (victory to the Mother). Groups chant in unison, adding line after line:

Say it softly: *jay mātā dī!*
Say it loudly: *jay mātā dī!*
Say it with love: *jay mātā dī!*
People in the front: *jay mātā dī!*
People in the back: *jay mātā dī!*
English people also: *jay mātā dī!*

Everybody say: *jay mātā dī!*
Remover of troubles: *jay mātā dī!*
Śerāṅvālī: *jay mātā dī!*

The first stop on the route is Darśanī Darvāzā, a stone gate from which one gets the first view of the mountain. Passes are checked here. Second is Bān Gaṅgā, the sacred stream in which many pilgrims bathe, so named because this is the spot where the Goddess shot her arrow (*bān*), causing a river to flow. A small temple to Vaiṣṇo Devī is here. Third is Caraṇ Pādukā, where a temple has been built around the Goddess's still-visible footprints. Pilgrims stand in the same spot Vaiṣṇo Devī did when she turned around to catch a glimpse of her pursurer. Fourth is Ādikumārī, the fifteen-foot cave where the Goddess meditated. The cave is barely wide enough to accommodate one pilgrim slithering through on his or her stomach, but the smoothness of the rock makes it easier than it looks. Inside is an alcove where a priest sits cross-legged, reciting prayers. This is the main stopping place along the route; a spacious plot of land holds a temple, water tank, tea stalls, restaurants, and overnight accommodations for one thousand people. Fifth is Hāthī Mathā, a face of the mountain that looks like the forehead of an elephant. Sixth is Sānjhī Chat, the highest point on the track (7,215 feet). From here the path begins a gradual descent first to the Bhairo temple, which pilgrims bypass, and then to the main temple, the *darbār* of Vaiṣṇo Devī. A new road built by the Dharmarth Trust circumvents the Bhairo temple completely, so that now pilgrims must make a special effort to visit it.[3] The *darbār* area is a large complex of shops, restaurants, dormitories, and enclosed areas with piped-in water for bathing. Just outside the cave is a square platform with seating room for about one hundred people. Waiting time for entering the cave is usually several hours, considerably more during the Navarātras. Pilgrims enter the cave single file, stepping over the rock said to be Bhairo's body. They must slither through a dark, narrow passageway ankle deep in ice-cold water. At the end of the ninety-foot tunnel, three steps lead to a room barely large enough to hold four or five crouching people. Here the pilgrims experience the fulfillment of their journey in the *darśan* of the three *piṇḍīs*. They make their offerings and are quickly ushered outside, where they receive part of their offerings back as *prasād* from one of the attending priests: a *biṇḍī* on the forehead, a scarf around the head, a red string around the neck, and some small coins that are said to ensure wealth if kept with one's money. From here the pilgrim hurries back down the mountain (possibly making the no longer compulsory stop at the Bhairo temple) to catch a bus for home or another pilgrimage place.

Intentions and Actions

What motivates a person or group to undertake a pilgrimage? Some devotees have a custom of going every year to a particular place or places, some go as a group with their guru or other religious organization, some go because their relatives or friends have gone, some go out of curiosity, some to make or fulfill a vow, some to conduct life-cycle rites, some for "peace of mind," and some because they feel called by the Goddess. The specific reasons for undertaking a pilgrimage are as numerous as the pilgrims themselves, but the element underlying all these reasons is the belief that pilgrimage is *efficacious,* that whatever results one desires will come about through the grace of the Goddess.

Through reading pilgrim guidebooks and talking with pilgrims, it becomes obvious that it is not merely the mechanical performance of the pilgrimage that produces results, but the attitude of the devotee. One must approach the pilgrimage with the proper *bhāvanā* (feeling or sentiment). Once the pilgrim has formed the intention (*saṅkalpa*) to undertake a pilgrimage, then he or she is obligated to do so. On the journey one's thoughts should be directed toward the deity. In premodern times pilgrimage was done primarily on foot, with parties singing devotional songs along the route. Nowadays buses have become the primary means of transportation, eliminating some of the rigor and asceticism. Still, I was told, one should cultivate physical, mental, and ritual purity through fasting or at least avoiding meat and liquor, abstaining from sexual activity, avoiding arguments, sleeping on the ground, and wearing clean clothing. Women should not undertake pilgrimages during their menstrual periods. A bath is obligatory before entering the temple and may be taken at the river or tank adjacent to the temple, at the rest house or pilgrims' hostel where one is staying, or, if the journey is not too far, at one's home. In any case, the pilgrims will at least wash their hands, face, and feet and remove their shoes before entering the temple. The Goddess is said to respond to the emotion of the devotee and will forgive minor ritual errors as long as the devotee is sincere and has faith. On the other hand, she will punish those who show disrespect as in the following anecdote, which I heard from several different devotees:

> A group of college boys were making a pilgrimage to Vaiṣṇo Devī. Instead of chanting *jay mātā dī* [victory to the Mother] along with the other pilgrims on the steep climb up the mountain, the boys began to joke and chant *jay pitā dī* [victory to the Father]. The other pilgrims became nervous and tried to make them stop, but they persisted. After a while, the Goddess came out of the sky in the form of lightning and turned them into stones.

The primary reason pilgrims give for going on pilgrimage is to receive *darśan,* and indeed, this is the sine qua non of a pilgrimage, regardless of the more specific purpose for undertaking the journey. *Darśan* means "seeing the divine image,"[4] participating in the power of the deity by viewing him or her in a manifest form. At pilgrimage places, *darśan* of the Goddess means, usually, viewing her in the form of a *piṇḍī* or a *mūrti.* A *piṇḍī* is a lump of stone, resembling somewhat a Śiva-*liṅga,* which is believed to have been self-generated (*svayambhū*) on the spot. It is believed to be imbued with *śakti,* that is, to be a manifestation of the Goddess herself. While the worship of stones as male and female deities is common throughout India, the term *piṇḍī* seems to be unique to the Panjab Hills cult. The Goddess is also worshiped in the form of a *mūrti,* an iconic image that is "enlivened" with her power.[5] Often these *mūrtis* are said to have appeared miraculously or are "discovered" buried in the earth after being seen in a dream.

When pilgrims arrive at a temple, the first thing they do after bathing is go for *darśan,* and only then do they perform any other rituals for which they have come. They approach the deity, make their offering, and receive part of it back as *prasād.* The standard offering at Goddess shrines is a red flag (*jhaṇḍā*), red powder (*sindūr*), small metal umbrella (*chattra*), and a coconut tied with a loosely woven red thread (*maulī*). This type of paraphernalia is not associated with shrines of the major male deities and may have some connection with animal sacrifice.[6] Red is an auspicious color associated with the blood of life, and thus is the color for a bride's clothing. Bridal symbolism is also evident in the red powder offered to the Goddess, for the powder is worn by brides on their wedding day and also by married women as a sign of auspiciousness. The flag and the umbrella are emblems of royalty and martial prowess, as the Goddess is also a queen and warrior. Other types of offerings include sweets, flowers, cash, red scarves (*cunnī*), and more expensive items such as jewelry or a crown.

The temple priest (*pujārī*) accepts the offerings on behalf of the deity and recites in a mixture of Hindi and Panjabi a request or supplication, called *ardās,* which follows this basic formula: "So and so's [the pilgrim's] *ardās* of x rupees offered at your feet. O Devī, make their pilgrimage successful, fulfill their wishes, keep their children healthy, give them blessings. Victory to the true court!" The pilgrim stands with palms together or prostrates in front of the deity, then receives from the priest a portion of the offering, usually some sweets and flowers and a *maulī,* which is tied around the neck. This is the *prasād,* or "consecrated leavings," which the deity has blessed and returned to the worshiper. Pilgrims will consume some of the *prasād* and distribute the rest to other pilgrims, to beggars, or to friends and relatives after returning home. I have often seen pilgrims handing out *prasād* to everyone in the vicinity, without regard to caste. Since it comes from the deity, it is the purest form of food and can be shared by anyone. *Prasād* should not be disposed of except in a body of water.

Popular songs praise the Goddess with such epithets as Vardātī, Grantor of Boons. Many, if not most, pilgrims to Goddess temples have made and fulfilled a vow (*sukhnā, manautī*) at one time or another. A vow takes a form such as this: "If you grant me x, I will visit your temple at y place and offer z." The favors pilgrims ask for are normally of a personal nature such as curing a disease, obtaining employment, ensuring a successful marriage match, winning a lawsuit, giving birth to a (usually male) child, passing an examination, or just general well-being. These are a few examples of vows pilgrims told me about:

> I started worshiping Devī when I had given the exam [State Account Services]. Fifteen days before the results came out, in a dream I went past a temple to Devī and did prostrations [*praṇām*]. She told me to take the *prasād.* Seven days before the results came out, I saw in a dream a stencil of the results with my name written on the list of those who had passed. (male, Kayasth caste, age about thirty)

> I have no particular reason for making this pilgrimage. But my mother-in-law, who is with me, wishes to recover from a mental illness. (female, Kayasth caste, age twenty-eight, wife of above)

> I got all my children from Mansā Devī. In my family, we go there for blessings after marriage and have the first head shaving of our children done there. On this pilgrimage, I just ask that everyone in my family remain in good health and that we all have peace of heart and faith. (female, Agrawal caste, age about thirty-five)

> I have been ill with cancer for a year. My daughter made a wish that if I got better, she would send me to Vaiṣṇo Devī, so that is why I have come. After climbing Vaiṣṇo Devī yesterday, I feel even better. (female, Sikh Khattri, age fifty)

> I have been to all the Goddess temples several times. My father was a staunch Arya Samajist and did not worship Devī. But when I was in the sixth class, I had tuberculosis and my mother took me to Vaiṣṇo Devī. She made a vow that if I were cured, my father would take me back there the following year. When we got back I was completely cured, so my father took me, and I have gone back every year since. In 1934 when I got my B.A., I promised I would go to Vaiṣṇo Devī if I was successful in the exam. I got first place in English. I got several jobs through her grace. Once my family lost all its wealth, and Devī came to the rescue. Now my son-in-law is sick and confined to bed. All diagnoses have failed. He has reduced from 72 to 42 kgs., so I have come to request his cure from Vaiṣṇo Devī. (male, Rajput, age seventy-three)

> This time I have come with no special wish. I planned this visit just to see the places in the hills. In the past I remembered Devī only whenever I was in trouble. I never remembered her out of faith, only out of greed. Now I have developed full faith. Devī is very generous and kindhearted. She fulfills your every demand. (male, Arora, age twenty-eight)

The most extreme form of fulfilling a vow is to cover a certain predetermined distance to the temple by prostrating one's body each step of the way. Pilgrims who choose this method, called *daṇḍautīs,* are a common sight along roads leading to Goddess temples, particularly during the Navarātra. A less strenuous way of fulfilling a vow is by making an offering in a particular temple. At Jvālā Mukhī, pilgrims often vow to make a special offering at the *sejā,* an elaborate and impressive ceremony for which this temple is especially known, in which the Goddess is put to bed. This takes place after the evening *ārtī* has been performed in the main shrine to the flames. At about 9:00 P.M. attention shifts to the Sejā Bhavan, a large room across the courtyard from the main shrine containing images of various forms of the Goddess, including the ten Mahāvidyās. The Sejā Bhavan is used during the day for recitation of sacred texts, singing of devotional songs, and resting. At night a cot is placed in the middle of the room, and pilgrims sit around it. The priests drape it with several layers of cloth while another priest performs *mudrās* (sacred gestures) and recites Sanskrit verses. Then several of the priests leave the room while another *ārtī* is performed in the main shrine. They return a few minutes later with an old man carrying a gun and remove the Goddess's jewelry from a locked chest, placing it in the proper position on the bed. The jewelry includes a crown, several necklaces, toe rings, four ankle bracelets, bracelets, bangles, and silver slippers (which the priest touches to his forehead before placing on the bed). A *yantra* (mystical diagram) carved on silver is also placed on the bed. Three pillows are placed in such a way as to resemble a head and two arms, and two small pillows are propped up on the inside of the two side pillows to resemble breasts. A pink *kurtā-pājāmā* outfit, which serves as the Goddess's sleeping garb, is laid out on top and covered with several large scarves. Laid on top is a final scarf offered by a pilgrim fulfilling a vow, along with items for the Goddess's personal use: *sindūr,* glass bangles, nose ring, henna, mirror, comb, toe rings, *biṇḍī,* blouse, and red ribbon. The priests lead the singing of a Sanskrit hymn from the *Saundāryalaharī* and then allow the people to approach and make cash offerings. The temple is closed immediately after this. Two or three of the priests and the man with the gun sleep in the room to protect the jewelry. In the morning the Goddess is awakened with a reading of the *Devī Māhātmya.* The priests say that the bedclothes are always wrinkled.

As Bhardwaj has stated, the prominent Devī shrines specialize in helping people with their personal problems.[7] Bhardwaj therefore argues that the worship at Devī temples is more "material" and less "spiritual" than those to the high male deities such as Krishna and Śiva. While agreeing that vows are a chacteristic feature of Goddess worship, I have come to question the distinction between material and spiritual. Goddess worship is not any less sacred or spiritual for being oriented to "this-worldly" concerns. In Śākta theology the material world is a manifestation of the Goddess, so the desire for material benefits does not contradict feelings of devotion (*bhakti*) or the ultimate goal of liberation.

All of the Goddess shrines in this study are known as being

traditional places for the performance of *muṇḍan,* the first head shaving of a child. Usually it is done for a boy, and sometimes for a girl, at the age of two or three. This ceremony, also called *cūḍakarman,* is counted among the major *saṃskāras* (life-cycle rites) that go back to Vedic times. Some families have the *muṇḍan* done at home; others have it done at a particular Goddess shrine. For example, many residents of Uttar Pradesh will have it done at Kāṅgṛevālī Devī, while Panjabis traditionally go to Jvālā Mukhī or one of the other temples. Some families do not have a customary place for *muṇḍan* but will make a vow to have it done in a certain place if the child lives that long.

The ritual itself is quite simple. The parents offer some money to the temple priest, who performs a *pūjā* to the Goddess. Then a man of the Barber caste shaves the child's head, after which the child is given a bath and dressed in new clothes. The priest then brings the child to get the Goddess's *darśan* and puts a *tilak* (auspicious red mark) on his forehead. The hair is considered to be an offering to the Goddess and is ultimately disposed of by burning or throwing into a body of water.

The question of when and why *muṇḍan,* as opposed to other life-cycle rites, became associated with Goddess shrines has not been sufficiently investigated. The *muṇḍan* can be seen as a vow fulfillment; that is how many informants explained it to me. If a devotee has asked the Goddess for the birth of a child, and that request has been fulfilled, the family will return to the shrine to conduct the *muṇḍan* as a thanks offering. It would seem, moreover, that the *muṇḍan* is a kind of symbolic sacrifice.[8] The mythic motif of offering a human head to the Goddess, which I will discuss further in chapter 4, and reports of devotees' cutting out their tongues to offer to the Goddess are ubiquitous. Thus, it does not seem too farfetched to see the hair offering as symbolic of a head offering, especially taking into account the element of vow fulfillment that is implicit in the performance of *muṇḍan* at Goddess shrines.

In contrast to such famous Śākta shrines as Vindhyavāsinī in eastern Uttar Pradesh and Kālīghāṭ in Calcutta, where the ancient practice of animal sacrifice continues unabated, at the Panjab Hills shrines it has been, to the best of my knowledge, almost completely eliminated. Every temple in this study, with the possible exception of Vaiṣṇo Devī, whose name reflects her vegetarian nature, has allowed the practice in the past. The Goddess, as the giver of life and death, is strongly connected with blood symbolism. The sacrifice of a buffalo (or the less expensive goat) is a reenactment of Devī's mythic killing of the buffalo demon.

Today at some places animal sacrifice (*balidān*) is allowed outside but not inside the shrine. When questioned, many of the temple priests exhibited strong ambivalence about the issue. For example, in 1983 a priest at Jvālā Mukhī informed me that animal sacrifice is not and never was practiced there; when pressed he said that it had been practiced previously but that the temple committee had decided to discontinue it five to seven years before. The reason given for stopping the practice was that many of the devotees disapproved and that it is not necessary. S. M. Bhardwaj, who visited Jvālā Mukhī in 1968, writes that goats were actually sacrificed in an enclosure after being offered symbolically in front of the sanctum and that a stream of blood could be seen coming from the enclosure.[9] Fifteen years later, I saw no evidence of animal sacrifice but did see goats offered symbolically and given over to the temple without being killed. Symbolic sacrifice is done in the following way: The devotee brings the goat into the temple courtyard, makes a supplication to the Goddess, then dumps a pail of water over the animal. If the animal shakes, that means the Goddess has accepted it. If actual sacrifice was being done, the goat would then be slaughtered, but in a symbolic sacrifice it is led away alive and given to the temple priests.

There are several reasons for abandoning animal sacrifice. The most important is the influence of Vaiṣṇavism, which forbids meat eating and animal sacrifice, in the Panjab Hills from about the seventeenth century on. A related factor is that with the increasing popularity of Vaiṣṇo Devī, the other temples are following suit in forbidding animal sacrifice although in other respects they remain close to their Tantric and Śākta roots. The general atmosphere engendered by such reform movements as Sikhism and the Ārya Samāj as well as Western values has also been hostile to animal sacrifice. Still another factor is changing patterns of patronage. Goddess temples were traditionally patronized by Hindu rulers of the hill states. As Kṣatriyas, these rulers were meat eaters and were not unduly concerned if animal sacrifice was conducted at the temples. Now the temples depend on generous donations from wealthy pilgrims, many of whom are of the merchant castes, which are traditionally vegetarian and opposed to animal sacrifice. It is perhaps to attract these pilgrims and to avoid offending their sensibilities that the shrines are discontinuing animal sacrifice or allowing it only in a very low-key way.

The shrines of Jvālā Mūkhī, Kāṅgṛevālī Devī, and Nainā Devī have traditionally had a stronger connection with animal sacrifice than have the other shrines. These shrines (as well as many other smaller shrines in the area) are under the control of *pujārīs* of the Bhojkī caste. Although they consider themselves Brahmins and wear the sacred thread, they are considered to be inferior by other Brahmins, who will not intermarry with them. Although many of them will now deny it, they have a reputation for consuming meat and liquor. The Bhojkī have in recent years attempted to raise their status through learning Sanskrit, establishing Sanskrit colleges, and abandoning animal sacrifice.

To say, however, that the move away from animal sacrifice is "Sanskritization" would be an oversimplification. After all, the most revered of all Sanskrit texts, the Vedas, enjoin animal sacrifice. Besides, it is generally recognized, even in the Sanskrit Śākta texts, that animal sacrifice is a traditional part of Goddess worship.[10] One temple priest at Kāṅgṛevālī Devī, the most well versed in Sanskrit and Sanskritic rituals of all the priests I met and an expert on Tantrism, used this argument, saying that he himself had performed animal sacrifice. He further explained that Vaiṣṇavism and Śāktism are two separate paths, each of which has its own rules. He said that when a goat is sacrificed to the Goddess, it is cooked and distributed as *prasād*. All will eat it, except for Vaiṣṇavas, who will only smear a drop of the blood on their foreheads. Another priest, this one at Nainā Devī, said that a goat is sacrificed there twice a year, and that this is the proper procedure (*vidhi vidhān*) for worshiping the Goddess. He also maintained that animal sacrifice is still carried out, albeit secretly, at all the Panjab Hills Goddess shrines.

Although actual animal sacrifice is no longer (if it ever was) central to the cult, the imagery still remains in the symbolic goat offering, the coconuts, and the red flags and strings.

Another characteristic feature of Goddess temples that immediately strikes the observer is the prominence of young, unmarried, prepubescent girls (*kanyās* or *kumārīs*) who are given free run in the temples. The Goddess is considered to be both virgin and mother, often choosing to manifest herself in the form of a virgin girl, so by extension all *kanyās* have a share in her sacred status. I have often seen these girls playing tag in the temple courtyard or huddled in a corner playing a game of jacks. Such sights are not seen in temples to the major male deities. The girls may be of any caste and are often the daughters of *pujārīs* or other local residents. During the festival season they come to the temples from miles around. They line the approaches to the temples and play in the temple courtyards, often harassing pilgrims to give them money. No one scolds these girls, for they are considered to be representatives of the Goddess. There is an attitude of playful indulgence toward them. After all, their divine status is short-lived; after their marriage they will not lead such carefree lives.

The worship of *kanyās* is considered to be extremely pleasing to the Goddess, and almost every pilgrim will perform it with a greater or lesser degree of formality. It is usually done after receiving *darśan* and is considered an adjunct to other rituals such as fire sacrifice (*havan*). The most informal type of *kanyā pūjā* is simply to give a few of the girls some sweets and a few coins and touch their feet. On a more elaborate scale, nine girls (representing the Nine Goddesses) are fed a meal of *pūrīs* and sweets and given a *ṭīkā* on the forehead, a red scarf, flowers on their head, a string on their wrist, and a larger amount of money. I once witnessed at Cintpūrṇī a *kanyā pūjā* done by a wealthy business family for 150 girls; 9 were chosen to get the full offering, while the rest received sweets and two rupees each.

All the temples have a place for performing *havan* (fire sacrifice), which is done according to the Śākta method with the accompanying recitation (*pāṭh*) of the *Durgā Saptaśatī (Devī Māhātmya)*. Although the temple priests may perform this or have it performed for them for their own benefit, it is not considered one of the services that they perform for pilgrims. Pilgrims wishing to have one performed bring along their own *paṇḍit* or make arrangements with one locally. Usually there are Brahmins not formally associated with the temple who are available to recite the *Durgā Saptaśatī* for pilgrims for a fee.

My discussion of pilgrimage has so far described the experience from the point of view of the pilgrim, that is, someone who is passing through for a short period of time and will be returning home. Besides the Goddess herself, there are those for whom a pilgrimage place is home. I will make a brief mention of them here. Of course, there are the local residents of the town or village, farmers, craftspeople, shopkeepers, restaurant owners, and the like, many of whose livelihood is dependent upon pilgrim traffic. And then there are the temple priests. The duties of the temple priests fall into two main categories, the care of the deity herself and the performance of services for the pilgrims. In the first category, the priests are required to perform the daily round of *pūjā* for the deity; this is independent of the pilgrim and is usually done behind closed doors. The schedule, which varies slightly from temple to temple, includes bathing the *piṇḍī* or *mūrti*, dressing and decorating it, offering cooked food (*bhog*) two or three times a day, performing *ārtī*, and putting the deity to bed for the night. These activities would continue on a daily basis whether or not any pilgrims visited.

The duty of the temple priests to pilgrims is to accept their offerings to the Goddess, say the *ardās* (supplication), officiate over special rituals such as *muṇḍan*, and show them around the temple and tell them stories about it. Some priests provide housing for their clients, especially at places such as Nainā Devī that do not have other pilgrim accommodations. Some families have a traditional relationship with a particular priest that may go back generations. Records of these relationships are kept in large, red registers called *bahīs*. At each visit the priest records the name of the pilgrim, names of others in the party, father's and grandfather's names, place of residence, amount of money or other gift offered, and any special rituals done. The relationship between the priest and the pilgrim is one in which the priest acts as an intermediary between the deity and the pilgrim.

Pilgrimage places are gathering spots for all sorts of religious specialists in addition to those officially in charge of the temples. As *śakti pīṭhas*, Goddess temples particularly attract Tantric *sādhus* and *yogīs*, many of whom spend their lives traveling from one pilgrimage place to another. At Jvālā Mukhī, the Gorakhnāth order has control of part of the temple, as discussed in chapter 2. Most of the Goddess temples have nearby shrines or tombs of local saints that house resident holy men, some of whom have reputations as healers or spiritual teachers. Pilgrims have an opportunity to interact with these holy men, thereby enriching their experience further.

Unlike Varanasi and Hardwar, pilgrimage centers associated with death and funeral rites, the Goddess shrines do not seem to attract large numbers of elderly people who move there with the intent to live out their lives in a sacred place. Nevertheless, one does come across people who came as pilgrims and ended up staying for good. One of these stands out in my mind, and I cannot resist telling his extraordinary story here. He was a middle-aged man who struck up a converation with me at one of the open-air restaurants on the path to Cintpūrṇī. As he was addressed respectfully by the restaurant staff as *Paṇḍitjī* and spoke with authority about the Goddess and her worship, I at first assumed he was one of the temple priests. Describing himself as an "outsider," a Maithili Brahmin from Bihar state, he proceeded to relate how he had come to reside at Cintpūrṇī.

He had been employed in the chemical department of a large company located near Ujjain in Uttar Pradesh when he became severely ill due to exposure to some chemical. He spent time in a hospital, having sold off his land to pay for treatment, but no doctor was able to diagnose his illness. Finally, he was forced to resign from his job and return home to Bihar. But there no one treated him with respect. His money was running out, and he had the constant worry of how to pay for his daughter's upcoming marriage. Unable to bear the insults and with no hope of recovery, he decided to commit suicide. His plan was to drown himself in the tank of a nearby Śiva temple.

Stealing out of his house at 11:00 P.M., after everyone had gone to sleep, he encountered a holy man (*mahātma*) on the road. Thinking that he was about to breathe his last, he decided it would be a good idea to speak with the holy man first and told him the whole story. The holy man dissuaded him from committing suicide, saying that it is a grave sin in the Hindu religion. Instead, he said the Brahmin should go to Himachal Pradesh, to the temple of the Goddess Cintharṇī, who takes away all worries, and that she would cure him. The holy man then vanished from that spot and was never seen again. The Brahmin went home, borrowed some money from a friend, leaving some with his children, and set off on foot for the Madhubani railway station, ten kilometers away. He did not know how he could make it there in the middle of the night, but a rickshaw happened to pass by and gave him a ride. Somehow, he made it by train to Ludhiana in the Panjab and from there took a bus to Cintpūrṇī.

At the temple he found a place to sit and, crying, began to recite the *Durgā Saptaśatī*. From that time on he did not suffer any more illness. He remained at the temple for nine days, cooking his own food on a stove he had brought with him and sleeping in a place the *pūjārīs* provided for him. At the end of nine days, he said to the Goddess, "I have recited your *pāṭh* for nine days. I had some money with me, but now I have spent it all. I don't have any money and can't continue to live in your *darbār* like this. Give me permission to leave." It was then 10:00 A.M., and he was planning to leave on the noon bus when a man from Taran-Taran, a paper manufacturer, asked him to perform a *havan* for him. He agreed to do so, provided he could finish it in time to catch his bus. The paper manufacturer had all the necessary materials with him, so the Brahmin was able to perform the *havan*. The paper manufacturer gave him fifty-one rupees and insisted on taking him to a restaurant to feed him. Then the paper manufacturer began to pour out his troubles concerning the difficulty in arranging his daughters' marriage; he asked the Brahmin to help him out by staying on for some time to do the *Durgā Saptaśatī* recitation for him. A few other people also asked him to do recitations, and he ended up staying for forty more days. On the fortieth day he was approached by a wealthy industrialist from Chandigarh who employed him to do recitations and *havans* for several more months, paying him four thousand rupees. That was still not enough to get his daughter married, so once again he asked the Goddess for help. Immediately, he was approached by a wealthy industrialist from Ludhiana, who upon hearing about the Brahmin's troubles asked him to make a list of what things he needed for his daughter's wedding and then provided all those things plus some money. The Brahmin went home, got his daughter married, then returned to Cintpūrṇī.

When I met him, he had been there about three years. A local restaurant provided him his meals and tea for free, and he had a constant flow of clients for whom he would perform recitations, *havans*, and astrological readings. He told me that the *śakti* of this place is only for those who have faith. He came here with faith, and the Goddess fulfilled all his wishes and granted him peace.

Communitas Revisited

Pilgrimage is a ritual that requires passage through space as well as through time.[11] Pilgrims leave the familiarity and relative mundaneness of their homes to venture out into a sacred zone where more direct communication with the Goddess is possible and where ritual actions take on a more intense quality. As Victor Turner has pointed out, there is an initiatory quality to pilgrimage in which the pilgrim moves from a familiar to an unfamiliar place and then is reintegrated into the familiar setting again, but only after having undergone a transformation. The time spent at a pilgrimage place is similar to the "liminal" phase of an initiation in which the usual norms of society are suspended and the pilgrim experiences a sense of "communitas" with other pilgrims.[12] As a devotee of the Goddess would say, "All are equal in the Mother's *darbār* [royal court]."

Many of the activities practiced at Goddess temples are of an individual or family nature and differ little in form from the same ritual done at home. For example, although *muṇḍan, havan,* recitation of *Durgā Saptaśatī,* and the like can all be done at home, performing them at Goddess temples which gives them even more efficacy.

Other activities have a more communal nature and contribute to the quality of "communitas" that Turner has described. On pilgrimage people have a chance to meet and mingle with other types of people with whom they would not come in contact in their daily lives. Status and hierarchy are temporarily put aside. On a group pilgrimage such as that arranged by a religious organization or nowadays by tour companies, seating is without regard to caste. Goddess temples in any case have always had low-caste clientele and have, so far as I have been able to ascertain, never refused entry to untouchables. Pilgrims experience a feeling of unity and camaraderie, singing devotional songs while riding together on the bus, approaching the temple on foot, or sitting in the temple courtyard. Some may join a spontaneous group of ecstatic dancers. Sometimes a whole village or neighborhood will take up a collection to donate a painting, image, or large flag to a temple and will form a procession to bring it there. The all-night communal ceremony called *jagrātā,* which will be discussed in chapter 4, is often held by a group of people at a pilgrimage place.

Similarly, at Goddess temples, the feeling of unity is reinforced by the communal meal called *laṅgar.* This meal, considered to be the *prasād* of the Goddess, is provided once or twice a day by the temple or sometimes (especially during the festival season) by a charitable organization. Pilgrims of all castes, Hindus and Sikhs, together partake of this meal, which is served by volunteers as an act of devotion to the Goddess. The word *laṅgar* comes from Sikhism, and its practice at Goddess temples is probably due to Sikh influence and the more relaxed attitude toward intercaste dining found among Panjabi Hindus. However, even those high-caste Hindus who would not normally dine with lower-caste people will do so at the Devī's *laṅgar,* because her *prasād* is pure and cannot be polluted.

I did see much of what Turner would term "communitas" on pilgrimages to the Goddess temples. Unrelated groups of pilgrims would strike up friendships, and many people told me stories about how they had been helped by strangers. Even I, a nosy foreign woman with a camera, was always welcomed as a fellow pilgrim, as one who had been "called" by the Goddess, never as an outsider who did not belong.

In June 1983, I was fortunate enough to participate in a week-long group pilgrimage to several Goddess temples, organized and led by a Chandigarh religious leader known as Bābājī. I was already acquainted with Bābājī, a guru in the Nāth Sampradāy, an order of practitioners that in the Panjab is closely associated with the worship of the Goddess. He calls himself a *gṛhasth-yogī,* that is, a yogic practitioner who is also a householder. He is also a government employee. In addition to leading about twenty *jagrātās* per month, he holds two major Hindu gatherings per year and leads a yearly pilgrimage to the major Goddess temples. I had paid several visits to his home and had attended *jagrātās* at which he and his *maṇḍalī* (singing group) had performed. It was at one of these *jagrātās* that my research assistant, Man Siṇgh, and I heard that there were openings in this upcoming pilgrimage and decided to sign up. At that point in my fieldwork, I had already visited all of the temples in this study several times, had participated in numerous rituals, had collected stories and songs, and had interviewed dozens of pilgrims. I jumped at the chance to go on this pilgrimage, since it would give me the opportunity to observe the interactions of a large, cohesive group of pilgrims. While the rituals we did at the temples followed the general pattern described earlier, it would be useful at this point to give a very brief account of our journey in order to convey some of the rhythm and flavor of traveling with such a group.

When Man Singh and I arrived at Bābājī's house at about 9:00 P.M. on the night of departure, a large crowd had already gathered in the adjacent open field. Bābājī, cutting a striking figure in his long hair, beard, and flowing saffron robes, was moving about giving last-minute directions. His assistant, a young woman renunciant known as Bahnjī (sister), was carrying a clipboard and handling the logistics. A loudspeaker had been set up outside to broadcast instructions to the waiting pilgrims. We were told that the buses would be arriving soon and that no one should try to board until their names were called with the seat assignment. We were also told that we should all behave properly and cooperate with each other; no one should argue, and anyone with a complaint or need should go directly to Bābājī. From time to time the announcer, one of Bābājī's close disciples, would lead the crowd in chants of *jay mātā dī!* The buses, three of them, arrived after some time, and a few names were called. For reasons unknown to me, this system broke down almost immediately, and people began to climb into the buses. Man Singh and I, eager to obey all the rules, sat there and waited for our names to be called. Finally, when we realized that we were the only ones not on the bus, we asked what we should do. We were then given the last two seats. The three buses were all full, with the total number of passengers at over 150.

In the course of our seven days together, we visted six major Goddess temples, with a few brief stops for other sights and shopping along the way. Much of our time was spent, of course, getting from one place to another, and most of us kept our original seats throughout, so that each bus became a kind of miniature community unto itself. While on the bus we sang devotional songs, especially at the beginning of each day and as we approached each sacred destination. In between we would chat with nearby passengers, read, look out the window at the spectacular mountain scenery, or attempt to catch a few winks of sleep.

The group of pilgrims was extremely diverse, a mixture of young married couples, families with children, single men and women, and elderly people. A wide range of castes was represented, from Brahmin to Blacksmith, with Rajputs and merchant castes such as Khattri, Arora, and Baniya being most numerous. With few exceptions, all were Panjabis and about a fourth were Sikhs. Everyone lived in Chandigarh, except for a few relatives of people living in Chandigarh who had come from out of town. The most important common denominator was a connection with Bābājī. Some were his family members or disciples; others said that they were friends of his family or disciples and liked him but were not his formal disciples. The bus owner also brought his wife and sons. Some had heard about the pilgrimage and decided that it would be a convenient way to see all the temples. Many remarked that it was auspicious to go on a pilgrimage with a *satsang,* a group of like-minded devotees. Some had gone on a pilgrimage with Bābājī before, others were coming with him for the first time. Most had previously gone on pilgrimage to the same temples on their own. As I would have expected, all the pilgrims I spoke with said that their main motivation was devotion to the Goddess, though many also had taken vows.

Our first destination was Vaiṣṇo Devī. We rode the whole night on the bus, making several stops on the way for water, latrine (in fields along the roadside), and breakfast. Some people bathed in a river along the way, men in their underwear, women in their *sārīs* or *salvār kamīz,* though some of the older women took off most of their clothes. By the time we reached Katra, the base camp for Vaiṣṇo Devī, it was about noon. Bābājī had arranged for several rooms at a pilgrims' hostel near the main bazaar, where some people rested and took baths, while others ate lunch in the bazaar. Small groups of people gradually set off on the climb. Bābājī's assistants had taken orders on the bus for *prasād* packages at twelve rupees each. The packages would be given to us at the main shrine, so that we would not have to carry them ourselves. We accompanied Bābājī and Bahnjī to the bazaar to make arrangements for buying and transporting the *prasād,* and also for Bābājī to get some tennis shoes and a walking stick. We reached the main shrine area at about 7:30 P.M., most of us exhausted from the hot, strenuous climb and lack of sleep. I had gotten to know many of the pilgrims by that time and went off with a group of women to bathe and change clothes. Our group was scheduled to have *darśan* at 10:00 P.M., and as the time grew nearer the mood became more and more exhuberant. Bābājī had gotten permission from the temple *pūjārīs* for me to photograph the *piṇḍīs,* something I had never attempted on my previous visits. When the crucial moment arrived, squatting in the dark, narrow cave with hundreds of people lined up behind me shin-deep in icy water, I was so nervous that I could not make my flash go off. After *darśan* we went off in small groups to eat in various open-air restaurants near the shrine, and about midnight stretched out blankets on the *dharmsālā* floor and fell asleep. At 5:00 A.M., Bābājī's assistants, who seemed never to sleep, woke us up to climb back down the mountain. When we reached Katra, we returned to the same pilgrims' hostel, where Bābājī had arranged for a feast (*bhaṇḍārā*) for our group.

Leaving Vaiṣṇo Devī in the afternoon, we stopped along the way in Jammu to see the impressive Raghunāth temple and do some shopping. We continued on through the night, stopping for dinner and a brief nap and to see the Śaivite cave at Triloknāth, arriving at Cāmuṇḍā Devī in the morning. There we stayed for two days, with group activities centered around evening *satsangs,* singing devotional songs, and feasts provided by Bābājī. One afternoon the "ladies *maṇḍalī*" led by Bābājī's wife, Kṛṣṇājī, performed devotional songs in the temple hall. The bus owner arranged an optional excursion to nearby Dharmsala; those wanting to go had to pay extra. Bābājī and his close disciples stayed behind, as did Man Singh and I, taking advantage of the first real leisure time to do informal interviews with some of the pilgrims we had not spoken with before. One of the pilgrims, a man who had lived in Great Britain for some years, took an interest in our work and helped us with the interviews.

On the sixth day we went to Kāṅgṛevālī Devī, where we all marched in one big procession through the street to the temple, Jvālā Mukhī, where Bābājī led us in an hour of devotional singing, and to Cintpūrṇī, where we spent the night. On the final day we made a brief stop at Nainā Devī and then returned home to Chandigarh. At Cintpūrṇī there was no special program, as Bābājī spent most of his time preparing a delicious *kaṛhī* and rice dinner for the whole group. Instead, people went to the temple for *darśan* in small groups, wandered around the bazaar, and did some shopping. The most popular items were mango *papaṛ,* a dried mango puree that is a specialty of the area, and bangles. Some of the older women instructed me to buy some glass bangles, because that is the auspicious thing to do at a place of pilgrimage. I had already bought glass bangles in Kangra, so I bought mother-of-pearl bangles at Cintpūrṇī. I noticed at Cintpūrṇī that tempers were beginning to get a bit frayed. We had been eating, sleeping, bathing, and riding in the bus together for almost a week, and people were beginning to think of the comforts of home. What was most irritating was that, of the two pilgrims' hostels we were staying in, one did not have any latrines and the other's latrines were locked up, because there had been no water for over a week. As we were on the side of a steep mountain, there were no large fields that could be used. Bābājī diffused the situation by getting permission for us to use the latrines at another pilgrims' hostel.

The journey had its humorous moments as well. Our bus trip had been remarkably uneventful, given the propensity of Indian buses to break down and the high accident rate on the narrow, winding mountain roads. Everyone commented on this, saying that we were under the protection of the Goddess and Bābājī. The only mishaps on the road were occasional bouts of motion sickness; the unfortunate young woman in front of me sat with her head hanging out the window more often than not. A few people had expressed concern that my presence as a foreigner might attract the unwanted attention of the authorities, but no one even bothered to check my passport. We were on the way to Nainā Devī, approaching the stretch of road that runs past the Bakra Dam, a restricted area where photography is forbidden. Knowing that there was a checkpoint ahead, Bābājī stopped the buses and sent a message back to me that I was to remain inconspicuous and not say anything when a guard came through looking for cameras. I followed his instructions, not wanting to hold up the whole group. As it happened, the bus I was on was passed through with no problem. But on Bābājī's bus, when the guard asked if anyone had a camera, a small boy yelled out, "I do, I do," waving a plastic toy camera, a souvenir from one of the temple stalls, in the air. The guards, not content to confiscate the toy, held up Bābājī's bus for over an hour while they tried to decide what to do. The absurdity of the situation struck everyone as hilarious, and we all took the delay in good spirits.

I saw much on the group pilgrimage that would support Turner's thesis that pilgrimage serves a social function and fosters a sense of commonality among diverse groups of people. But at the same time, based on my observations and conversations with the pilgrims, I would have to say that that is not its only, or even its primary, significance. Pilgrimage is an intensely personal experience, so much so that individual pilgrims traveling together for convenience or companionship may have vastly different understandings of what it all means and may not even tell each other their private reasons for undertaking the pilgrimage.[13] Even on the group pilgrimage I have just described, for most of the pilgrims, the pilgrimage had a personal or family significance that had nothing to do with the group as a whole. Also, a pilgrim's experience may differ greatly at different times in his or her life. At times it may be more social, at other times more personal. For example, one pilgrim told me that his first visit to Vaiṣṇo Devī was a last-ditch attempt to cure his tuberculosis, after more conventional treatments had failed. After his cure, which he attributed to the Goddess's grace, he became her devotee and now sees pilgrimage as a form of *sādhanā,* or spiritual discipline. Another pilgrim reported that she initially visited Jvālā Mukhī out of curiosity, because all her friends were doing so. Only after receiving *darśan* did she undergo a personal transformation and become a devotee of the Goddess, so that now she regularly undertakes pilgrimages.

A pilgrimage place is a physical, geographical place where the Goddess has manifested herself in a particular localized form. It is a place imbued with power and as such attracts pilgrims who come with specific desires they wish to have fulfilled or just to experience and participate in that power. It is both in the world and removed from the world, a transition zone between the realm of gods and the realm of humans. Goddess temples lie on the fringes, removed from populated areas, in mountains that have mythical associations. Stories of modern-day miracles abound; almost every pilgrim I spoke with claimed to have witnessed a miracle or knew someone who had. Thus, it is appropriate to conclude this chapter with a miracle story current in the oral tradition:

> Once a husband and wife and their small daughter were climbing the mountain to Vaiṣṇo Devī. They were planning to ask the Goddess for a son. On the way, their daughter fell into a ravine, and they could not find her. The wife refused to go for *darśan,* saying that she had come to get another child and instead had lost the one she had. The husband wanted to get *darśan.* He went up and started looking for his daughter in the jungle. Suddenly, he came upon her sitting with a lap full of dried fruits and eating contentedly. Her father, overjoyed to find her safe, asked if she wasn't afraid being alone in the jungle. The daughter replied that she was not alone, that a girl with a big dog [the Goddess with her lion, which the girl mistook for a dog] had made friends with her and given her something to eat.

4

Waking the Goddess

The Jagrātā *as Ritual Performance*

Come, Mother, to my house,
O Mother who saves the world,
Come, Mother, to my house.

Without you no good comes to me.
Throughout the world, your name is true.
Mother, I chant your name.
O Flame One, I dedicate myself.
O Lion One, I dedicate myself.
O Mountain One, I dedicate myself.
Come, Mother, to my house.

Come to my house.
Mother, may I prosper.
With a pure heart I remember you.
O, I am small, Mother,
surrounded by worries.
I sacrifice myself at your feet.
Come, Mother, to my house.[1]

Wake up, Mother, wake up!
Bringing offering lamps, I come to your door,
In my hand an ocean of Ganges water to bathe,
In my hand gold-threaded cloth to adorn,
In my hand a dish of saffron,

to place a *tilak* on my Mother
Wake up, Mother, wake up!

In my hand a basket of flowers,
to offer flowers to Mother.
In my hand coconut and dates,
to offer food to Mother.
Wake up, O Mother, wake up![2]

We have seen in chapters 2 and 3 how the Goddess manifests herself at various places of pilgrimage and how devotees travel long distances to visit her in those places. In this chapter we discuss the Devī *jagrātā,* in which the Goddess comes to visit her devotees in their homes or communities. The Panjabi word *jagrātā,* also *jāgā* or *jāgraṇ* (Sanskrit: *jāgaraṇa*), means an all-night vigil, usually to worship a deity. In the greater Panjab it generally refers to a Devī *jagrātā,* a ritual performance held to gain the favor of the Goddess and to obtain some material benefit or repay her for one already received.[3] Structurally, the performance of a *jagrātā* is the counterpart to pilgrimage. On a pilgrimage, devotees travel long distances to visit the Goddess in places where she is manifested in iconic or aniconic form. In the *jagrātā,* devotees invoke the Goddess to visit them in their own homes or communities in the form of a flame (Hindi–Panjabi: *jot;* Sanskrit: *jyoti*), which is lit at the beginning of the ceremony and kept burning all night.

The *jagrātā,* which as a performance genre probably dates back several hundred years, is held in both villages and cities but in its more elaborate and commercialized form has become a "craze" in the cities. The contemporary Devī *jagrātā* is a compelling example of a traditional cultural performance adapting to modern conditions. In this chapter I explore the dynamics of the ritual process of the *jagrātā,* the significance of its charter myth, and the symbolism behind the two central motifs of fire and wakefulness. I then conclude with some observations on the contemporary relevance of the Devī *jagrātā.*

The Ritual Process

Two basic types of *jagrātās* are held in contemporary Panjab—those sponsored by a private individual or family for a relatively small audience and those sponsored by an organization or wealthy donor for the general public. The first type, held either inside the home or in a tent on a nearby vacant plot, is usually in fulfillment of a vow or in celebration of some important family occasion such as a marriage, birth of a child, recovery from a serious illness, moving to a new house, winning a lawsuit, or passing an examination. Generally only one party of performers is engaged for this type of *jagrātā*. Often, especially among the urbanized middle classes, printed invitations are sent out to friends and relatives as they would be for a wedding. However, since the place where a *jagrātā* is held becomes temporarily consecrated as Devī's temple (*darbār,* or "royal court"), anyone is welcome to attend, and often neighbors hearing the singing will stop by to pay their respects to the Goddess and greet the hosts.

The other type of *jagrātā,* called Viśāl Bhagavatī Jāgraṇ, is held on a much grander scale and advertised widely in newspapers and on billboards. Several groups are hired to perform in succession, the decorations are more lavish, and as many as ten thousand people may attend. The Viśāl Bhagavatī Jāgraṇ, a relatively recent phenomenon, is usually an annual affair held by a religious or secular organization to invoke the Goddess's blessings and obtain merit. Groups as diverse as the Sanātan Dharm Sabhā, Shiwalik Breweries, and the Motor-Rickshaw Drivers' Union sponsor an annual Visāl Bhagavatī Jāgraṇ.

Traditionally, the most popular day for *jagrātās* is the eighth day (*aṣṭamī*) of the bright fortnight of each lunar month, the day sacred to Devī in her various manifestations. Nowadays, due to the standardized workweek, Saturday night is also popular. During the autumn and spring Nine Nights festival, scheduling is so tight that they happen any night of the week.

In order to be called a *jagrātā,* the ceremony must last all night, must have a lighted *jot,* and must conclude with the telling of "The Story of Queen Tārā." Another type of performance genre that is closely allied to the *jagrātā* is the *kīrtan, bhajan,* or *caukī*. In these, a *jot* is lit at the beginning, devotional songs are sung, and consecrated food (*prasād*) is distributed at the end. A *kīrtan* or *bhajan* session is usually held for several hours in the afternoon and is particularly popular among women. A *caukī* is basically the same thing but is held for three or four hours in the evening. A *jagrātā* meets all the requirements for these performances, but the reverse is not true. On one occasion I witnessed a woman approaching the leader of a performing group to book them for a *caukī* she had vowed to hold. This particular group did not usually do *caukīs*, so the leader talked her into having a *jagrātā* instead, since it would fulfill her original vow and then some.

Jagrātā performers, known collectively and individually as *maṇḍalī*, form groups of five or more members who conduct the necessary rituals, sing devotional songs, and tell stories. *Maṇḍalīs* do not generally consider themselves to be professionals but are amateurs who participate out of devotion to Devī. They do receive donations from sponsors, and some have a set fee, but the earnings from a *jagrātā*, divided among all the members after paying transportation and other expenses, do not amount to much. Most have other full-time occupations. The *maṇḍalī* is an intermediary between the sponsor and Devī. In some cases sponsors consider the head of the *maṇḍalī* to be their guru or spiritual preceptor. In other cases the *maṇḍalī* is asked to perform on the basis of its musical or storytelling expertise.

The leader and organizer of a *jagrātā maṇḍalī* is called the *pradhān*, while the spiritual head is called the *mahant*. Often these are the same person. Some *maṇḍalīs* do not have a *mahant* in their own group but consider a person in another *maṇḍalī*, often in another town, to be their *mahant*. Thus, a *mahant* may have several *maṇḍalīs* in different places acknowledging him as their head. Like classical music lineages, *jagrātā maṇḍalīs* are loosely grouped into *gharānās*, or schools,[4] but nowadays many *maṇḍalīs* are springing up without a *gharānā* affiliation. A person joins a *maṇḍalī* by approaching the *mahant* and accepting him as one's guru. One may also join informally by asking to play an instrument or sing at a forthcoming *jagrātā*. An activity that reinforces the coherence of such a fluid group is a yearly pilgrimage undertaken by the *maṇḍalī*, which often puts money aside for this purpose. I have seen many of these groups, often on bicycles, at the major Goddess shrines.

The cosmopolitan composition of *maṇḍalīs* is striking. Among the dozen or so *maṇḍalīs* I interviewed in Chandigarh, and the many others I observed there and in Delhi, a wide variety of castes, occupations, and ages was represented. All of the *maṇḍalīs* with whom I spoke stressed the mixed composition of their groups and the unimportance of caste in the worship of Devī. Traditionally, certain castes such as Brahmins (priestly caste) and Mehrās (a musician caste) were associated with *jagrātās*. Nowadays, all castes are represented among Hindus, Sikhs, and occasionally even Christians.[5] The majority of members are male, but there are some women, especially vocalists. Most are householders, though I did meet one renunciant (*saṃnyāsī*) who headed a *maṇḍalī*.[6] Several *maṇḍalīs* were connected with the Gorakhnāthīs, a Śaivite sect with strong connections to the Devī cult; two of these were led by householder Gorakhnāthī *yogīs* who had large followings. The leader of the oldest *maṇḍalī* in Chandigarh and one of the most knowledgeable about Devī cultic lore was in fact a Sikh.[7] He is the only one I met who was initiated into *jagrātā* performance through his family tradition, being a member of the Mehra caste. Another, less traditional, *maṇḍalī* head, belonging to the Khattri (merchant) caste became involved in *jagrātās* purely through his own interest. His *jagrātā* activities dovetailed nicely with his business in light, electrical, and loudspeaker rentals.

The devotional songs sung at a *jagrātā*, like those sung at pilgrimage places, are called *bheṇṭān* (Panjabi plural of *bheṇṭ*, or "offering"). Their lyrics cover various topics, such as the Goddess's majestic power, her exploits in killing demons, her various temples and manifestations, and the grace and favor she bestows on her devotees. The songs sung to traditional folk tunes in often somewhat archaic language are called *pakkī* (pure, firm) *bheṇṭān*, while the modern type with devotional lyrics sung to popular film tunes are called *filmī bheṇṭān*.[8] The latter especially abound in popular bazaar pamphlets and cassette tapes with titles such as "Latest Hit *Bheṇṭān*." Particularly popular are *bheṇṭān* sung by Narendra Chanchal, a well-known playback singer in Bombay films who got his start as a small-time *jagrātā* singer in Amritsar. He became famous by singing in the Vaiṣṇo Devī sequence of the Hindi film *Āsā*. He is still in great demand as a *jagrātā* performer, though his fees are beyond the reach of most people, and tapes and pamphlets of his *bheṇṭān* are sold everywhere. The *maṇḍalīs* I interviewed had various attitudes toward the use of film music. A few traditionalists rarely perform film tunes.[9] Some said they did not like to perform them but did so because of popular demand. Others said that the *pakkī bheṇṭān* are more difficult to understand, so they have to sing the more accessible *filmī bheṇṭān*. An opinion often expressed was that religious practices have degenerated since the "old days" but that it is better to worship Mātā with film songs than not at all. A few—

such as the renunciant who said, "Now there is even disco in the *darbār*"—were unabashedly enthusiastic about the use of film music, saying that entertainment does not have to conflict with devotion. Many *maṇḍālīs* write and sometimes record their own *bheṇṭān*. All keep their own personal diaries filled with words to their favorite *bheṇṭān,* which they have written, read in a book, or heard from another singer.

Musical instruments used at a *jagrātā* vary according to the size, expertise, and taste of the *maṇḍalī*. Traditional instruments include *ḍholak* (drum), *cimṭā* (tonglike percussion instrument), *chaiṇe* (cymbals), and *gāgar* (water pot). Nowadays the harmonium, congo drum, and sometimes even the saxophone and guitar are also used. The effect is a combination of indigenous and Western sound that is riveting, to say the least.

The elements of a *jagrātā* are varied and flexible according to the practices of a particular *maṇḍalī* and the wishes of the sponsor. The following description includes ingredients that are generally considered necessary for a successful *jagrātā*. When a person decides to host a *jagrātā,* he or she approaches the head of a *maṇḍalī* to fix the date and discuss the various materials needed for the rituals. The larger *maṇḍalīs* have a typed or printed handout sheet that lists these materials (*sāmagrī*) and other necessary instructions. Nowadays, at least in the cities, loudspeakers and microphones are part of the necessary equipment and may often be rented through the *maṇḍalī*. When the date has been decided, the sponsor sends to the head of the *maṇḍalī* a red cloth containing saffron-colored rice, raw sugar, a red thread, and 1¼ rupees. This offering, called *ḍal,*[10] is both an invitation from the sponsor and a contract with the Goddess. When I asked *maṇḍalīs* about the significance of *ḍal,* all were adamant in stating that once they accept the *ḍal,* they are obligated to perform the *jagrātā* on that date, even if a death occurs in their family, an event that usually prevents Hindus from performing auspicious rituals. Even if the sponsor cancels or postpones the *jagrātā,* the *maṇḍalī* is bound to perform it somewhere else at its own expense. Failure to do so would result in dire consequences—according to one informant, seven bad rebirths.

The *jagrātā* begins at about 9:00 or 10:00 P.M. at night and continues until about 6:00 or 7:00 A.M. The sponsors set aside a room in their house or set a tent outside as the *darbār*. All must wash their hands and take off their shoes before entering. The sponsors often rent a large poster, which may have electrically moving parts, depicting Śerāṅvālī on her lion and perhaps other gods such as Hanumān, Bhairo, Śiva, or Gaṇeśa. Particularly popular is a graphic representation of the famous devotee Dhyānū Bhagat offering his head on a platter to the Goddess. These images, however, are largely decorative. The ritually significant image of the Goddess is the aniconic *jot,* a flame burning on a heavy cotton wick set in a container of flour dough (which to me looks like a small pie) and fed with ghee throughout the night. As they enter or leave the *jagrātā* area, devotees bow before the *jot* and make cash offerings.

The first thing that happens in a *jagrātā* is a *pūjā* (worship), performed either by the *mahant* of the *maṇḍalī* or by a Brahmin priest brought in for the occasion. Gaṇeśa (the god of beginnings), the nine planets, and Devī are worshiped. The *mahant* or priest then ties protection cords on the sponsors' wrists and puts an auspicious red mark (*tilak*) on their foreheads.

The next step is the "empowerment of the flame" (*jot pracaṇḍ*). *The mahant,* uttering *mantras,* holds a lit piece of cotton hanging from a stick above the *jot* until the flame drops down and ignites the wick inside the *jot.* This is a dramatic moment that takes place amid cries of *jay mātā dī* (Victory to the Mother) and *jaykārā Śerāṅvālī dā: bol sāce darbār kī jay* (Śerāṅvālī's victory cry: say, victory to the true court). It is at this point that the *jagrātā* actually begins, for with the empowerment of the *jot,* Devī has appeared among the congregation in flame form (*jvālā rūp*). With the transformation of an ordinary room or tent into Devī's *darbār,* mundane space has become sacred space. The sanctity of the place lasts only as long as the *jagrātā;* afterward it reverts to its original mundane status.

After the *jot pracaṇḍ,* the singing of *bheṇṭān* begins. At least the first two are of the traditional *pakkī* type and include praises of Devī and all the gods, beginning with Gaṇeśa. After these, film tunes may be introduced. Audience members are encouraged to sing along and to respond in between songs with the proper slogans such as *jay mātā dī* or *jotāṅvālī mātā terī sadā hī jay* (O Flame Mother, your eternal victory).

At any point during the *jagrātā,* a devotee may come forward and make an *ardās* (supplication–offering)[11] through the *maṇḍalī.* He or she hands the *maṇḍalī* some cash, whereupon the *maṇḍalī* announces, "X rupees *ardās,* so and so's *ardās* at Mā's auspicious feet; may his or her wishes be fulfilled." The *maṇḍalī* is acting as an intermediary between the devotee and Devī; it is in effect accepting offerings on her behalf. At the same time, the money is being given in part out of appreciation for the *maṇḍalī*'s performance. These offerings are either divided among the members, used for expenses, or given to a temple or charitable cause.

Consecrated food of sweets or salty snacks and tea may be served to the audience several times throughout the night after being offered in front of the *jot*. The singing of *bheṇṭān* is interspersed with speeches and stories told by the *maṇḍalīs*. These may include anecdotes about personally witnessed miracles performed by the Goddess, moral and social teachings,[12] announcements for organized pilgrimages, stories about the origins of Devī shrines, and other stories from Purāṇic and folk sources. Some of the more popular stories include Dakṣa's sacrifice and the founding of the *śakti pīṭhas*, the killing of Mahiṣāsura and other demons, and the wedding of Śiva and Pārvatī. About halfway through the *jagrātā*, the four watches (*pahars*) of the night are explained in either verse or prose: If one worships Devī during the first watch, one gains the light of intelligence (*buddhi prakāś*); in the second, food and wealth (*ann-dhan*); in the third, devotion (*bhakti*); and in the fourth, liberation (*mukti*). Following this is a poetic recitation of the sixteen *kalās* (arts or sports) of Devī, apparently the sixteen successive entities arising in the universe.[13] This cosmogonic sequence sets the stage for the more immediate charter myths of the present age that follow.

Next the sponsors offer coconuts to Devī by holding them over the *jot* until they burn slightly. Later the coconuts will be broken and given out to the audience as consecrated food. At this time, one of several stories is told to explain why coconuts are offered. The most popular and well known of these stories, already summarized in chapter 3 in connection with the Jvālā Mukhī temple, is that of Dhyānū Bhagat, the semilegendary sixteenth-century devotee who cut off his own head and offered it to the Goddess, then received a boon from her that in the future a coconut would suffice. The second most popular "coconut-explaining" story is that of Nandā and Nandalāl, which will be summarized in chapter 5. I have heard one other, which I summarize here:

> At one time in Calcutta, Kālī organized a sacrifice to which the 330 million gods were invited. All the seers and sages came as well, and Guru Gorakhnāth while wandering around also showed up. Now, as you

> know, at Mā Kālī's feet coconuts are also offered. Some devotees cut off a goat's head and offer it. Some devotees like Dhyānū cut off their head and offer it. Some devotees like Śambu cut off their tongue and offer it.[14] Some devotees cut their fingers and offer drops of blood at Mā's feet. According to each one's faith, in Mā Kālī's *darbār* a sacrifice is given. Now, Guru Gorakhnāth was a follower of the Vaiṣṇo belief, and he considered taking life to be a sin. So, Mā Kālī asked him, "you didn't bring an offering to my *darbār?*" He replied, "I consider taking life to be a sin, so I have not brought anything to your *darbār* to offer." Kālī then told him to leave. He replied that he would neither leave nor offer a sacrifice. So, Mā Kālī became angry and through her *śakti* turned Gorakhnāth into a goat. Since Guru Gorakhnāth is an incarnation of Śiva, he was able with his *śakti* to turn Mā Kālī into a fly and suck her into his stomach with his breath. Without air or water, Mā Kālī began to writhe in his stomach and pleaded to be released, saying that he would not have to give her a blood sacrifice. He said that he would do so on the condition that any Vaiṣṇo devotee would be able to offer a coconut and that she would consider it equal to a head. She agreed, and Guru Gorakhnāth released her and changed her from a fly back to her own form. Kālī changed Gorakhnāth back to his own form. So from that time coconuts began to be offered in Mā's *darbār,* and those who offer them reap the same fruits as Dhyānū Bhagat when he cut off his head and offered it.[15]

These stories reflect the tension between blood sacrifice and vegetarian offerings so evident in the Goddess cult.

A phenomenon that may occur at a *jagrātā,* as well as in other contexts, is divine possession by the Goddess. Possession is signaled by glazed eyes, rhythmic circular head movements, ecstatic dancing, and speaking with the voice of Devī, who is said to be "playing" in that person. Often it happens that a devotee, usually a woman, enters into a spontaneous possession trance. Although such possession, I am told, may occur at any time, the occasions on which I have witnessed it were well into the night during periods of intense singing and drumming. In some cases, such possession becomes formalized in certain women who, as Mātās (Mothers), become central figures of their own cults in which they are worshiped as manifestations of the Goddess herself. These Mātās are featured at their devotees' *jagrātās,* where they are worshiped along with the *jot,* becoming possessed in the early part of the morning before the telling of "The Story of Queen Tārā." A more detailed discussion of possession in several contexts is the subject of chapter 5.

The most important part of the *jagrātā* is the telling of "The Story of Queen Tārā," the charter myth, without which the *jagrātā* is not considered complete. It is either recited in prose or sung in verse so that it will end just before daybreak. It may take anywhere from one to three or more hours to narrate, depending on how many songs are interspersed and how many episodes are included. A summary and discussion of the story appears in the next section.

After the telling of "The Story of Queen Tārā," the *jagrātā* ends with an *āratī,* the waving of lighted oil lamps clockwise around the *jot,* with the accompanying song "Jay Ambe Mātā." Some optional rituals at this point include *havan* (fire sacrifice) and *kanyā pūjā* (worship of small girls). The sponsors present the head of the *maṇḍalī* with a red turban and a sum of money such as 151 or 201 rupees. The *jot* is extinguished, and there is a final distribution of consecrated food consisting of *halvā* (farina pudding) and *canā* (spicy black chick-peas). The size of the audience is largest for about the first two hours at night and again in the morning, when many people drop in for the final rituals and food distribution. However, it is considered most efficacious to sit through the entire *jagrātā* without sleeping.

"The Story of Queen Tārā"

The following is a somewhat condensed summary of the story based on several Hindi and Panjabi versions that were available to me:[16]

> Once there were two sisters, Tārā and Rukman,[17] who were observing the "Eleventh Day Vow."[18] Inadvertently, the younger sister broke the fast ahead of time by eating meat.[19] Tārā cursed her to become first a vulture, then a lizard, and then to live in a low-caste house in her next three lives. Rukman was immediately repentant, and Tārā assured her that she would have a chance to redeem herself by virtuous acts.
>
> In the next birth, Rukman was born as a vulture in the Himālayas.[20] Then she gave up that life and was reborn as a lizard. Meanwhile, Tārā was reborn in heaven as a nymph. At this time the five Pāṇḍavas, during their period of wandering in the forest, held a great sacrifice (*yajña*) to which they invited the 330 million gods and goddesses.[21] When they

invited Ṛṣi Durvāsā, he, out of pride, refused to attend, because all the other deities had been invited as well. Out of spite, he took the form of a bird and when no one was looking, dropped a poisonous snake into the pot of rice pudding that was to be served at the feast after the sacrifice. The lizard saw this happen. So, when the Pāṇḍavas, along with the 330 million gods and goddesses, approached the pot to eat the rice pudding, she jumped into the pot. All the gods cursed the lizard for ruining the feast, saying that she would be reborn into a low-caste house. Then they emptied out the pot and saw the snake. They said, "This is not a lizard but some goddess who has sacrificed her life to save ours." A curse once uttered cannot be taken back, so they modified it by saying that in her next birth she would be born in a royal house, but would have to live in a low-caste house.

So, the lizard was born as the daughter of King Saparaś. Tārā, her sister from a former life, had already taken birth in the same house and had been married to King Harīcand.[22] When Rukman was born, the astrologers said that she would be harmful to the king and that he should have her killed. The king refused, saying that it is a grave sin to kill a maiden (*kanyā*). The astrologers then advised him to have a box made and inlaid with gold, put the baby girl inside, and set the box afloat in the river. Anyone finding it would then have the wherewithal to bring up the girl. The king agreed, and the girl was set afloat in the box.

As the box was floating down the river, a Brahmin saw it and tried to retrieve it, but it kept moving away from him. He called a sweeper who was passing by and told him to retrieve the box. They made a deal that the Brahmin would get the outside of the box, while the sweeper would get what was inside. The box floated right to the sweeper. When it was opened, the sweeper was overjoyed to see a beautiful baby girl inside, for he and his wife had remained childless for many years. The couple named her Rukman[23] and brought her up lovingly. When Rukman came of age, they married her to a sweeper boy in the very same city where her sister Tārā was married to King Harīcand.

Rukman's mother-in-law used to work as a sweeper in Queen Tārā's palace. As she was getting old, Rukman took her place. On her first day at work, Tārā took her aside and explained to her that they were sisters in both a previous and the present birth and told her the circumstances leading to their present difference in status. Tārā told Rukman that she should worship Bhagavatī Mātā in order to make her life successful. Rukman asked how to do this. Tārā replied that Devī fulfills all wishes and that one should worship her by having a *jagrātā* performed.

Rukman made a vow, saying, "O Mātā, if by your grace I get a son, then I will have a *jagrātā* performed for you."[24] In the tenth month, by Devī's grace, a beautiful son was born in her house. Time passed, and Rukman forgot to have the *jagrātā* performed. When the child was five years old, he came down with smallpox. Rukman went to Tārā to bemoan her fate. Tārā reminded Rukman of her unfulfilled vow. So Rukman again vowed that if her son recovered, she would definitely hold a *jagrātā*. By Bhagavatī's grace, the boy recovered the next day.

When Rukman went to the *bhaktas* [devotees] in the temple to ask them to perform a *jagrātā* in her home, they refused on the grounds that they were Brahmins and she was a lowly sweeper. She kept insisting, and finally they said, "We will come if Queen Tārā also agrees to come to your house and eat your *prasād*." Rukman explained the situation to Tārā, and she readily agreed to attend the *jagrātā*.[25]

The night of the *jagrātā* approached. That day Sain the barber informed King Harīcand that his wife, Tārā, was planning to attend a *jagrātā* in a low-caste home. The king refused to believe such a thing about his wife, but to be on the safe side, he cut a small slit in his finger and rubbed it with red chilies so that he would not fall asleep that night.[26] It was getting later and later, and still the king did not fall asleep. Tārā prayed to Mātā, and finally a cool breeze blew, putting the king to sleep. Tārā jumped up and seeing that the palace was surrounded by guards, tied a rope to the skylight and climbed out.[27] On the way, she met a thief, but through the grace of Mātā was able to overpower him. In her haste, she left behind a slipper and a torn piece of clothing.

Tārā arrived at Rukman's house while the *jagrātā* was going on and told the people there to offer *bhog* and distribute *prasād*. So they offered *bhog* and distributed *prasād*.[28] Tārā put hers in her bag. Seeing this, the devotees asked, "Why did you do that? If you don't eat your *prasād*, we won't either." Tārā replied, "I am taking this home for the king. Now give me my *prasād*." She took the *prasād* and ate it.

Meanwhile King Harīcand had awakened and followed Tārā to the *jagrātā*, meeting the same thief on the road. He also found her slipper and took it with him. To his amazement, when he arrived at the *jagrātā*, the slipper had miraculously left him and joined its mate outside the *darbār*. He stood outside the door watching what was going on. As Tārā was leaving, he accused her of ruining their *dharm* and destroying his lineage. He demanded that she open her bag and show him what was inside. When she opened the bag, the cooked food[29] had miraculously changed into flowers, uncooked rice, betel nut, and cloves. The king, astounded, asked how this happened. Tārā replied that it was Devī's grace. When they arrived home, Tārā lit a fire without flint or matches. The king, even more amazed, asked, "Tell me the way [*panth*]. How can I get a direct vision [*pratyakṣ darśan*] of the Mother? I will do anything."

Tārā told him that it wasn't easy, but still he insisted. So, she told him that he would have to sacrifice his favorite blue horse. He took out his sword and killed the horse. Then she ordered him to sacrifice his beloved son. He then killed his son. Next she told him to cut up the horse and the boy, place them in a cauldron, and cook them. He did this as well. Finally, she told him to dish out the food on five plates: one for Mātā, one for himself, one for the horse, one for the son, and one for her. When he complied, she told him to start eating his share. The king, bound to his word, started to eat, but tears welled up in his eyes.[30] The horse and the son both came back to life. Devī granted him his *darśan* appearing before him on her lion. King Harīcand worshiped her and begged for forgiveness. Mātā forgave him and then disappeared.

The king praised Tārā's devotion and built a temple to Devī at her request.[31] Queen Tārā, King Harīcand, and Rukman lived out their lives happily and ultimately attained liberation [*mukti*]. Whoever reads, tells, or hears this story will have all his or her wishes fulfilled.

Sacrifice and Pollution

Unlike other stories that are told and sung in several contexts, "The Story of Queen Tārā" is told only within the context of the *jagrātā*. There are numerous versions in Hindi and Panjabi. As far as I know, it is not mentioned in any Sanskrit text. Like the story of Dhyānū Bhagat, it has come down through oral tradition and has only recently been printed in popular bazaar pamphlets. The only known literary mention to the story, and a somewhat obscure one at that, is a four-line reference in the writings of the Sikh poet Bhāī Gurdās, a fifteenth-century contemporary of Guru Arjan, the fifth Sikh guru.[32] Some *maṇḍalīs* include these verses in their narration of "The Story of Queen Tārā"; others have mentioned them to me in conversation. Whether or not Bhāī Gurdās was referring to the same Tārā and Harīcand, the fact that *maṇḍalīs* perceive it to be so leads them to believe that the Tārā story originated or became incorporated into the *jagrātā* around the time of his writing. It also provides another connection between Sikhism and the Goddess cult. No one I interviewed could tell me the original source of the

Śerāṅvālī in Vaiṣṇo form, flanked by Bhairo and Hanumān. Popular bazaar print. (Introduction)

Kālī, statue in folk style at Mansā Devī temple. (Introduction)

Kālī emerging from the forehead of Śerāṅvālī. Painting at Kālkā temple, Kalka, Haryana. (Introduction)

Devī as Mahiṣāsuramardinī, killer of the buffalo demon. Silver carving at Kāṅgṛevālī Devī. (Chapter 1)

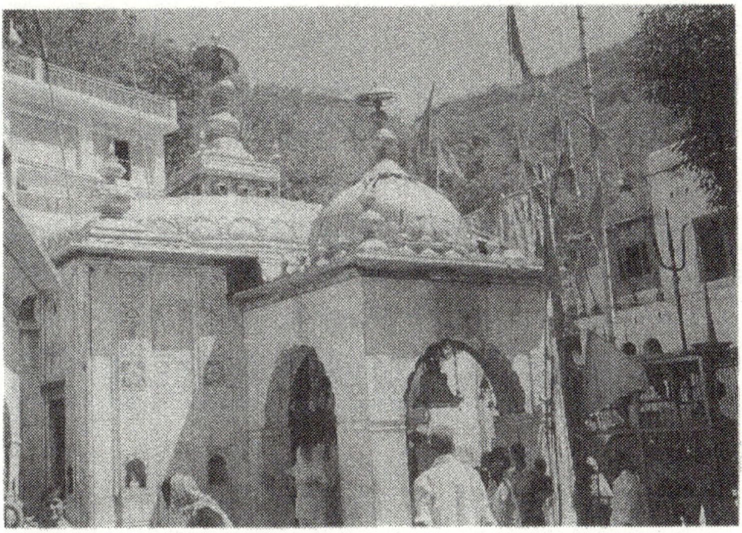

Jvālā Mukhī temple, entrance to the shrine containing the flames. The gilded roof was donated by Maharaja Ranjit Singh. (Chapter 2)

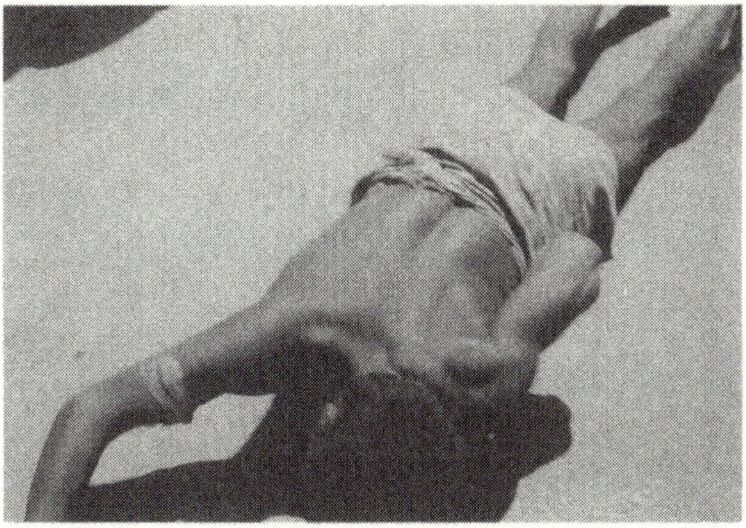

Daṇḍautī pilgrim prostrating himself on the route to Mansā Devī temple. (Chapter 3)

Kanyā at Vaiṣṇo Devī applying an auspicious mark (*ṭīkā*) to a pilgrim's forehead. (Chapter 3)

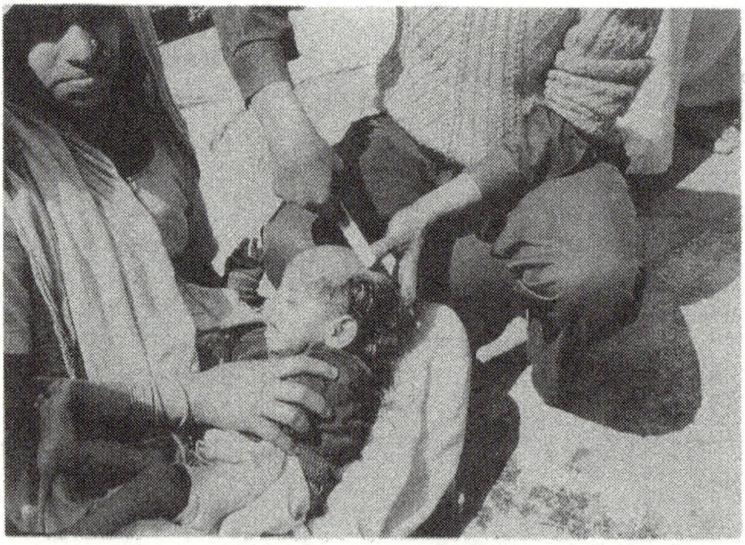

Muṇḍan, first head shaving of a child, at Kāṅgṛevālī Devī temple during the spring Navarātra. (Chapter 3)

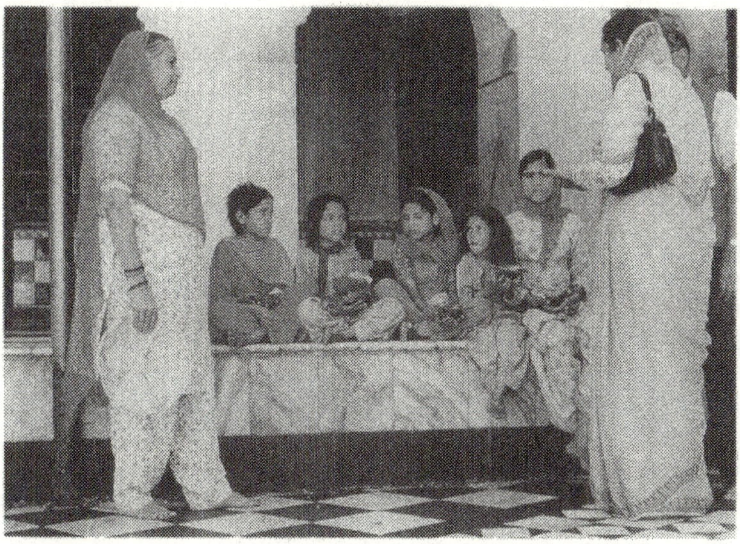

Kanyā pūjā, the worship of small girls as manifestations of the Goddess, at Jvālā Mukhī. (Chapter 3)

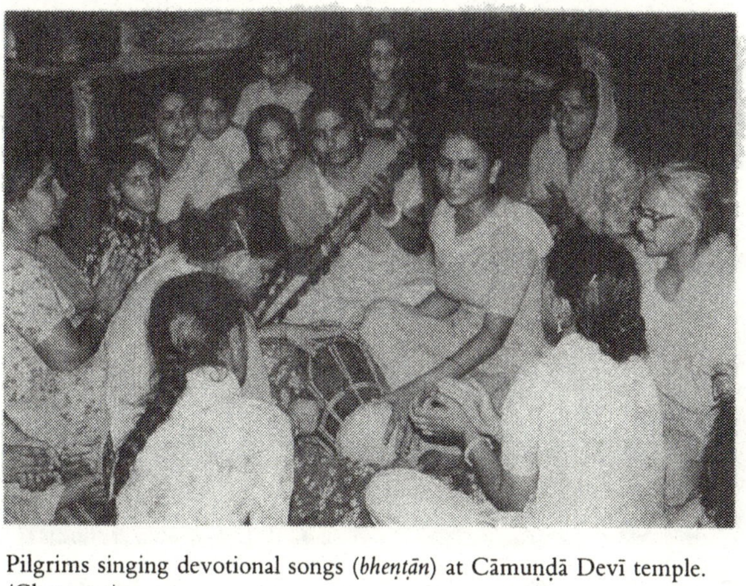

Pilgrims singing devotional songs (*bheṇṭāṇ*) at Cāmuṇḍā Devī temple. (Chapter 3)

Communal meal (*laṅgar*) at Jvālā Mukhī temple. (Chapter 3)

Pilgrims dancing at Cintpūrṇī temple during the spring Navarātra. (Chapter 3)

Jagrātā maṇḍalī performing at a *jagrātā* in a suburb of Chandigarh. The Mahant is in the center. (Chapter 4)

Ten-armed Devī killing a demon, flanked by Hanumān and Bhairo. Popular poster at a Viśāl Bhagavatī Jāgraṇ. The caption in Devanagari script is *jay mātā dī*. (Chapter 4)

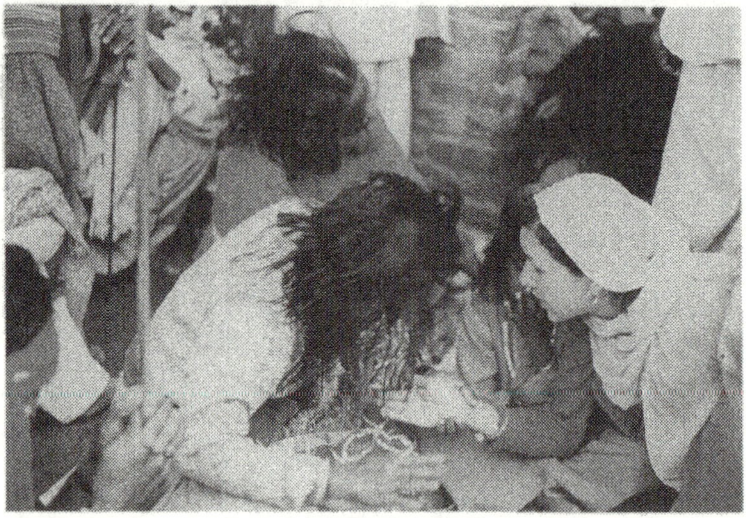

Possession at a pilgrimage place, Jvālā Mukhī, during the spring Navarātra. The woman on the right has approached the possessed woman for advice. (Chapter 5)

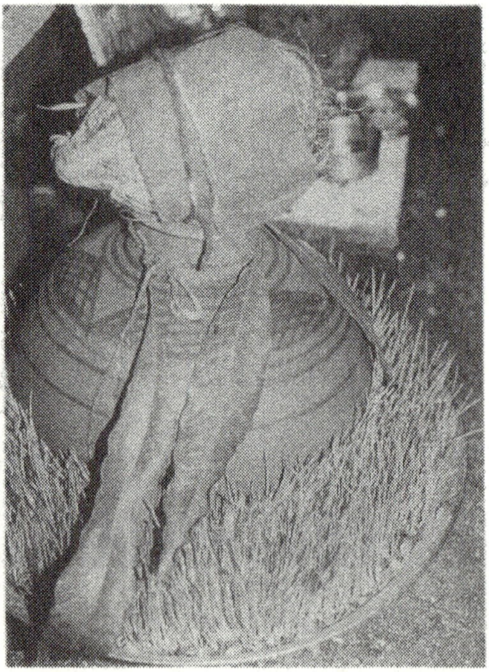

Barley sprouts on the eighth day of the Navarātra at Gumti village, Haryana. (Chapter 5)

The younger Mātā with Goddess image at Navadurgā temple in Gumti, Haryana. Both have been given new clothes as an offering by devotees of Gumṭivāle Mātā. (Chapter 5)

Poster announcing Ūṣā Bahn's program. (Chapter 5)

Painting in popular style being donated by a group of pilgrims at Cintpūrṇī temple during the Sāvan Aṣṭamī festival. (Chapter 6)

Santoṣī Mātā temple at Mani Majra village, Haryana, near Chandigarh. This temple was formerly called Annapūrṇā. (Chapter 6)

story, although many informants had wondered about it themselves. One religious leader in Chandigarh placed an advertisement a few years ago in the *Panjāb Kesarī*, a Hindi-language newspaper published in Jullunder, challenging anyone to name the (Sanskrit) source of "The Story of Queen Tārā." No one replied, so he concluded that it is a *dantkathā* ("tooth," or folk, story) of no special significance. However, when the leader of the *maṇḍalī* with which he is attached tried to omit the story from his *jagrātās,* there was such an uproar among his clients that he was forced to reinstate it.

Devotees consider the Tārā story to be true and significant as a didactic story regardless of whether it actually happened or whether it has any textual basis. According to the head of a *maṇḍalī* in Chandigarh,

> *Tārārānī kī kathā* is not found in any history [*itihās*]. In the old days, they used to play *ḍholak* [a drum] and sing *bheṇṭān* all night. *Tārārānī* was made up, and it developed as a custom to keep people awake and to show the greatness of Devī for propagation [*pracār*]. Its purpose is to show how strong *bhakti* is, to show the power of devotees and the power of Devī. Also, before that, people used to say that one shouldn't go into the house of a sweeper and eat there, but Tārā was such a *bhaktinī* that she went there. There used to be *bhog* of meat and wine. In those days, it used to be Kālī's *jagrātā;* now they call it Vaiṣṇo Devī's. Actually, there is [traditionally] only *pāṭh* [recitation of the *Devī Māhātmya*] for Vaiṣṇo. There is [traditionally] no *jagrātā* for Vaiṣṇo, only for Kālī.

Another *maṇḍalī* head explains the significance of "The Story of Queen Tārā" as follows:

> In the Kali Yug, the custom started of telling "Tārārānī." It used to be that a golden pitcher and the like were used, and only rich people had *jagrātās*. In the Tārārānī story, when Tārā told Rukman to have a *jagrātā,* she substituted cheap things for expensive things. This opened the way for all people to have *jagrātās*. . . . The episode of the *balidān* [sacrifice] is used to prove Devī's power so that the king would believe in her. Devī brought the goat alive that had been used for *prasād* and changed the meat into dried fruits. The king promised to do whatever Tārā said if she would tell the secret of how the light was lit. So he had to sacrifice his son. The idea is that everything belongs to and comes from Devī. *Balidān* means getting rid of your ego. One has to extinguish the self. One shouldn't say, "This is mine."

Two themes that stand out very clearly in the story and in these two interpretations of it are self-sacrifice and pollution, both of which are placed within the context of *bhakti.*

In "The Story of Queen Tārā," there are two instances of self-sacrifice. The first is when Tārā's sister Rukman, reborn as a lizard, jumps into a boiling pot of rice pudding in order to save the lives of others and obtain merit for a better rebirth. The episode takes place at the Pāṇḍavas' *yajña,* also a sacrifice.[33]

While the Tārā story itself is not found outside the greater Panjab, the motif of self-sacrifice by jumping into rice pudding is encountered in other contexts. A story is told in a fifteenth-century Indian Sufi collection about a cat that listened to the religious discourses of a *shaikh* and performed various marvels, including jumping into a boiling pot of milk in order to prevent his master from being poisoned by a snake that had previously fallen in it.[34] The same motif is found in a story from Nepal in which a female dog, like Rukman as lizard, contaminates rice pudding in order to prevent snake poisoning, thus atoning for a ritual infraction as a human in a previous life.[35]

The second sacrifice in the story is when Tārā's husband, King Harīcand, is compelled to kill his own son and horse, parts of himself as it were, in order to get a vision of Devī. An amazingly close parallel to this episode is the South Indian story of the "Little Devotee" in which a devotee cuts off his son's head to provide food for a wandering ascetic who turns out to be Śiva himself.[36] However, unlike the Little Devotee, Harīcand undergoes a transformation from nonbeliever to believer, a transformation mediated by his wife, Tārā, which culminates in the vision of which he is not worthy until he is prepared to sacrifice his own self. As the second *maṇḍalī* leader put it, "*Balidān* means getting rid of your ego." Most devotees see the image of offering one's son as in the Tārā story or one's own head as in the Dhyānū Bhagat story as a metaphor for dedicating oneself entirely to Devī. However, there are cases in which these stories are taken and acted upon quite literally. It used to be not uncommon for devotees to cut out their tongues and offer them to Devī. This practice is not unheard of even today; the priests at Goddess temples tell stories of having witnessed people's tongues grow back after they had cut them out and offered them. A more extreme example is cited by David M. Wulff from an Indian newspaper article:

> In 1972 in Jullunder, the Punjab, a father decided to sacrifice his three sons to the Goddess as a means of assuring the peace of the soul of his own father, who had died some fifteen years before. A night-long vigil of song and prayer [presumably a *jagrātā*] culminated in the death and dismemberment of the one son, three and a half years old, who had not escaped. The boy's uncle had proclaimed that the Goddess would restore his life after the sacrifice.[37]

It is worth noting that Tārā is never asked or expected to make any sacrifice. She remains a static character undergoing no transformation or conversion. Even though it is her son as well as the king's, her nonattachment is so well cultivated that she does not see his death as a sacrifice. She is already the perfect devotee, a natural *bhaktinī*. As such, she fits A. K. Ramanujan's description of the woman saint.[38] He says that because *bhakti* itself is inherently antistructural and women—along with low-caste men—are relatively unstructured participants in society, they do not need conversion as do their high-caste male counterparts. Tārā experiences no internal struggle; she has only external obstacles to overcome. Tārā's problem is not to undo the entanglements of caste and status, for she has already transcended them within herself and does not feel bound by them, but rather it is how to get around her husband's objection to her attending a sweeper's *jagrātā*. King Harīcand, on the other hand, must break down the high-caste notions of purity, duty, and propriety to which he is attached. For this reason, the prominence of women and low-caste characters in the story is not surprising. Tārā, who has transcended her high-caste status (or never put much stock in it in the first place), acts as Harīcand's guru in initiating him into the worship of Devī. She clearly places her duty to Devī, and even to her sister Rukman, above her duty to her husband. She is hardly the model of wifely submission extolled in the Hindu *śāstras*. Rukman also acts independently of her husband by having the *jagrātā* performed at her own initiative. She looks to Tārā for cues and validation of her actions, certainly not to her husband, who is not even named. Her husband plays no further role in the story than to provide Rukman a socially acceptable context in which to have a child.

"The Story of Queen Tārā" displays a strong concern about issues of high and low caste, purity and pollution. It comes out overwhelmingly in favor of the view that the power (*śakti*) of the

Goddess makes caste irrelevant, as there is no high or low in Devī's *darbār*. However, the notion that impurity is connected with low-caste status is not ignored in the story. In fact, it seems to be implied that the law of *karma* works at least to some extent according to conventional notions of ritual purity and status hierarchy. Rukman is brought up in a low-caste house as a result of her polluting deed of breaking a fast by eating meat in a previous life. However, Tārā's deliberately exposing herself to the same pollution shows that devotion to Devī overruns pollution. The Goddess prefers Tārā and Rukman, who have broken the rules of ritual purity, over Harīcand, who until the end has kept his purity intact but has remained undevoted.

A story with similar overtones is told in Bengal in connection with Bipadtarinī, a goddess who is worshiped by women and children in times of crisis. In that story a queen was fascinated by the fact that her low-caste friend ate beef and wanted to see what it looked like. As the friend was showing her the meat, the queen's husband rushed in to kill her. The queen prayed to the goddess Durgā, and when the king tore at her clothes to see what she was hiding, all he could find were red flowers.[39]

Still another story is told in Puri, Orissa, to explain why food from the Jagannāth temple is shared among all castes. In this story Jagannāth and his brother Balabhadra banish the goddess Lakṣmī from the temple for accepting a food offering from an untouchable but then undergo starvation for twelve years until they finally are reduced to begging food from an untouchable woman who turns out to be Lakṣmī in disguise. Frédérique Marglin observes that the story illustrates how the concepts of auspiciousness and inauspiciousness crosscut and undermine the concepts of purity and pollution.[40]

The importance of *śakti* in overcoming pollution and status inequalities is clearly pointed out in "The Story of Queen Tārā," as it is in the Orissan story. Yet in the Tārā story, a tension between vegetarian and nonvegetarian remains, reflecting a general anxiety about meat eating and blood sacrifice. It is either implied or directly stated that the food offered at Rukman's *jagrātā* was meat, but it is not clear whether this offering was approved of or not. Devī changed the *prasād* into "pure" vegetarian foodstuffs, but it remains ambiguous whether she did so in order merely to protect Tārā and demonstrate her power to Harīcand or because she also prefers such offerings. The informant quoted above refers to a *jagrātā* in which meat is offered as "Kālī's *jagrātā*" and one in which vegetarian food is offered as "Vaiṣṇo's *jagrātā*." Many of the devotees who spoke to me about the story assumed that it had become current around the time that *jagrātās* started being dedicated to the Goddess in her Vaiṣṇo aspect rather than her Kālī aspect. A similar shift in style of worship is also depicted in the Dhyānū Bhagat story in which Devī proclaims a vegetarian offering, the coconut, to supersede a blood sacrifice. This story, one should remember, immediately precedes the telling of the Tārā story in the performance of the *jagrātā*. As a matter of fact, all the *jagrātās* I attended had only vegetarian offerings to Devī. It is also a fact, however, that many Panjabi Hindus and most Sikhs eat meat. Perhaps the emphasis on vegetarian offerings is a concession to intercaste dining, as vegetarian offerings offend no one. At the same time, there seems to be a recognition that although blood sacrifice is polluting and immoral, at least from the high-caste and, incidentally, modern point of view, it is still considered traditional in Goddess worship and that Devī—at least in her Kālī aspect—likes it. Thus, an ambiguity remains.

Waking and Burning

Why is a nightlong vigil so important in the worship of the Goddess, and why is a flame the object of worship in that vigil? In exploring these questions, it becomes clear that staying awake and the burning flame are closely connected.

The concept of waking or wakefulness is central in Hinduism as in many religious traditions. In fact, it could be called a root metaphor for the Hindu religious experience. The state of enlightenment, for example, is often compared to being awake as opposed to being asleep or deluded. Deities who are active in the world, as opposed to being otiose, are said to be "awake" (*jāgrit*). Images of gods and goddesses in temples are ritually "put to sleep" each night and "awakened" each morning. Viṣṇu, who sleeps during the rainy season, is "awakened" at its end by a special festival, whereupon certain activities such as weddings, which have been suspended, can be resumed. Similarly, in Bengal the goddess Durgā is awakened each fall with the *bodhana* ceremony in preparation for the beginning of the Navarātra festival. All-night vigils of one kind or another are common in Hindu and Buddhist practice, particularly as part of an intensive spiritual discipline (*sādhanā*) for ascetics and *yogīs*. Gautama the Buddha (which means "awakened one") himself attained enlightenment at daybreak after staying awake all night, and his meditative experiences during the several watches of the night are an important part of his spiritual biography. On the popular level, an example that comes most readily to mind is the yearly festival of Śivarātrī, falling in February and March, in which the god Śiva is worshiped all night.

The Sanskrit word *jāgaraṇa,* a synonym for *jagrātā,* comes from the root *jāgṛ,* which means to be awake, to watch over, or to be attentive or intent on something. It can also, when said of a fire, mean to go on burning. Waking, from the point of view of the devotee, is a form of self-denial or asceticism. Various forms of denial in popular practice include fasting (the denial of food); *brahmācarya* (the denial of sexual activity); walking barefoot on pilgrimage (the denial of comfort); and in this case waking (the denial of sleep). The *jagrātā,* however, unlike some other forms of denial, is a communal activity. Drinking the strong tea and eating the sugary snacks given out as *prasād* or consecrated food, singing devotional songs, and listening to stories together as a group reinforce everyone's ability to stay awake. Besides being a denial of sleep, wakefulness itself is a positive quality, being associated with such attributes as wisdom and lucidity of mind. By staying awake, devotees help themselves and please the Goddess.

In a *jagrātā* it is not only the devotees who are being kept awake but also the Goddess herself, here in the form of a flame. We have seen that the Sanskrit root *jāgṛ* and its derivatives can refer to a fire continuing to burn. Lyrics in the devotional songs sung at *jagrātās* play upon this meaning with references both to the devotees' staying awake (Mahārānī, *terī raīṇ jāgāṅge* [Great Queen, we will stay awake your whole night]) and to keeping the flame awake (*terī jot jagāvāṅge* [we will keep your flame awake]). The refrain of another popular song is *jāgo,* Maiyya, *jāgo* (wake up, Ma, wake up). The flame is often referred to in Panjabi as the *jagdī jot,* the waking flame. The devotees keep the flame awake by singing devotional songs and feeding ghee to the flame. Thus, one purpose of the *jagrātā* is to keep Devī awake, that is, accessible, approachable, and active in the lives of human beings.

As to why the flame in particular has been chosen to represent Devī in the *jagrātā,* the immediate answer would be that the flame represents the deity as she is manifest at the famous pilgrimage site Jvālā Mukhī in Kangra District, Himachal Pradesh, where, according to its charter myth, the "flame tongue" of Satī fell at the time of her dismemberment. Thus, the *jot* at a *jagrātā* could be viewed as the flames of Jvālā Mukhī in "portable" form.[41]

At the same time, fire itself is an archaic and multivalent symbol in Indian religion, going back to the Vedic fire sacrifice. The connection of a goddess with fire is also an ancient motif. As I have noted previously, the "seven tongues" of Agni, the Vedic fire god, came to be identified with feminine deities (*Muṇḍaka Upaniṣad* I.24), perhaps even with the Seven Sisters. In Panjabi the word *jot* can also refer to the *ātman,* or soul; it could thus be interpreted as the *śakti* or power that resides in all beings. While aniconic representations of goddesses are common throughout India, their representation as a flame is not so common. The *dīpa* or lamp, is standard in all forms of Hindu *pūjā,* but it is usually an item offered to the deity, not a representation of the deity itself.

Ann Gold makes an intriguing reference to the worship of the goddess Hing Lāj in the form of a flame in Rajasthan. Apparently this is an esoteric rite held only by householder Nāths on the eleventh night after a death, in place of the exoteric flour-ball offerings given on the twelfth morning. The Nāths hold a *jāgaraṇ* and sing *bhajans* that interweave themes of Śāktism and *nirguṇa bhakti* theology. In keeping with the *nirguṇa* (formless) theme, they worship no image other than a flame that is kept burning all night.[42] Hing Lāj is a goddess whose main shrine in Baluchistan (now in Pakistan), like Jvālā Mukhī, is said to have an eternal flame. Although the ceremony Gold describes is different from the Panjabi *jagrātā,* which is exoteric and as far as I know is never performed in the context of death rites, the similarity in the image of the flame, the all-night vigil, and the connection with Nāths, who also play an important role at the Jvālā Mukhī temple, is striking. It may well be that these two ceremonies stem from a common tradition that developed in the Tantric centers of medieval northwest India.

Modernization of Ritual

Jagrātās are becoming increasingly popular, especially in urban areas. In Chandigarh alone there are a few dozen *maṇḍalīs*; in Delhi they number in the hundreds. As a performance genre, the *jagrātā* is especially suited to urbanized popular religion with its intercaste appeal, low level of ritual snobbishness, and entertainment value. The upsurge in *jagrātās,* however, is not an isolated phenomenon; it is consistent with the relatively recent revival of Devī worship and pilgrimage to Devī shrines. Informants indicated that people hold *jagrātās* and worship Devī more because she grants boons and because it is appropriate to worship her in the Kali Yuga. Old symbols are being renewed and transformed to suit the demands of changing societal values and sensibilities. For example, the message of the Tārā story is consistent with and provides a religious basis for the modern ideals of anticasteism and anticommunalism.

While examples of Sanskritization can clearly be discerned in the Goddess cult as a whole and in the *jagrātā,* modernization is also quite evident, as discussed more fully in chapter 6. The *jagrātā* is an excellent example of a popular religious performance genre, drawing on both classical and folk traditions. Technological innovations such as mass printing, loudspeakers, movies, cassette tapes, and the like all play a part in the transmission of cultic lore. It is now common for a *maṇḍalī* to read or hear various versions of "The Story of Queen Tārā" or other stories and then compose his own version. Many *maṇḍalīs* publish their own pamphlets or record their own music for the propagation of the cult. These innovations have not detracted from the religious significance of the cult, as one can see by the fervor displayed by devotees. In fact, secular artifacts are picked up and made religious. Film songs are made sacred by their dedication to Devī. Loudspeakers and microphones have been made indispensible items in the paraphernalia of worship. Images of the Goddess have gained a new dimension by the addition of electrically moving parts. The Devī *jagrātā,* which has now become a product of popular culture, belies the notion that modernization and commercialization necessarily lead to a decline of the sacred. Rather, modern means are appropriated to facilitate access to the Goddess and communication among devotees.

5

The Play of the Goddess

Possession and Participation

The most dramatic way in which the Goddess manifests herself to her devotees is through possession of human, usually female, vehicles. It was my own experience of observing such possession, recounted in the introduction to this book, that brought home to me in a very concrete fashion the immediacy with which devotees experience the Goddess's presence and which led me to take seriously the notion of the Goddess as an agent herself, rather than as simply a disembodied symbol or projection. Many scholarly studies of possession have struck me as rather patronizing, attempting to account for possession as a purely psychological or sociological phenomenon, not something that "really happens."[1] I wonder if it is possible, if not to "explain" possession, at least to approach a better understanding of it by going beyond theories of individual or collective pathology, which are inadequate as interpretive models. As Peter Claus has stated,

> The psychological and sociological "preconditions" sometimes identified as the causes of possession may only be secondary features. In order for psychological states to be interpreted as possession and in order that sociological preconditions set the stages for such states, there must be precise ideological correlates that anticipate precipitation of the phenomenon.[2]

In neither psychological nor sociological explanations is much attention paid to the spirit or deity possessing the person, it being regarded at best as a convenient epiphenomenon. This seems to me a grave omission, since from the point of view of the participants and the tradition, the spirit or deity is the most important actor. For the devotees in a cult, the crucial concern is not just that a person is possessed, but who or what is possessing the person and for what purpose. For this reason, I am viewing Goddess possession not as an isolated phenomenon but as a religious expression within the theological and ritual context of the Goddess cult and popular Hinduism in general.[3] To that end, I approach Goddess possession in this chapter from several different angles. Moving from the general to the specific, I start out with a discussion of indigenous terminology, moving on to a description of the occasions and context of Goddess possession, then following up with two individual case studies. This ethnographic expedition then leads me back to consider a sacred narrative that among other things, is about possession.

Semantics of Goddess Possession

I am concerned here specifically with divine possession within the Goddess cult, not with unwanted possession by malevolent spirits or ghosts (*bhūt-pret*) nor with related phenomena of sorcery, witchcraft, and black magic that fall under the general category of *jadū ṭonā.* Susan Wadley has made the distinction that in a village in Uttar Pradesh, the afflicting spirit "rides" while the invited spirit "comes."[4] Gananath Obeyesekere states that in Sinhalese, *āvēsā* is the term used to describe those possessed by evil spirits; *ārude* is for those possessed by a deity, adding that "psychologically, they tap the same propensity: culturally they are radically different."[5] Similarly, in the Panjab, possession by an evil spirit must be exorcised by force or appeasement, while possession by a benevolent deity such as Śerāṅvālī or Bābā Bālak Nāth[6] is usually encouraged and cultivated, even if not at first initiated. Possession by an evil spirit is seen as an affliction or punishment, while possession by the Goddess is seen as a gift, a sign of grace, a positive, albeit awesome and often troublesome, appearance.

But what exactly is possession? To describe this cross-cultural phenomenon, the following definition is as good as any: "any complete but temporary domination of a person's body, and the blotting out of that person's consciousness, by a distinct alien power of known or unknown origin."[7] Yet the word "possession" is inadequate except as a very rough gloss that I use advisedly to describe a complex set of related phenomena. Several phrases in Hindi and Panjabi are used in the context of the Goddess cult to describe these phenomena. Also, terminology varies throughout India; here I am concerned with terms used in the area of northwest India, where I conducted fieldwork.

One term I frequently encountered was *pavan*, or "wind, breath." When a person is possessed, it is said that the *pavan* has come to her or entered her. Her hair, no matter how tightly bound, is said to open up and fly freely due to the force of the *pavan*. The state of possession is characterized by glazed eyes, a change in voice, and the head whirling around in circles with hair flying loose. Under normal circumstances, a woman's hair would be bound or tied up and braided, not allowed to hang loose. Paul Hershman, in a discussion of hair symbolism among Hindu and Sikh Panjabis, mentions one context of the expression *val khūle* (loose hair) as being "a woman possessed who in a trance whirls her head with her hair flying free."[8] In this instance the Goddess is said to have taken on *pavan rūp* (wind form). *Pavan* is a subtle, invisible form intermediate between the unmanifest Goddess and her full manifestation. It is a form characterized by motion and breath, which the Goddess takes on in order to move from one place to another or to display her power without becoming fully visible. For example, in several versions of "The Story of Queen Tārā," discussed in chapter 4, the word *pavan* appears as a form of the Goddess. When King Harīcand's wakefulness prevents Tārā from attending the sweeperess's *jagrātā*, Tārā prays to the Goddess, whereupon a cool breeze (*pavan, havā*) blows and puts the king to sleep. An informant discussing the story with me referred to this episode as Tārā praying to "the goddess of the wind." Later in the story, after the king had witnessed the transformation of meat offerings into vegetarian ones, he wanted the Goddess to enter his palace. According to an oral version of the story, Tārā prayed to the Goddess and "hearing Tārā's supplication, Mā Jagadambā [Mother of the World] set out. Taking on wind form [*pavan rūp*], she reached the palace. Hearing Tārā's supplication, Mā took on wind form and came and sat on Tārā's head."[9] Then she sat on Tārā's tongue, and chiding the King for trying to test her, told him to sacrifice his horse and son. I have also found references to the Goddess entering Tārā in wind form in written Hindi verse compositions of the story.[10]

While *pavan* is a major expression relating to possession, it has a somewhat broader meaning as a form of the Goddess. It can also refer to an invisible thought form. A *sādhu* who acts as a *pujārī* at a Durgā temple told me that he had been called there by the Mātā, who had come to him in the form of *pavan*. Whenever he forgets to do some work, she comes into his mind in the form of *pavan* to remind him. He says that when this happens, she enters his mind through the breath in his mouth and that he sees her in his mind.

Another term used in connection with the possession phenomenon is the verb "to play" (Hindi: *khelnā;* Panjabi: *kheḍnā*). It refers to the wild and "playful" head and body movements of the person being possessed. The Goddess is said to be "playing" in that person, as in the expression, "the Goddess plays in X." Sometimes it is stated with the vehicle as the agent as in "X started playing." A slightly different but related use of "play" is found in devotional songs (*bheṇṭān*) evoking the image of small girls (*kanyā, kañjak*) representative of the Goddess in her virgin aspect playing in the temple courtyard.[11] These songs represent the sweet and lovable aspect of the divine play, evoking *vatsalya bhāva* (parental love)—one of the modes of *bhakti*—in a way similar to that found in the cult of the child Kṛṣṇa. These expressions are all tied in with general notions of divine play in Hinduism.[12] In various stories connected with the Goddess, her actions are described as play (*khel*), drama or sport (*līlā*), and art or fabrication (*kalā*). All of these terms are used roughly interchangeably to suggest the Goddess's exuberant but seemingly (to humans) purposeless creativity.

The person possessed is called *savārī* (vehicle), as in "the vehicle of Kālī" or the "vehicle of Vaiṣṇo Devī," meaning that the Goddess in a particular form rides on or inhabits the vehicle and speaks through her. *Savārī* also is used in the sense of the "riding" or "mounting" that the Goddess does as in the expression *savārī rūp,* meaning the Goddess appearing in the form of a possessed person.

The most ambiguous word used in connection with possession and somewhat removed from its everyday usage is *caukī*. In ordinary usage in both Hindi and Panjabi, a *caukī* is a square platform or seat. As I have encountered the word, it means something like a possession session or performance. If during a *jagrātā* a planned possession takes place from, say, 2:00 to 4:00 A.M., that period of time will be called the *caukī*. A *caukī* is also an evening performance similar to a *kīrtan* or *bhajan* in which the Goddess is worshiped with songs and music with or without possession taking place. In this sense, *caukī* seems to mean a performance or ritual in which gifts of song, flowers, sweets, incense, and the like are offered to the Goddess. Both of these usages seem to evoke a sense of the Goddess being seated on a platform granting *darśan* and receiving offerings from her devotees whether in the context specifically of possession or not. In still another usage, *caukī* refers by extension to the possession trance itself, as in the statement "the *caukī* of the Goddess enters her." Other expressions used in connection with possession are *śakti ānā* (coming of power), *praveś* (entering), and *jībh par/te baiṭhnā* (sitting on the tongue).

Contexts of Possession

In reading about South Asia, one often gets the impression that possession and related ecstatic behavior are part of the "little tradition" and thus confined to the lower castes and the poor and uneducated in rural areas.[13] So I was somewhat surprised to discover not only how prevalent the phenomenon is in the cult of Śerāṅvālī but how widespread it is throughout the population. I have seen Goddess possession in both village and urban settings, among low and high castes (including Brahmins), the poor and the rich, the uneducated and the educated. I have seen Sikhs as well as Hindus in possession trance. Possession by the Goddess, while occurring in both sexes, is more frequent among women, while possession by a male deity such as Bābā Bālak Nāth is more frequent among men.

There is considerable variety in possession experiences, in their intensity, duration, and frequency. There is also considerable variation in the degree of recognition, respect, and encouragement given to possession vehicles by other members of society.

Unplanned, uncontrolled possession occasionally occurs in a nonritual context. I have not seen this type of possession but have heard reports of young girls "playing" for hours on end without warning. Such after-the-fact descriptions are part of the hagiographies of women who later achieved some control and regularity over their possession and have come to understand it in terms of the theology and religious practice of Devī *bhakti*. At the time of the initial possession, however, there may not have been recognition or acceptance by the vehicle or others that the possessing deity was the

Goddess. Often sorcery (*jādū ṭonā*), insanity (*pāgalpan*), or possession by a malevolent spirit (*bhūt-pret*) are initially suspected because of their similar symptoms.

Unplanned, uncontrolled possession may occur in devotees in a ritual context such as a *jagrātā, bheṇṭ* singing, or pilgrimage. While the music is playing and drums beating, a person may spontaneously start to shake, roll the head, or dance. No one seems particularly surprised or disturbed when this happens; in many cases it is an isolated event in a person's life. However, such spontaneous possession experiences do often progress into regular or planned ones and become part of a person's devotional and spiritual practice. The initial experience may be repeated and develop into a periodic pattern. I came across an example of this type of development while interviewing a man of the Kāyasth caste from Chandigarh on a group pilgrimage to the major Devī temples. In a discussion of his long-standing devotion to the Goddess and the miracles she had performed for him, he volunteered the information that he had recently started to "play," describing his experience as follows:

> I do *pūjā* twice a day. When I go to a *jagrātā,* I get the *caukī.* I see Devī seated on a lion, and my head starts spinning around. Bābājī [his guru] told me to offer a coconut at Mansā Devī. This has been happening for five or six months now. I got it last night during *pūjā* time. I get a feeling of wind [*pavan*] overwhelming me like a whirlwind and see the image of Devī. I am not afraid of this experience. I sit in front of a flame [*jot*] every day and concentrate. The *pavan* comes when I am listening to a beautiful *bheṇṭ*. At first my wife worried that I would become a *sādhu* and forsake the world, but now she and the children realize what it is.[14]

This informant's description of a vision (*darśan*) of the Goddess followed by the wind is typical of possession experiences. The vision of the Goddess along with the statements she makes while inhabiting her vehicle are the major signs distinguishing Devī possession from possession by other deities or spirits.

Possession is also found to be planned, controlled, and even orchestrated in a performance situation. There seems to be a progression from initial spontaneous possession to more controlled and regular periodic possessions. A woman may start to become possessed on a certain day of the week, such as Tuesday or Friday, or on the *aṣṭamī* (eighth) day of the bright fortnight of the lunar month. When this becomes known outside her family, people may come on these days to sing *bheṇṭs,* offer her gifts, and ask for her help as an oracle or healer. The woman may start to hold *caukīs, kīrtans,* or *jagrātā* in her home on a regular basis or be invited to participate in these events at others' homes. She may build a small shrine or temple and/or start making pilgrimages with her devotees to Devī temples. In this way, a small cult begins to form.

During the spring and fall Navarātras and the ten-day festival during the month of Sāvan (July–August), pilgrimage places such as Jvālā Mukhī, Cintpūrṇī, and Nainā Devī are besieged by these women, called Mātās (Mothers) and their entourages from villages and towns all over the greater Panjab. These parties come laden with red flags and other offerings. They bring their own drums, cymbals, and other musical instruments—nowadays even a cassette tape player—and set up "stage" in the temple courtyard. After lighting incense and a lamp, they start drumming and singing, and the Mātā begins to "play." People in her entourage and other pilgrims at the temple approach the Mātā to worship, make a small cash offering, and ask for a prophecy or favor. At any given time during the festival season, and occasionally at other times as well, one can see several of these performances going on at once amid the other temple activities: *pūjās, ārtis,* ecstatic dancing and singing, *muṇḍans* (ritual head shaving of children), *kanyā pūjā,* pilgrims eating and distributing *prasād,* priests reciting the *Devī Māhātmya,* and the general clamor and shouting of *jay mātā dī*. In the next section, I will discuss a few Mātās of this type.

The goddess Śerāṅvālī is like the great gods Viṣṇu and Śiva in terms of her degree of power, purity, and universality. At the same time, she shares characteristics such as accessibility, immanence, and intimacy with the lesser deities and saints.[15] While the great gods of the Hindu pantheon do not generally possess their devotees, the lesser godlings do. When I asked informants why the Goddess possesses people, while Viṣṇu and Śiva do not, they agreed that this is the case, but they usually were unable to provide a reason. One informant, the secretary of a newly built Bābā Bālak Nāth temple in Chandigarh, gave the following explanation:

> Bābā Bālak Nāth and Devī can both enter either a man or a woman. Just as there are different branches of the government, so do different gods have different functions. Full *avatārs* do not enter. Viṣṇu, etc., does not enter. Mā is *śakti;* she is everywhere. Therefore, she does not fall into the category of *avatār*.[16]

The general understanding of possession is that the Goddess plays in people and speaks through them as a means of helping her devotees and showing them her *śakti*. It can also happen that she wishes to castigate those who have committed some evil or that she has a demand that she expects her devotees to fulfill. It is not unusual for new temples to be built or old images to be "rediscovered" as the result of a command from the Goddess in *savārī rūp*. A small temple in a village that is now part of the city of Chandigarh was built in the late nineteenth century after a young girl became possessed by the Goddess and told the villagers that building a temple would be the only way to eradicate a severe epidemic. A Nainā Devī temple was built on a hillside outside Kalka in 1950 on the orders of the Goddess, who entered a small girl and commanded those listening to dig up an ancient image of Nainā Devī that lay buried and forgotten there.

There are various explanations as to why some people get possessed and others do not. Some say it is due solely to the divine play of the Goddess. Others say it is the fruit of *karma* or because of a *saṃskāra* (mental impression or predisposition) from a past life. Others say it is the reward for faith and devotion to Devī. Sometimes it runs in a family; the *śakti* is passed from generation to generation. Or it can be the result of spiritual practice (*sādhanā*) in which one attempts to bring on possession as a means of identifying with the Goddess.[17] Purity is also cited as a requirement for a suitable vehicle; she should not eat meat, drink liquor, or be unchaste. That is why young girls below the age of puberty and unmarried women are thought to be especially suitable vehicles for the Goddess.[18]

Charges of chicanery, commercialism, and exploitation are not uncommon, even among those who consider themselves devotees of Śerāṅvālī. An informant who grew up in a village near Jullunder told me that in his childhood during the yearly pilgrimage to Cintpūrṇī fights would break out between rival parties over whether or not a possession was legitimate. He summed it up as follows:

> When one camp goes for reverence, and the other for commercial purposes, there is a clash. An example of commercial intent is when a group holds a *jagrātā* and a girl becomes possessed [Devī *khelnā*]. This is often a fake, and some groups have several women who regularly stage these possessions. My father had a friend with a red turban who had tests for distinguishing real *khelnā* from fake. He would take a *sangal* [iron rod]

> and prod her with it. An even more foolproof method is to put lighted *dhūp* [incense] under the person's nose. If the possession is real, she will not flinch. There was a group who used to come to Cintpūrṇī every year from about 1950 to 1955 who would stage possession. They would do this every night. We did not mind it if they did it on their own, but they used to do it in public when other *jagrātās* were going on. Then fights would break out. Our group would not let them have a session inside the temple, because they were using it as a regular business. They would also have *jagrātās* at their home and made quite a bit of money out of this.[19]

The same informant recalled a case of what he considered to be a valid spontaneous possession. A *jagrātā* to which four different *maṇḍalīs* had been invited was taking place. During the *jagrātā*, a young woman started to "play." She had always been a devotee of Devī and had recently been married into a family that ate meat and drank liquor. During her *caukī*, she was tested by a *mahant* from one of the *maṇḍalīs*, who put lighted incense under her nose and struck her with a metal bar. She did not flinch. She spoke as Devī and ordered all drunk people to leave the *jagrātā*. After this the young woman was so drained that she had to remain in bed for two months. Her in-laws were so shaken by the experience that they became vegetarians and teetotalers.[20]

Other tests are mental rather than physical. People will ask the possessed person questions in order to test her clairvoyance. For example, they might ask how much money is in someone's pocket. Thus, there is a certain amount of skepticism as to the validity of possession, at least as regards individual cases.

Apotheosis and Institutionalization

In Hinduism there is no clear dividing line between divine and human; gods can become humans and humans can become gods. There are numerous forms of worship of deified humans such as ancestors, heroes, *satīs, yogīs, siddhs,* and *nāths.* A similar phenomenon is the worship of certain women who are regularly possessed as Mātās or living goddesses, as manifestations of Śerāṅvālī. Such a woman is said to embody the *śakti* of the Goddess during her *caukī,* that is, to become a human icon. The sanctity of the possession experience carries over into her normal life, and she gradually becomes a religious specialist and object of worship. This process occurs with varying degrees of institutionalization. Here I present accounts of two such cases that, while not necessarily representative, can provide glimpses into this phenomenon.

Gumṭivāle Mātā: A Family Tradition

My first encounter with Mātājī and her niece occurred quite by accident. It was in October 1982 when I visited Jayantī Devī, a small hilltop temple in the Panjab Shiwaliks about an hour's bus ride from Chandigarh. I was accompanied by my friend Manjit, a research scholar in social anthropology at Panjab University. When we arrived at the temple, we found a group of about fifteen people seated inside singing devotional songs. Of these, there were three women who seemed to be particularly significant, an elderly woman in a plain cotton sari and a middle-aged and a very young woman dressed identically like Panjabi brides in bright red *salvār-kamīz* and *cunnī*. The elderly and middle-aged women took turns leading the singing in Hindi and Panjabi; the elderly woman would recite verses from time to time in Sanskrit from the *Devī Māhātmya*. The young woman sat quietly throughout the session with her head bowed, eyes glazed, and body swaying from side to side; she seemed to be crying. When the singing was over, the whole party went into another room for their *laṅgar* (communal meal), and the temple *pujārī* distributed *prasād*. At that point I began doggedly to question the *pujārī* about the temple and its history, legends, and festivals. He obligingly told me what I wanted to know and allowed me to photograph several images. But Manjit was intrigued by the "red ladies"; she could hardly wait to ask about them. What we found out opened up new doors of inquiry for me that would probably have remained closed had it not been for Manjit's persistence and enthusiasm. The *pujāri* did not know anything about these women, since they were just there for the day from Chandigarh, but he introduced us to one of their major devotees, whom I will call Mr. S. Later I became well acquainted with Mr. S. and his family, who were extremely knowledgeable about the ritual and lore of the Devī cult and kept me informed of important performances and functions.

Mr. S. explained that the two women dressed in red lived in village Gumti near Shahabad Markanda (in District Ambala, Haryana), where they have their own temple. When the elder was five years old, she got a boon from Durgā, and Mātā entered her. She is unmarried. The younger woman is her niece, who was entered by Kālī Mātā due to a blessing from her aunt. The elderly woman who accompanied them is Devkī Mātā, a saintly and respected lady from Chandigarh who is active in organizing religious functions. She does not, however, become possessed. Through later conversations with Mr. S., with other devotees, and with the Gumṭivāle Mātās themselves and through observing them in ritual and nonritual contexts at their home and on their subsequent visits to Chandigarh, I was able to piece together a general picture of their lives and cult.

The two Mātās belong to a well-to-do Brahmin peasant family that originally lived and owned land near Lahore, West Panjab. The elder Mātā's mother had started getting the *śakti* after her marriage. She passed it on to her daughter, who started "playing" at about age five. After the partition of 1947, the whole family moved to the Haryana village, where they now live. The mother died on the way in Amritsar after drinking some polluted water. The daughter, who at the time of our meeting was about forty-five, had passed on the *śakti* to her brother's daughter nine years earlier, when she was about seven years of age. The child used to fight with her brothers and sisters. One day her aunt said to her, "Kālkā, don't fight." From that time on, she would get the *pavan* of the goddess Kālkā, another name for Kālī. Her aunt gets the *pavan* of Vaiṣṇo Devī, so the two balance each other. The niece is referred to as Choṭī (little) Mātā or Devtā, while the aunt is called by the honorific Mātājī. Mātājī has some control over her possession, while the younger is still very inexperienced. Neither of the two women is married; both say that celibacy makes it easier to maintain the purity necessary for a vehicle of the Goddess. They both have a guru, Rāmānand Svāmī, a *saṃnyāsin* who lives near Kurukshetra.

Many of Mātājī's followers are refugee West Panjabis like herself—some of whom knew her mother—who have settled in Chandigarh, Ludhiana, Ambala, Delhi, and other places in East Panjab and Haryana. Gradually, the local people have started to visit her, too, as they hear about her powers and miracles. The native Haryanavis tend to identify her with Bālā Sundarī, a goddess enshrined in nearby Nahan, Himachal Pradesh, who is the tutelary goddess of many families in the area. West Panjabis tend to identify her with Vaiṣṇo Devī, but both groups say that the two goddesses are both aspects of Mahādevī, the Great Goddess.

Besides general *darśan,* the reasons people visit Mātājī fall into three categories: prophecy, healing, and material gain. During her *caukī* (which will be described below), Mātājī "tells things" such as when would be a good day to begin an enterprise, whether or not one will succeed in an endeavor, whether or not one should trust a certain person. Sometimes she makes such predictions in response to a question; other times she volunteers the information. The devotees tell a story about a man whom Mātājī told not to go on a trip. He went anyway, and his train collided with another one near Ambala. Once she volunteered the information to Mr. S. that in his past life he had been an M.A. student in a particular village who had committed suicide because of failure in the exam. Upon inquiry, Mr. S. found out that there had been such a person in that village. Also, Mātājī will castigate someone if there is something she does not like. For example, if during the *caukī* there is a menstruating woman in the crowd, she will tell her to leave.

Healing and granting material welfare are both called boons (*var*). People come to Mātājī for these while she is in her normal state of consciousness as well as when she is in her *caukī*. Her devotees make offerings of sweets, flowers, money, and the like to her, taking some back as *prasād*. This *prasād* is supposed to have healing power. I have seen many people bringing small packets of cloves or cardamoms to be blessed, or bottles of water, which Mātājī holds in her hands for a few moments, toying with the lid, and then hands back. The spice or water is then consumed at home to cure whatever disease the person has.

Numerous stories have grown up around Mātājī's healing and wish-granting powers. A woman from Ambala said that she used to come to Gumti once a month for a *jagrātā*. Then for about seven years after her husband's death, she did not make her monthly visit, although she would come from time to time when her child had an exam. After some time, she developed an ulcer and swelling on her face. Around this time, she went to another village to visit some relatives. There she met a fortune-teller who told her that she had forgotten to worship Mā, that she used to go somewhere and should go back. After this she came to Gumti to meet Mātājī, and her problems went away. Others attribute their marriages, jobs, and success in examinations to Mātājī's grace.

At first, Mātājī had only one small room in which to receive devotees. There is also some talk that in those days, her elders did not approve and tried to put obstacles in her way, but because of pressure from devotees and out of fear, they allowed her to continue and did not force her to marry. Her following gradually grew. The biggest watershed in the institutionalization of her cult was in 1969, when her temple was built and an image of her late mother consecrated. The temple is to the Navadurgā (nine Durgās).[21] According to Mr. S., the temple was built according to the blueprint specified by Kālī, who entered Mātājī and, speaking in Bengali, said that she had come from Calcutta with instructions.[22]

Now Mātājī and her niece are installed in a large compound at one end of the village. The entrance is marked by a large gateway with "Śrī Prabhāveśvarī Navadurgā Mandir" written on the top (Prabhāveśvarī is Mātājī's given name), leading into a compound containing living quarters, cattle sheds, and guest rooms. They face a large courtyard, on the south side of which is the temple, consisting of one large, square room. The central image is of Durgā–Śerāṅvālī flanked by Hanumān and Bhairo.[23] On the walls surrounding the Durgā image are carved images of the nine Durgās, with the addition of Sarasvatī on one end and Kālī on the other. West of the temple is a *havan kuṇḍ,* or pit, where fire sacrifices are performed by a Brahmin during the Navarātra. Directly opposite the temple on the north side of the courtyard is an elevated platform with an image of Śiva. On the west side of the courtyard is a large audience hall (*darbār*) in which there is a large wooden platform where the two Mātās sit during their *caukī* and *jagrātās.* At the back of this hall is a doorway leading to their private rooms. Adjoining their sitting room is a small shrine housing the image of Mātājī's mother. Behind these rooms is a large open area edged by several rooms and sheltered verandas, which is used as an outdoor kitchen and eating area during special functions.

The people who currently live in this compound are Mātājī, Devtā, Devtā's mother and father, a servant who takes care of the animals, and a *pujārī* for the temple. The *pujārī,* a *sādhu* with long, matted hair, was at the time I met him fifty-seven years of age. He said that he had been known as Bābājī since childhood and that he was a native of District Nadiya, West Bengal. He left home at an early age to sing *bhajans,* wandering here and there and worshiping Kālī at Kalighat in Calcutta. He is originally a Brahmin but gave up his caste after becoming a *sādhu.* He has a guru, Svāmī Padmadās, who is still living in Bengal. Bābājī has been living in the Haryana area for over thirty-five years, speaks Hindi and some Panjabi, but claims to have forgotten his native Bengali. Before he came to serve in Mātājī's temple, he was staying at Kurukshetra, the famous pilgrimage place not far from Mātājī's village. One day he was singing *bhajans* at a temple to Śerāṅvālī at Kurukshetra when Gumṭivāle Mātā's form appeared in front of him and called him to Gumti.

Mātājī's establishment is obviously an expensive one to keep up. Most of the funds come from devotees, while some come from her family's farm income. She owns a car, and her devotees have bought her a refrigerator and telephone and sponsor her trips and pilgrimages. However, it is still an informal association. Devotees may come and do *sevā* (service) at the temple, but there is no formal hierarchy among them. Mātājī maintains control over all the affairs of the temple. A few years ago, one of her close devotees tried to form a temple committee, but Mātājī refused, saying there was no need for it. Mātājī makes a point of not discriminating among devotees; she welcomes people of all castes. Once when she found out that her relatives were giving out more *prasād* to relatives and less to others, she told them to distribute it equally. It is said that they broke out in a rash that did not heal until they did so.

While welcoming all castes, Mātājī at the same time places strong emphasis on certain Brahminic or "Sanskritic" practices. All food prepared on the premises or brought and offered to Mātājī is strictly vegetarian. Devotees explain that the emphasis on vegetarianism is because Mātājī is the Goddess in Vaiṣṇo *rūp*. Even though Devtā gets the *pavan* of Kālī—who is generally carnivorous—she is still under Vaiṣṇo influence (*prabhāv*). When Mātājī went to Calcutta, she refused to go inside the famous Kālī temple there, because goats were being sacrificed. Although Mātājī has had little formal schooling, she is articulate and has an extensive vocabulary in Panjabi and Hindi. She has great respect for the Sanskrit language, regularly sponsoring readings from Sanskrit texts and Sanskritic rituals.

The rituals and functions surrounding Mātājī can be divided into the following categories: daily, monthly, biannual, annual, and occasional. Daily rituals include the morning and evening *pūjā* and *ārtī* conducted in the temple by the *pujārī*. These are similar to the routine worship services found in many small temples. Mātājī and Devtā also perform their private devotions and receive devotees informally throughout the day. In the evenings from about nine until twelve o'clock, a *caukī* is held when the two Mātās are in residence. Devotees who live nearby bring their musical instruments and sing devotional songs. One of the devotees lights a *jot* in front of Mātājī and Devtā, who are seated on the wooden platform in the audience hall. Both become possessed, receive offerings, and answer questions. At the end of the evening, the devotees perform *ārtī,* and the Mātās distribute *prasād.*

Every *aṣṭamī,* the eighth of the bright half of the Hindu lunar month, they hold a *jagrātā.* The date of the next *jagrātā* is always written on a blackboard inside the courtyard, since the dates of the English and Hindu calendars do not coincide. The *jagrātā* is similar to the general type described in chapter 4, except that the focus of attention is on the two Mātās. Although electric lights may be used to decorate the outside of the building, no loudspeakers or moving *mūrtis* are used. The only objects of worship are the *jot* and the two Mātās. Devotees gather, light the *jot,* and sing *bheṇṭs* for several hours before the two appear. By Mātājī's order, they sing only the more traditional *pakkī bheṇṭs,* not the popular type set to film tunes. The Mātās make an entrance at about 2:00 A.M., go into a trance, and start to "play" as in the daily *caukī.* The singing continues during their possession, but "The Story of Queen Tārā" cannot be told until after the possession is over. At a *jagrātā* I attended at Gumti, the *caukī* lasted so long that the telling of the story—at most *jagrātās* an elaborate and lengthy oral narrative—was condensed into a single balladlike song.

The biannual festivals at Gumti are the autumn and spring Navarātras, which are universally celebrated in the Goddess cult in temples and in private homes. The Navarātras take place on the first nine nights of the bright fortnight of the lunar month Kārtik (September–October) and at the same time in the month of Cait (March–April). During these times, Mātājī stays in retreat and does not give *darśan* until the eighth. She stays shut up in a room, fasting and meditating, seeing no one except a single female devotee (Mrs. S. in recent years), who waits on her. On the first day of the Navarātra, a water pot (*kalaś*) is established in the shrine room containing the image of Mātājī's mother; barley is planted around it and allowed to sprout for nine days, as is commonly done in temples and homes. Each day a *paṇḍit* comes to recite the *Devī Māhātmya,* performing a *havan* on the tenth day. On the eighth night a *jagrātā* is held as on all other *aṣṭamīs,* but on a grander scale, and is called *baṛī* (big) *aṣṭamī*. The decorations are more elaborate, and as many as two or three thousand people attend. A *laṅgar* starts early in the evening at which several hundred people are fed. On the tenth day, after the *havan,* the barley sprouts (called *khetrī*) are taken to a nearby river and immersed.

The annual festival at Gumti is the Mūrti Sthāpanā Divas, celebrating the installation of the Navadurgā temple and Mātājī's mother's image on May 29, 1969. There is a nine-day recitation of the *Devī Bhāgavata Purāṇa* in Sanskrit, culminating on May 29 with a *havan*. Some devotees (not necessarily Brahmin priests) perform the recitation each morning and evening, keeping the text wrapped in a red cloth in the Navadurgā temple next to a *kalaś* with barley sprouts planted around it. It is obvious that the celebration of this annual festival has been patterned after that of the traditional Navarātra, although it is not identical in all details, the *Devī Bhāgavata Purāṇa* being substituted for the *Devī Māhātmya* and a higher degree of informality occasioned perhaps by having lay recitants rather than a *paṇḍit*. When I attended the celebration in 1983, the *havan* was not held on that day but was rescheduled for a day or two later, because the *Devī Bhāgavata Purāṇa* recitation had started a day late that year. A carnival-like atmosphere pervaded. Visitors had set up several stalls outside the compound to sell ice cream, tea, pakoras, and other snacks. Devotees provided free ice water inside. Several hundred people came and went, visiting the temple, going for audience with Mātājī in her back room, and chatting with friends. A lavish *laṅgar* consisting of thick *capāttīs, dāl,* cooked squash, sweet rice, and salty rice was provided all afternoon. A wedding-type band played in the courtyard in the afternoon, while some of the women, mostly the very young and elderly, danced. Some important devotees from Chandigarh had brought new clothes for the main Durgā image in the temple. First they dressed Devtā in a new red *colā* (gown) and *cunnī* (scarf) and then dressed the image in identical clothing.

On that day I also met another Mātā who stays with Mātājī from time to time and comes to visit on special occasions. She was a seventeen-year-old Baniyā (merchant caste) from a village near Kurukshetra. She goes by the name of Bhadrakālī, after the goddess who enters her. She has been getting the *pavan* since she was about eight years old. A *Satyanarāyaṇ kathā*[24] was going on in a friend's house when she fell down and started shaking. Her family took her first to the hospital and then to the Kālī temple in Patiala. There she received a "direct vision" (*sākṣāt darśan*) of Devī. After that she started coming to Gumti to meet Mātājī. Mātājī identified her goddess as Bhadrakālī and refused to accept the girl as her disciple, saying that Bhadrakālī is the most senior of all the manifestations of the Goddess. "Bhadrakālī" has continued an informal association with Mātājī, however, and performs *caukī* from time to time at Gumti. She has also become a disciple of Mātājī's guru, Rāmānand Svāmī, whom she met through Mātājī when he came to Gumti for a *bhaṇḍārā* (feast). Bhadrakālī gets the *caukī* every Saturday. She mentioned that her father used to get the *caukī* of the goddess Bālā Sundarī but that now he gets it very seldom. Bhadrakālī considers this to be her life's work and does not plan to marry. She would like to pass the power on to someone else when she gets older. Although she does not have much of a following today, her validation by Gumṭivāle Mātā and her participation in functions at Gumti may lead to future cult development.

Besides presiding over functions that take place at Gumti, Mātājī and her niece are often on tour. They go on pilgrimage to Goddess temples with groups of devotees several times a year and are frequently invited to perform at *jagrātās* or *caukīs* in their devotees' homes in various towns and cities. Nowadays they get more invitations than they can handle. A small group of devotees coordinates their travel arrangements and accommodations. When they come to Chandigarh for a *jagrātā*, the *maṇḍalī* that is also invited is the Durgā Bhajan Maṇḍal led by Gopāl Singh Pāl, who has been a devotee of Mātājī's for many years. I attended several *jagrātās* in and around Chandigarh at which the Gumṭivāle Mātās were the featured attraction. They all followed the same general pattern as the one I describe here.[25]

The *jagrātā* was held in the home of Mr. and Mrs. A., a lower-middle-class Aroṛā family, on the occasion of their son's birthday. A tent had been set up outside to accommodate the seventy-five to one hundred guests who attended. The major decoration was a large poster board image of Dhyānū Bhagat offering his severed head to the eight-armed Goddess seated on a lion. It had electrically moving parts so that Dhyānū's arms and head moved forward in a gesture of offering, and the lion's head and tail and Devī's arms moved. On the right side was a painting of Bhairo with Śiva above him; on the left was Hanumān with Viṣṇu above him. In front was a table with fruit, flowers, incense, sweets, a water pot (*kalaś*), and red scarves (*cunnīs*) surrounding a *jot* that was lit at the beginning of the *jagrātā*.

Before the *jagrātā* started, I was taken into a room inside the house where the two Mātās were seated on a bed receiving devotees. All others were seated respectfully on the floor. People would approach, bow and touch their feet, perhaps exchange a few words, and receive some sweets from one of the Mātās as *prasād*. Some would leave right away; others would sit down for a while and chat quietly with other devotees. A few women were massaging the Mātās' feet.

Meanwhile, the *jagrātā* started at about 11:30 with the initial *pūjās, jot pracaṇḍ*, and *bheṇṭ* singing. At about 2:00 A.M. the younger Mātā (Devtā) came out dressed in a pink *salvār-kamīz* and a pink-and-silver *cunnī*. The elder Mātā remained inside the house. Later some devotees explained to me that because Devtā is "in training," it is she who appears alone in out-of-town *jagrātās*. Devtā sat down on a sheet-covered wooden platform next to the *jot*. People then came up in single file to place garlands around her neck and touch her feet. At first she sat demurely with her head covered and bowed while the *bheṇṭ* singing continued. Gradually, her head bent lower and lower until it was almost touching her knees. After a while, she started to shake, at first slightly, then violently. Then her head started to rotate in a rhythmic fashion. By this time her *cunnī* and all the garlands around her neck had fallen off. Her hair became completely loose and flew about wildly as her head whirled around and around. This continued for about an hour amid *bheṇṭ* singing and cries from the audience of *jay mātā dī* (victory to the Mother) and Gumṭivāle Mātā *terī sadā hī jay* (O Mother from Gumti, your eternal victory). Gradually, she started to calm down and finally sat still, her eyes wandering and unfocused. A few close devotees looked after her, putting a red shawl around her shoulders when she appeared to be cold. At one point she started grasping at the red-and-black sheet beneath her. Mr. S. and another devotee brought out a cream-colored sheet and exchanged it. Later, he explained to me that she had found the black stripe to be disturbing, since Kālī does not like the color black, only red or pink.

At about 4:00 A.M. Devtā gave permission for the "The Story of Queen Tārā" to begin. Since it cannot start until the *caukī* is over, it sometimes has to be abridged to fit into the remaining time. Even so, the version the Durgā Bhajan Maṇḍal told on this occasion was longer and more complete than those I have heard other *maṇḍalīs* perform. Devtā distributed *prasād* at the appropriate part of the story. Toward the end Mr. S. told the *maṇḍalī* to finish telling the story, because the elder Mātā was going to come out. A few minutes later Mātājī made her entrance, wearing the same type of clothing as Devtā and sitting next to her on another platform. Everyone lined up for her *darśan,* and she handed out marigolds as *prasād.* After the story was over, the congregation performed *ārtī* to the two Mātās and to the *jot,* and there was a final distribution of the traditional chick-peas and *halvā.*

A New Universalism: The Cult of Ūṣā Bahn

Like the cult of Gumṭivāle Mātā, the cult of Ūṣā Bahn (Sister Ūṣā) depends on the personal charisma of a woman vehicle of the Goddess, but it has a higher degree of formal institutionalization and conscious theatricality.

I first found out about Ūṣā Bahn when I saw her picture on a poster in a booking agency for pilgrimage tours in Old Delhi. The proprietor turned out to be a fervent devotee of hers and told me that she has headquarters in Agra and Delhi, that Kālkājī (another name for Kālī) becomes manifested in her, and that she grants all one's wishes. He added an intriguing detail: every *aṣṭamī* her tongue comes out to a length of twelve or thirteen inches.

A few months later, Ūṣā Bahn came to Chandigarh while on an extensive tour of pilgrimage places and cities where her devotees live. I was able to interview her and the *mahant* of her organization and to attend a *jagrātā* and a *kīrtan* at which she performed.[26]

Ūṣā Bahn's organization, the Śrī Vaiṣṇo Bhajan Maṇḍal, is located in Agra, with a branch in Daya Basti, Delhi. She presides over a temple in Agra called Śrī Ūṣeśvarī Mahākālī Mandir[27] and is also building a hospital there for the poor. Every year since 1961, she and her entourage have gone on a biannual organized pilgrimage to Vaiṣṇo Devī and other Devī temples, stopping along the way to perform *kīrtans* and *jagrātās* at temple *dharmsālās* (rest houses) and homes of devotees. When they reach the temple of Jvālā Mukhī, they light a *jot* from the eternal flame there and carry it with them for the rest of the pilgrimage, using it as a *jot* in *jagrātās* along the way. The pilgrimages each last about three months and are organized so that she returns to Agra just before the Navarātra for a large procession and a grand *jagrātā* called Viśāl Bhagavatī Jāgraṇ. During the nine days of the Navarātra, she retires to a room where she sits without moving or eating, holding a pot of sprouting barley in her lap.

I was able to find out only a few details about Ūṣā Bahn's life. She was born in Lahore in 1946 of a well-to-do Panjabi Khattrī family.[28] At partition in 1947, her family moved first to Delhi and later to Agra, where her father owns a printing press. Her initial possession occurred when she was seven or eight years of age; she played continually for sixty-four days. She was recognized as a vehicle of Kālī and gradually started attracting followers, mainly among the West Panjabi refugee community settled throughout East Panjab, Haryana, Delhi, and Uttar Pradesh. As with Gumṭivāle Mātā, there are numerous accounts of miracles attributed to her. According to the *mahant* of the Śrī Vaiṣṇo Bhajan Maṇḍal, in 1965 a man in Delhi cut out his tongue to test her *śakti* and she joined it back together. He also told of several other cases of tongue cutting and rejoining.[29] It is believed that during a *jagrātā* she hands out red powder (*sindūr*) and always manages to have enough to go around.

Ūṣā Bahn has never married and acknowledges no human guru. She has taken the *jot* as her central symbol and considers it to be her guru. She believes that her cult is universal, because the *jot* or sacred flame is found in all religious traditions. She has combined in herself the roles of both Mātā and guru. She is called Mātājī by her devotees and bases her authority on being a vehicle of Kālī. At the same time, she takes a much more active role in teaching and propagation than does Gumṭivāle Mātā. Rather than the red "bridal" or "goddess" clothing that the Gumṭivāle Mātās wear, she sports *saṃnyāsī*-like orange or saffron-colored clothing. While the Gumṭivāle Mātās take a silent and passive role in the *jagrātās*, Ūṣā Bahn takes a more vocal and active role, leading the singing, giving sermons, and telling stories.

The first time I saw Ūṣā Bahn was in Chandigarh at the home of Devkī Mātā, the saintly lady whom I had previously met accompanying the Gumṭivāle Mātās to Jayantī Devī. I had found out that Ūṣā Bahn, on the way back from her biannual pilgrimage, was performing a *kīrtan* there that afternoon; I arrived just as it was over. A crowd of women was lining the driveway, and there was a busload of people in front. A woman ran through the crowd, ringing a bell. Behind her followed several people carrying a *jot*—encased in a silver and glass box—in a palanquin on their heads. Then Ūṣā Bahn herself emerged from the house shouting slogans such as "*jay mātā dī*" and "*jay* Jvālā Mukhī" and giving blessings to devotees who touched her feet. She got into the bus with her entourage, who had accompanied her from Agra. I was told that they were going to another devotee's house to rest before proceeding to that evening's *jagrātā*, which would be held in Mohali (a Chandigarh suburb) at the home of still another devotee.

When I arrived at the middle-class Panjabi Baniyā home at about 10:00 P.M., the *jagrātā* had not yet started. A tent had been set up on an empty lot next to the sponsor's house. A stage had been set up in front of large posters of Vaiṣṇo Devī, Kālī, Hanumān, and Bhairo. A water pot wrapped in a scarf and topped with a coconut stood on the right-hand side. The crowd fluctuated from about eight hundred to one thousand and was about two-thirds women. Loudspeakers were spaced throughout the tent. There were about seven musicians, one of whom was a Sikh, who had come with Ūṣā Bahn from Agra.

Ūṣā Bahn had already arrived and was receiving devotees inside the house. I was impressed by her presence as a small, vigorous woman who speaks with wit and confidence in both Hindi and Panjabi. She looked fresh and alert in spite of the fact that she had been traveling constantly for over six weeks, going from one *jagrātā* or *kīrtan* to another with very little sleep. She is well versed in Purāṇic and oral literature and is very interested in spreading the truth about the Goddess, expressing concern about misunderstandings and "false stories." She said that she has been to the shrine of Vaiṣṇo Devī many times; at one time she went once a month for about fourteen months in order to find out the true story of the Devī's arising and life. She has been to the village where Vaiṣṇo Devī first appeared and is still worshiped today. She told me that her conversations with people there have led her to believe that some of the legends told about the place are false, particularly those that cast aspersions on the character of Bhairo.[30] It cannot be true, she argues, that Bhairo had evil intentions toward Vaiṣṇo Devī. If he had, then why would she give him a boon that he would be worshiped there? His name would not even be mentioned. He is actually, she instructed me, one of the nine Nāths or Siddhs, a disciple of Gorakhnāth. Furthermore, Ūṣā Bahn argued, Vaiṣṇo Devī did not kill him; rather, he had a fight with Laṅgur Vīr (Hanumān), her bodyguard. Ūṣā Bahn said, with her customary wit, that the popularly accepted stories about Bhairo illustrate one of the problems with the Hindu religion (*sanātan dharm*), that people can write anything they want and get away with it.

The *jagrātā* started at about 10:30 with devotees bringing out the *jot* amid the fanfare of ringing bells and sounding conch shells. Since the *jot* had been carried unextinguished from Jvālā Mukhī, there was no *jot pracaṇḍ* (lighting or "empowering" the flame) as at other *jagrātās*. The devotees placed the *jot* at the center of the stage; throughout the night young women took turns fanning it with a chowrie. After a *pūjā* conducted by a hired Brahmin *paṇḍit* who travels with the group, the musicians started singing *bheṇṭs*.

Ūṣā Bahn made her appearance shortly before midnight, walking through the crowd dressed in a saffron-colored *salvār kamīz*, and seated herself next to the *jot*. Everyone in the audience lined up to receive a red *ṭīkā* on the forehead from her, after which she led the singing of a long *kīrtan* about devotion to the guru. She led a few other songs and told the story of the origin of Jvālā Mukhī. At about 1:30 there was a break in the program for *ardās*. Ūṣā Bahn left the stage at about 1:45 to bathe before the *caukī*. While she was gone, the members of the *maṇḍalī* added more ghee to the *jot* and continued to sing *bheṇṭs*. The antics of one devotee attracted considerable attention. Wearing a red suit with "Hanumān" written on it in Devanagari lettering, he jumped around, making faces like a monkey and blowing a horn. Others told me that four years ago when he joined Ūṣā Bahn's entourage, he could not speak at all, but that now he is able to speak a little. He is affectionately known as "Hanumānjī."

Ūṣā Bahn reappeared at about 3:30, dressed like Kālī, completely in black. She talked about the hospital she was building in Agra and took a collection for it. The devotees started singing *bheṇṭs* again, and shortly thereafter the *caukī* started. Ūṣā Bahn's head and upper body spun around and around with her long hair flying loose. From time to time she would stick out her tongue to a length of four or five inches and roll her eyes back. She would also stick her head into the flame with no apparent harm. While the *caukī* was going on, people in the audience would stand up, wave their arms in the air, and shout slogans in a manner that reminded me of a Christian revivalist meeting.[31]

After about half an hour, she stretched out her hands, and her attendants covered them with a black cloth. When they took the cloth away, her right hand was filled with *sindūr* (red powder). The crowd responded with shouts of *jay mātā dī* and the like, obviously considering this a miracle. She started giving out *sindūr* and rupee coins to the people assembled, calling them up one at a time. Several times she repeated the statement that there would be enough *sindūr* for everyone, reinforcing the rumor of her miraculous power. First she called me forward, giving me *sindūr* and telling her attendants to give me a rupee coin, which she called "a protection" (*ek rakṣā*). Then she called up various people according to their type of problem: those facing a lawsuit, those needing an operation, those having marriage difficulties, women whose brothers are in trouble, women having trouble getting their daughters married, those without children. Most of the people she told to wrap the coin and *sindūr* in a red cloth and worship it. To some she gave flowers or spoke a few words of advice. She gave one woman a coin to put around the neck of her small son who is affected by cold. She told one young woman that after quite a long time her planets were finally good. She told another woman, who had not been called up, to go back to her seat. After all those with problems had come forward, the rest of the crowd lined up to receive blessings. Meanwhile, some halwa and chick-peas were offered to the *jot* and distributed to the crowd as *prasād*.

This *jagrātā* was different from the usual type in that there was no offering of coconuts and no telling of "The Story of Queen Tārā." In fact, it is the only one I have ever seen or heard of that lacked these elements. The *caukī*, rather than being a segment inserted into the sequence of the *jagrātā*, actually took over the whole show. Later, the *mahant* explained to me that the Tārā story was not told because of the unbroken flame (*akhaṇḍ jot*) from Jvālā Mukhī. Ūṣā Bahn and her followers had made a vow to keep the *jot* lit until the day after the Navarātra, when they would tell "The Story of Queen Taārā" and then extinguish the *jot*.[32]

The next day, before leaving Chandigarh, Ūṣā Bahn appeared at an afternoon *kīrtan*, leading *bheṇṭ* singing and telling stories about the goddess Vaiṣṇo Devī. There was no *caukī*. She announced that there would be a *kīrtan* held every Saturday in Chandigarh by her local devotees to raise money for her hospital in Agra.

The degree of complexity in Ūṣā Bahn's religious organization can be briefly conveyed by summarizing the information given on a Hindi-language poster advertising a special function to be held in Delhi.[33] At the center of the poster is a calendar-type painting of Ūṣā Bahn dressed in orange robes, seated on a lion skin. Beneath her is written her name, Bahn Ūṣā Devījī. Flanking her are the words "the flame is all-pervading" (*jyoti sarv vyāpak hai*). Above her head is Śerāṅvālī–Durgā pictured inside a golden "halo." Above this is a gold pot holding a *jot*. In the four corners above Ūṣā Bahn's head are symbols of four religions, a Hindu temple with the Oṃ symbol, the Sikh golden temple with the Gurmukhī Oṃ, the Christian cross, and what appears to be a Muslim minaret. Above the painting are the words "Śrī Vaiṣṇo Bhajan Maṇḍal, Śrī Ūṣeśvarī Mahākālī Mandir" with the Agra and Delhi addresses. Beneath the painting is the following announcement:

> The grand procession of the vehicle [*savārī*] of the sacred Jvālā Jyoti will take place on Friday, September 17 [1982], and the 30th Viśāl Bhagavatī Jāgraṇ will take place on Saturday, September 18 and Sunday, September 19. O Beloved of Durgā, the Reverend Bahn Ūṣā Devījī of Agra, having given her servants the *darśan* of all the *darbārs,* having gone on pilgrimage by foot with the sacred Jvālā Jyoti will arrive in the city of Delhi on Friday, September 17 at the Sabzi Mandi Railway Station. The vehicle of the sacred Jvālā Jyoti will leave the [station] at 3:00 PM and arrive at Daya Basti Ground. Charming glimpses into the Grand Vehicle will be the special attraction. The famous Hindu Jīyā Band, Śarmā Band, and Jasvant Band will gladden your hearts with their sweet melodies. In celebration of the sacred flame, on the 18th of September at Daya Basti Railway Ground a Viśāl Bhagavatī Jāgraṇ will take place.

This is followed by a list of all the *jagrātā maṇḍalīs, mahants,* and performers—including the famous Narendra Chanchal—who will be on hand. Last is the statement: "All Durgā lovers should receive *darśan* of the Jvālā Jyoti and make their lives successful."[34]

Possession as Manifestation

There are various ways in which the Goddess manifests herself in the world, making herself available to her devotees. Possession, as we have seen in the cases discussed above, is one way that is visible, accessible, and allows verbal communication between the devotee and the Goddess as well as allowing the human vehicle to participate in her power. The importance of possession can be further explored when it is seen in the context of a larger narrative. The story of Nandā and Nandlāl, an oral narrative often told at *jagrātās,* illustrates the Goddess's various modes of manifestation and the place of possession among them. A summary of the story is as follows:

There once was a potter named Icchū Bābā who had a daughter named Nandā and a son named Nandlāl. He had an image of the Goddess that had been discovered and dug up from the earth. Every day Nandā and Nandlāl would worship the image by lighting a *jot,* singing *kīrtan,* and distributing *prasād.* The potter had an enemy who went to the contractor and told him that the land he had sold the potter had a valuable image on it and that the contractor should go and claim it. The contractor tried to get the image, but Icchū Bābā would not give it up. The case came to the village Pancāyat, which decided that the image should be put back on the spot where it was unearthed and that the image would go back by itself to its rightful owner. Icchū Bābā put the image on his head and took it to that spot, lamenting, "How can I take your name when you are no longer in my house?" On the way back, he met his children Nandā and Nandlāl. They said, "Why are you crying? The image has flown back and is in a niche in our house."

People heard about the miraculous image and started coming from near and far, saying that whatever you ask for you will get. The contractor became jealous and went to complain to Faruq Shāh Bādshāh in Delhi, saying, "A certain Icchū Bābā, a potter of village Narela, has lit a *jot* in front of an image of Mātā and has collected more money than is in your treasury." The Bādshāh then ordered his soldiers to bring the potter to court. When the soldiers arrived at Icchū Bābā's house, they found him very ill. Not wanting to be responsible for his death, they arrested the two children instead and took them to Delhi. Nandā lit the evening *jot* before she left and vowed that she would return by morning to light the morning *jot.*

The Bādshāh had the two children put in jail, saying that he would decide what to do with them the next day. Nandā and Nandlāl prayed to Mā: "Who will light your *jot?* If we your devotees die here, who will believe in you?" Then with the Great Mother's power, the Bādshāh's lion throne began to shake. In wind form [*pavan rūp*], Mā had come to the aid of her children. She put a trident on the Bādshāh's chest, telling him to release the children if he wanted to keep his kingdom intact. The

Bādshāh apologized to Mā and became devoted to her feet. He told his soldiers to take the children back to Narela village before morning.

When Nandā and Nandlāl reached the village, they found that their father had already died. They continued the same practices that their father had established—lighting the *jot,* singing *kīrtan,* and distributing *prasād*—but added a new one, making a pilgrimage on foot every year to Jvālā Mukhī. Years passed this way. Finally, Nandā died, becoming Mā's beloved forever. Nandlāl continued his duty year after year until finally he became too decrepit.

He made one last trek to Jvālā Mukhī, hobbling all the way. He cried so much that Mā's feet were bathed in his tears. Mā appeared directly before him and asked why he was crying. He said, "Don't you know? Because I will be unable to come to your *darbār* anymore." Mā replied, "Whenever you want my *darśan* light a *jot* at home and have a *jagrātā.* You will get my *darśan.*"

One year later, Nandlāl called all the devotees and announced that Śerāṅvālī would manifest herself at his *jagrātā.* Everyone assembled and waited expectantly. By 3:00 A.M. she still had not come. They started to taunt Nandlāl, saying that he was lying in his old age and trying to get money. Nandlāl beseeched Mā over and over to remember her promise and save his honor.

At this time, the Great Mother was aroused from sleep by these supplications. She mounted her lion and emerged from the cave. Her servant, Laṅgurvīr, asked where she was going in the middle of the night. She replied that a devotee had called her to his *jagrātā.* Laṅgurvīr said, "What a great devotee he must be if the Master of the Three Worlds is leaving her place to go to him. If he is a greater devotee than I who serve you night and day, I would like to get his *darśan.*" So she took him along.

Mā became wind form [*pavan rūp*]. When she reached Narela village, she said to Laṅgurvīr, "Laṅgurvīr, it is not right for us to go inside in our own forms. Why? Among the congregation seated there, there are those who are not devoted to my feet. There is one child, Nandlāl, who has lit my *jot.* He is attentive to my feet. Let us go and give him *darśan.*" Then Mā took the form of a five-year-old girl seated in the congregation. The girl's hair flew about wildly. When the girl started "playing," devotees started running away from there. Why? Because at that time, no one knew anything about "playing." Mā said, "Fear not, my children, I am here to take care of you, Nandlāl, to deliver you."

Mā gave her *darśan* to Nandlāl and asked, "What offering have you brought in honor of my coming?" Nandlāl had forgotten to bring

> anything, so he cut off his head and offered that. The Mother was pleased and joined it back to his body, offering him a boon. He asked that in the future, devotees should be allowed to offer something else instead of a head. So, Mā gave him the boon that in the future, she would accept a coconut and consider it a head. That is why in the Kaliyug, we offer coconuts to Mā. Therefore the coconuts being offered here [at this *jagrātā*] tonight are considered by Mā to be heads.[35]

This story illustrates the Goddess's epiphanies, the various forms in which she manifests herself and in which devotees experience her: the carved image found in the ground, the *jot* lit daily in household worship, the wind form that enters the Bādshāh's throne and makes it shake, the eternal *jot* at the pilgrimage place Jvālā Mukhī, the direct vision (*sākṣāt darśan*), and the wind form by which she travels from her cave dwelling to Nandlāl's house and by which she possesses the five-year-old girl. Of these, the *sākṣāt rūp* is the highest. It is the full epiphany reserved only for those who have demonstrated the highest faith by worshiping the Goddess in her other forms. All other forms are "disguised" epiphanies, so that the devotee must make a leap of faith to accept them as being the Goddess herself. In the story the Goddess does not appear before the entire *jagrātā* congregation in her *sākṣāt rūp*. Instead, she chooses to enter and speak through a five-year-old girl, knowing that a true devotee will recognize her. The others are afraid and run away. The *bhakti* element in the story is of course evident. It is interesting to note that no emphasis is placed on the small girl as a separate entity; she is completely identified as the Goddess. That is, she is the Goddess herself, rather than the recipient of the Goddess's grace. The emphasis in this story is on the relationship between Nandlāl (and earlier Nandā and Icchū Bābā) and the Goddess. The Goddess does not possess Nandlāl himself, because then no communication could take place. In typical *bhakti* fashion, Nandlāl's goal is not identity (*sayujya*) with the divine but rather nearness (*samīpya*) to the divine.

Conclusion

As indicated at the beginnning of this chapter, most scholarly discussions of possession have aimed at explanation rather than understanding. Explanation is an external approach, an attempt to define a phenomenon against a "rational" or an "objective" standard of truth that necessarily lies outside the worldview of the phenomenon itself. All attempts at explanation are bound to be reductionistic in that they assume that phenomena being explored are not valid in and of themselves but are only thinly disguised expressions of something else.

In a recent essay, Manuel Moreno argues for what he calls a "processual" view of deities rather than a "structural" view. The structural view sees deities as "'disembodied symbols' of social realities and human relationships."[36] The processual view, on the other hand, takes deities seriously as personal beings who interact with humans. While seeing the value of the structural view for illuminating aspects of social structure that are not readily apparent through observation, Moreno argues that it leaves out the dynamics of the interaction between deities and humans as Hindus themselves understand them: "This personalistic [processual] view is crucial to an understanding of established patterns of worship, both at the individual and collective level. At both levels we can observe the dynamics of a *mutually rewarding* [emphasis mine] reciprocity between divine and human persons."[37] I find Moreno's approach consistent with my own attempts to understand the phenomenon of Goddess possession.

Understanding begins with approaching the phenomenon on its own terms, by experiencing or reexperiencing it as do the participants themselves. An important part of understanding a religious phenomenon such as possession is to view it within the larger ritual and ideological context of the culture. Understanding implies an acceptance of what Paul Ricoeur has called the "hermeneutics of recovery" rather than the "hermeneutics of suspicion."[38] It is a stance that embraces a multiplicity of meanings rather than reducing them to a narrow explanation. In interpretation, however, there is no such thing as pure understanding. Any attempt to communicate one's understanding necessitates falling back to a greater or lesser degree on models of explanation. The word "interpret" literally means "to stand between," that is, to mediate or bridge the gap between two different worldviews. To a certain extent, one thing must be stated in terms of another. Thus, explanation can be used to enrich and lead to higher levels of understanding.

Goddess possession is a performance. The treatment of Goddess possession as performance is suggested in the indigenous context itself, both by the descriptions of the Goddess's actions in the mythic realm by such dramatic and aesthetic terms as *līlā* (play) and *kalā* (art) and by descriptions of her intrusion into the human realm as *khelnā* (playing). Unlike some religious performances, which are enacted by human beings to entertain and please the deity, the possession performance is characterized by the Goddess appearing as an actor herself, acting in concert with the human vehicle for the benefit of the audience, human devotees. Within this playful interaction, it is possible to view the phenomenon from at least three different perspectives.

From the theological point of view, it is the Goddess herself who controls the possession. She chooses it as her means of self-revelation and manifestation in the world of humans. It is one of several means, as illustrated in the story of Nandā and Nandlāl. Possession is her divine *līlā* (play), brought down to the human level. There is another caveat to this, however, in the theology of *bhakti*. The Goddess's immanence and participation in the lives of humans are grace, but this grace is in response to the longing of her devotees. Unless her devotees have faith, she will not reveal herself. The well-known saying "The *bhakta* [devotee] is greater than Bhagvān [God]" is relevant here. It is in response to the supplication of her devotees that the Goddess is induced to appear.

Thus, from the cultural or collective point of view, it is the audience of devotees who control the possession. In order for the possession to have a cultural meaning, it must conform to a preconceived ideology. A milieu in which the line between human and divine is seen as permeable and in which the individual self is not seen as an inviolable fortress is favorable to the acceptance of possession as a phenomenon. The devotees control the possession by confirming, acknowledging, interpreting, and structuring the experience. Songs, music, rituals, and question-and-answer sessions serve to transform what would otherwise be an individual subjective experience into a culturally meaningful phenomenon. For example, Ūṣā Bahn's "production" of *sindūr* is transformed into a miracle by the devotees' faith and expectations. As we have also seen, institutionalization and routinization of charisma further channel what begins as a subjective experience into a culturally shared and sanctioned experience. It is worth noting that in the greater Panjab area, since a popular Śāktism is the dominant Hindu

Collective understanding + agreeming

cult, Goddess possession is seen in a positive light. Possession-like experiences are then perhaps more likely to be interpreted as the grace of the Goddess rather than stemming from other sources.

Finally, from the individual point of view it is the human vehicle herself who controls the possession. Although possession seems to strike randomly and spontaneously, there may well be elements in the psychological makeup of certain women that contribute to their receptivity.[39] The power and authority that Mātās wield as religious leaders is almost unheard of in this patriarchal society. For women who make a career of it, such as Gumṭivāle Mātā and Ūṣā Bahn, divine possession is one of the few culturally accepted forms of avoiding marriage in a society that allows few avenues of self-expression for women outside marriage. In the cases we have outlined above, a common pattern emerges: the vehicle participates in the power of the deity, at first seemingly unwillingly. But gradually she is able to gain control over this power to a certain extent, to predict its coming, to prevent it from coming at times, and to bring it on at other times. Idiosyncracies in the Goddess's behavior during possession seem to emanate from the vehicle's personality. For example, Kālī, when present in Devtā, does not like the color black; it is the color of choice when she is in Ūṣā Bahn, who purposely wears black for the *caukī*. Just as the Goddess has a different localized identity in each of her temples, so does she have a different personality in each of her human vehicles. In some virtuosi, possession is used as a spiritual practice, or *sādhanā,* similar to yogic practices aimed at merging oneself with the divine.

Thus, the theological, cultural, and individual dimensions are mutually dependent and must be considered together. The Goddess, the audience, and the vehicle act and interact simultaneously in the "play" of possession.

6

The Goddess and Popular Culture

Contemporary Perspectives

A theme that has cropped up again and again in this study is the simultaneously archaic and contemporary quality of religious expression in the Goddess cult. Modern technology, urbanization, and mass media have introduced numerous changes in religious practice. Modern means of transportation, especially rail and bus, have made Goddess temples more accessible to larger numbers of people and have changed the dynamics of the pilgrimage process. A journey that used to be undertaken on foot with many stops along the way can now be made in a fraction of the time, eliminating many of the traditional stopping places. Pilgrimage is becoming both more popular and more streamlined. The ritual paraphernalia of the *jagrātā* now includes microphones, loudspeakers, and electronic *mūrtis*. Art of the mass-produced bazaar calendar print type has largely replaced folk art; even paintings commissioned for donation to temples are painted in this style. Mass-produced plastic statues of the Goddess grace the homes and dashboards of devotees. Even elegant marble statues in temples are, as a Western observer once quipped, "painted to look like plastic." The most popular devotional songs are now those sung to film tunes, and even "Devī Disco" has become the vogue. What do all these changes mean? Do they reflect a commercialization and decline of religious values, or are they simply a contemporary version of processes that have always taken place? Is the medium the message, or is this simply old wine in new wineskins?

In this chapter I explore these questions from several angles, looking at some of the ways in which modern popular culture intersects with the sacred. Beginning with a few remarks on how popular culture relates to classical and folk culture, I move on to a discussion of the popular pamphlet as a transmitter of religious lore in the Goddess cult. I then dedicate the bulk of the chapter to a case study of the "new" goddess Santoṣī Mā, whose fame and popularity have spread through the media of print and film.

The Classical–Folk Continuum

One of the key areas of focus in the study of Indian civilization has been the problem of levels. The Great Tradition–Little Tradition model has been articulated in a variety of ways, and although scholars are aware of its limitations, most appear to assume it implicitly, if only to point out exceptions to it.[1] Another version of this model that does not rely on the urban–rural dichotomy is the distinction between classical and folk culture, which focuses more on the mode of transmission than on the content. The Indian terms *mārga* (highway) and *desī* (country), denoting two strands of an artistic tradition, are roughly equivalent to classical and folk. Some examples of classical or high culture are texts and songs written in Sanskrit and canonical art. Their folk counterparts would be tales and legends told orally in a local dialect, folk songs, folk painting, and so on. These categories, of course, are not rigid; there is much overlap and interaction between the two. A third category is popular culture, which includes bazaar pamphlets, movies, and tapes in the standard regional language, film tunes, lithographs, and plastic images.

How does popular culture fit into the classical–folk typology? Is popular culture a product of modern times, or has it always existed? Joseph Elder points out that if mass culture (a term I take to be roughly equivalent to popular culture) consists of artistic products aimed at the general unrestricted public, then it is as old as society itself. Elder cites the historical continuity from the crude mass-produced icons of Harappa to the crude mass-produced icons of today.[2] Similarly, medieval *bhakti* poetry, spread largely by wandering bards orally, functioned much in the same way as modern mass media. The only difference is that the time it took to spread among the masses was much greater. Modern industrial technology is not a necessary condition for the existence of popular culture, but it allows popular culture to spread more quickly and easily. Also, while a few examples of popular culture can be found in premodern India, now they abound. Until recently, scholars took little interest in popular culture in India as a form distinct from elite culture and folk culture. It has been commonly assumed that popular culture necessarily reflects a process of secularization. Milton Singer was a pioneer in the study of the effects of urbanization on both classical and folk culture. His comments remain thought-provoking:

> The commercial mass media of film, radio, and print bring elements of a modern, secular culture with them into the cities and eventually into the towns and villages. Yet this trend has not displaced the traditional media or traditional culture. On the contrary, it is common to find such traditional institutions as temples adopting the tape recorder, the public address system, the radio, and the printing press for the popularization of prayers, devotional songs, and religious discourses. Traditional media are also employed to spread the "modern" messages of community development, sanitation, and industrialization.[3]

Singer further observes that urbanization and increased use of mass media do not result in secularization, but rather democratization of religious practice. This he attributes to the general shift toward *bhakti* that is less dependent on caste, ritual, and traditional *jajmān* relationships and lends itself to expression in the vernacular, popular media.[4] We have seen a similar ideology in the stories and songs of the northwest Goddess cult, which emphasize that the "call" of the Mother is open to all, regardless of caste. By the same token, in religious practices such as pilgrimage, the *jagrātā,* and the worship of charismatic leaders such as Mātās, caste boundaries are routinely transcended. While I believe it would be going too far to say that the modern popular media have brought about this democratization, I think it is fair enough to claim that these media, because of their universal availability, lend themselves to the propagation of ideas and religious forms that are already found in the tradition.

Popular Pamphlets

The popular pamphlets available at pilgrimage places and in bazaars in the towns and cities are one of the most important means of propagation within the cult. As Stuart Blackburn and A. K. Ramanujan point out, "The printed pamphlet plays a pivotal role in the folk–classical continuum as a medium into which both oral and written literature is adapted. Situated in the middle of the folk–classical divide, the pamphlet is something of an equalizer."[5] Many of the pamphlets on the Goddess draw on both the elite Sanskritic tradition and the local or regional folk traditions, joining them together in a highly self-conscious way. The most common Sanskritic story retold in the pamphlets is that of the *Devī Māhātmya,* especially the killing of Mahiṣāsura and the creation of Kālī in the Śumbha–Niśumbha episode. Other stories connecting the cult to the Sanskritic tradition are also recounted in many pamphlets. Two that are also depicted in calendar art are Rāma worshiping Devī during the Navarātra in order to gain the power to defeat Rāvaṇa[6] and Devī giving power to Arjuna to win the *Mahābhārata* war.

One pamphlet has arranged the various stories into a clever scheme, detailing Śerāṅvālī's *avatāras* in each of the four Yugas.[7] According to this scheme, in the Satya Yuga, three *avatāras* of the Goddess appeared and the three episodes of the *Devī Māhātmya* (the killing of Madhu and Kaiṭabha, Mahiṣāsura, and Śumbha–Niśumbha) occurred. In the Tretā Yuga, the *avatāra* called Vaiṣṇo Devī appeared and the part of her story that deals with Rāma occurred. In the Dvāpara Yuga, during the time of Kṛṣṇa there was no *avatāra* of the Goddess,[8] but she gave *śakti* to Arjun so that he and his brothers could win the war. Later they performed a horse sacrifice that figures in the Queen Tārā story. In the Kali Yuga, there were the stories of Vaiṣṇo Devī with Śrīdhar and Bhairo, Dhyānū Bhagat, Queen Tārā, and King Candradev.[9]

Another pamphlet focusing on Vaiṣṇo Devī[10] has used a different scheme to incorporate various stories; it has divided them into categories: (1) the birth of the Goddess, Purāṇic story (the three *Devī Māhātmya* episodes), (2) a history (*itihās*) and guide to the Vaiṣṇo Devī pilgrimage, (3) folk stories (*dant kathā*) and other related histories (Dhyānū Bhagat, Tārārānī, and King Candradev), (4) stories of the nine goddesses (three sets of nine are listed, the nine Durgās, the nine flames at Jvālā Mukhī, and the nine commonly worshiped today—Bhagavatī Satī (Pārvatī Devī), Durgā, Vaiṣṇo Devī, Jvālājī, Nainā Devī, Cintpūrṇī, Mansā Devī, Bālā Sundarī, and Kāṅgṛevālī Devī. Most of the pamphlets include devotional songs and *āratī* to various forms of the Goddess and lists of the 51 or 108 *śakti pīṭhas.*

Thus, the popular vernacular pamphlet can be seen as a continuation of the Purāṇic tradition, synthesizing local, regional, and pan-

Indian stories and practices and bringing them together in an intelligible form. Some scholars have suggested that popular pamphlets have resulted in increased standardization of myth and cult.[11] This is true to some extent, for "standard" myths about the shrines can be found in most pamphlets, often reproduced word for word with little regard for copyright law. On the whole, though, the pamphlets, whether anonymous or with named authors, remain very close to the oral tradition. Certain motifs and plots from the oral tradition do get picked up and become standardized in the popular pamphlet tradition, but there is still considerable room for variation and even creativity. The Purāṇic style of elaboration and interweaving such that every story is connected to another story continues in the popular pamphlet tradition. For example, one pamphleteer connects the stories of Dhyānū Bhagat and Queen Tārā with the Sanskrit *Devī Māhātmya* myth in an ingenious way which I have not seen elsewhere but that is typical of the Purāṇic spirit. He begins his verse rendition of the story of Dhyānū Bhagat, not in the time of the emperor Akbar where most versions start but back in the time of the *Devī Māhātmya,* at the point in the story when the king Suratha and the merchant Samādhi, having heard the full story of the Goddess, worship her clay image on the riverbank. The pamphleteer then has the Goddess appear before them and say:

King Suratha, reap the rule of the Kṣatrī line.
Merchant, I give you my devotion today.
In the next life, King, be known as Harīcand,
Through Queen Tārā's devotion gain my *darśan.*
Merchant, in the next life, become Dhyānū,
Sing my praises and spread my name.
I'll protect you both in every life,
In *jagrātās,* I'll fill my devotees' treasury.
That devoted Merchant when he took birth
Was called Dhyānū Bhakt, as the world knows.[12]

This version also chronicles the life of Dhyānū Bhagat, detailing his birth, childhood, travels, miracles, preaching against animal sacrifice, and a different version of his encounter with Akbar. According to this version, he was born in Nadaun village, was carried by the Goddess to Jammu, went to Kangra on foot, then to Jvālā Mukhī, and finally settled at Cintpūrṇī, where he disappeared at the age of thirty-five. I have not encountered these details anywhere else; the author is clearly drawing on a tradition, probably of the Amritsar area, different from that found in most pamphlets.

How do the pamphleteers choose their sources? I was able to speak with one pamphleteer, Mahant Omnāth Śarmā of Delhi,[13] who is well known as a writer of devotional songs and "histories" of the Goddess and as a performer of *jagrātās*. Śarmā presides over a small Kālī temple in New Delhi but is also employed full-time as a stenographer at Cottage Industries on Janpath. The sources of his authority are diverse and eclectic. He says that his *iṣṭ devī* is Vaiṣṇo Devī, although he was married in a Kālī temple. His guru is a woman, Śrī 1008 Śubh Mūrti Mātājī, who lives at Hardwar and Vaiṣṇo Devī. She is a *sādhu* and *brahmacārinī* who gets possessed by Devī during the Navarātras. His master (*ustād*) in music is Mahant Hīrā Lāl Hīrā, a classical singer who lives in Delhi. He is the *mahant* of his own *jagrātā māṇḍalī,* which belongs to the Kāśī Mātā *gharānā* style that originated in Lahore. Interestingly enough, although he is a Brahmin, several castes are represented in his *maṇḍalī,* even a sweeper who plays the *dholak.* There are also three Muslims who wear the *tilak* and believe in Devī. Remarking that the best god is the god who feeds you, he said that the Muslim god is not around; you cannot see him, but the Hindu gods and goddesses eat and wear saris, so they are more approachable. He has written hundreds of songs, some for Narendra Chanchal, and has also performed with Chanchal. He says that he prefers to sing songs in a light classical style but sometimes writes and sings in film style, to which he has no objection because it generates interest.

When I asked him how he gets his information for the stories he writes, he said that for "The Story of Queen Tārā," he read the well-known Caman Lāl Bharadvāj's version and heard versions from many other *mahants,* then composed his own, making corrections where he thought necessary. For him the main purpose of the story is to show that all are equal under Devī. When he writes about the Goddess temples, he goes to the places, meets the elders, gets all the stories from them, and then decides which stories are appropriate for the present time and society. He added that he uses these stories for the purpose of propagation (*pracār*) only, not for any personal profit. In a pamphlet on Nainā Devī he begins with an introduction on the importance of Devī *pūjā* and on the cultural significance of pilgrimage, saying that it was introduced by Śaṅkarācarya in the eighth century for the purpose of fostering cultural unity in India. Many people, he says, worship Devī without knowing the significance of doing so. He sees himself as a teacher and transmitter of culture, as can be seen from his introduction to the section "Worship and Major Sites in the Kali Yug" in the same pamphlet:

> Today in every area the greatness of the Mother is spreading, but before saying "Jay Devī" it is necessary for us to know who Mā is. Before finding this out, we have to look toward our religious books to find out where, when, and how the Mother arose. Come, dive into the Ganges of wisdom and ponder on the Mother *śakti* possessed of three *guṇas*. It can be said with certainty that the entire universe is based on *śakti.* In order to know her, she can be called by so many different names; it is necessary to know this also. Come, first let us ponder Mā's arising.[14]

Santoṣī Mā

No study of contemporary Hindu Goddess worship would be complete without taking account of Santoṣī Mā. This goddess has taken all of northern India by storm, and the greater Panjab region is no exception. In fact, my most vivid memory of my first visit to Vaiṣṇo Devī in 1978, besides the ice-cold water in the cave shrine, is the melody of the song "Jay Santoṣī Mātā," which played constantly in the roadside shops all the way up the mountain. When I asked devotees about it at the time, they replied that Santoṣī Mā is of course the same as Vaiṣṇo Devī, that they are both *śakti.*

The Santoṣī Mā phenomenon illustrates the continuity of the Goddess tradition in a modern context. Santoṣī Mā (Mother of Satisfaction) is somewhat different from other goddesses described in this study, for she is neither associated with any particular geographical spot as are Jvālā Mukhī, Nainā Devī, and so on, nor is she a goddess of Purāṇic mythology such as Satī and Durgā. She sprung, seemingly from nowhere, into prominence sometime in the early 1960s. Temples to Santoṣī Mā in Jodhpur (Rajasthan), Ujjain and Indore (Uttar Pradesh), Delhi, and Bombay are said to have been founded in 1963. Her cult received a further boost in 1975 with the release of the Hindi film *Jay Santoṣī Mā,* an immediate box office hit that still draws crowds today. She has intrigued scholars of Hinduism, who have hailed her as the "new goddess."[15] There is no known oral tradition of Santoṣī Mā. Rather, information about her comes from popular pamphlets in Hindi published as far east as Calcutta and as far west as Jodhpur.[16] According to these pamphlets, Santoṣī Mā is the daughter of Gaṇeśa and his wife, Riddhi-Siddhi.[17] Technically, this makes her the granddaughter of Śiva and Pārvatī, but most worshipers identify her as an aspect of the Great Goddess, saying that there is a reference to the Goddess as Tuṣṭi (satisfaction, contentment) in the Purāṇas.[18]

The major ritual associated with Santoṣī Mā is a *vrat* (fast, vow) performed on Fridays that has become her trademark. The *vrat* is relatively uncomplicated, requiring only that one should set up a water-filled pot (*kalaś*) with a dish of jaggery (*guṛ*) and chick-peas (*canā*) above it. The standard amount of the offering is $1^1/_4$ annas' worth, but this is not crucial, since as the pamphlets say, "The Mother hungers only for affection [*bhāvanā*]." Taking jaggery and chick-peas in one's hand, one should recite or listen to the story (*kathā*) of Santoṣī Mā and then feed the jaggery and chick-peas in the hand to a cow, distributing the rest as *prasād*. The water from the pot is then sprinkled throughout the house and over the *tulsī* plant. This *vrat* should be performed every Friday until the wish one desires is fulfilled. Then one must perform a final ceremony (*udyāpan*), consisting mainly of a special meal, including a fried bread (*khājā*), rice pudding (*khīr*), and chick-pea curry, fed to eight boys. One should also light a lamp with ghee and break open a coconut. The boys may receive any kind of gift except cash. The person keeping the *vrat* should take *prasād* and eat only one meal that day. The one prohibition associated with the Santoṣī Mā *vrat* is that the person keeping it should neither eat nor feed anyone any type of sour food, for that would anger Santoṣī Mā and dire consequences will ensue.

The story of Santoṣī Mā can be summarized as follows:

> There was an old woman who had seven sons, the youngest of whom was an idle good-for-nothing who naively thought that his mother loved him dearly. In fact, she was feeding him the impure leftovers of his elder brothers. When he was able to confirm his wife's allegations to this effect, he decided to leave home to seek his fortune. He left his young wife behind, telling her to fulfill her duty. He found employment with a gem merchant in a far-off land and eventually became very rich himself, completely forgetting about his wife in the process. Meanwhile, his wife was being badly mistreated by her mother-in-law and sisters-in-law.

> Not only was she forced to do all the menial housework, she even had to go out to collect firewood in the jungle. While engaged in this one day she came across a group of women performing the Santoṣī Mā *vrat*. She then prayed to the goddess for the return of her husband and performed the *vrat* according to the women's instructions.
>
> Thus enlisted, Santoṣī Mā reminded the husband of his wife's plight in a dream. Following the goddess's advice, he sold his business very profitably and returned home with gifts of cloth and jewelry. The next Friday, the heroine performed the *udyāpan* ceremony to thank Santoṣī Mā, only to have it sabotaged by an evil sister-in-law who encouraged her sons to ask for something sour to eat. The heroine refused to give them sour food, but unthinkingly gave them some money which they spent on sour food. Santoṣī Mā immediately became enraged, and as a result the husband was arrested on a charge of tax evasion.
>
> Once again the heroine performed the *vrat* and pleaded with Santoṣī Mā for forgiveness. When she did the *udyāpan* again, the nephews tried the same trick again, so this time she fed the sons of Brahmins and gave them fruit instead of cash. Her husband was released from jail, and nine months later she gave birth to a handsome son. Later on Santoṣī Mā decided to pay her faithful devotee a visit and, in order to test her faith, took on a ferocious form. The rest of the family, especially the mother-in-law and the conniving nephews, were terrified, but the heroine quickly recognized Santoṣī Mā and opened the door to the house for her. After she had explained who the goddess was, the wicked in-laws fell at Santoṣī Mā's feet and apologized for their misbehavior. The story ends with the entire family receiving Santoṣī Mā's grace.[19]

Santoṣī Mā's iconography as shown on popular posters and pamphlet covers is fairly standard. She is seated on a throne in lotus posture wearing a red sari and a headdress. Her arms hold a sword, a trident, and a golden bowl of what appears to be *khīr,* with the fourth arm extended in the *abhaya mudrā,* or fear-not, gesture. Often she is shown in a mountain setting with temples in the background, accompanied by her devotees and by a peacock and bull. Images of Santoṣī Mā in temples and homes, however, show less fidelity to this set iconography, with informants calling images Santoṣī Mā that in fact appear to be Durgā or Vaiṣṇo Devī. This fluidity of names and images is not surprising, being in keeping with the general tendency in the Goddess cult to view all (or most) goddesses as one.

Some scholars[20] have attempted to attribute Santoṣī Mā's popularity to some unique characteristic of hers that more especially suits her to modern needs and problems, especially those of urbanizing lower-middle-class women who constitute the bulk of her devotees. However, there is little about Santoṣī Mā that is new except her name. Her nature and behavior fit the general pattern of goddesses identified with the Goddess. Furthermore, there is no evidence to suggest that Santoṣī Mā is becoming more popular at the expense of more established manifestations of the Goddess. She is rather sharing in the bounty of the overall Goddess vogue. There is good reason for believing that Santoṣī Mā's rapid rise to fame has more to do with her widespread exposure through the media of print, film, and radio than with any special quality she possesses.[21]

Santoṣī Mā, while having her own "history" (as daughter of Gaṇeśa) and idiosyncracies (dislike of sour foods), shares many structural similarities with Śerāṅvālī that fit her for absorbtion into the Panjab Hills Goddess cult. The most important of these are her single, independent status, her benevolence with a flip side of fierce punitiveness, her accessibility to people of all castes, and her generalized concern with the mundane affairs and well-being of her devotees. Like Śerāṅvālī, she is both a virgin and a mother.

The most prevalent form of Santoṣī Mā worship in the greater Panjab region, as in most of north India, is the observance of the Friday *vrat. Vrats* in general are more commonly practiced by women than by men, and Santoṣī Mā's is no exception. In fact, it has become the most popular of women's *vrats,* practiced by housewives, students, and working women alike. Some of the reasons contributing to its current vogue include the fact that it is inexpensive and easy to keep, requiring only a small amount of jaggery and chick-peas, reading or listening to the story, and a single dietary restriction, the avoidance of sour foods. Also, like other weekday *vrats,* it is easier to remember than those falling on a lunar date (*tithi*). Keeping of the Santoṣī Mā *vrat* does not in any way conflict with the worship of Śerāṅvālī. On the contrary, images of the Goddess in her lion-riding form are often worshiped in conjunction with the Santoṣī Mā *vrat,* and those who keep it are also likely to be active in other aspects of the Goddess cult such as pilgrimage or *jagrātās.*

A recent phenomenon is the widespread Santoṣī Mā "chain letter," whose existence Stanley Kurtz reports in Nepal, Calcutta,

Uttar Pradesh, Rajasthan, Delhi, Madhya Pradesh, and Bombay.[22] I have heard numerous reports of these letters being circulated in the cities and larger towns of Panjab. I have one in my possession that a neighbor of mine in Chandigarh received. It is a carbon copy, handwritten in Devanāgarī script in a mixture of Hindi and Panjabi (such as is commonly spoken in Chandigarh and eastern Panjab generally). At the top is a crudely drawn figure, iconographically identical with Serāṅvālī but with the caption "Jay Santoṣī Mātā" written on either side. Entitled "The Miracle of Santoṣī Mātā," it reads as follows:

> A woman was worshiping in Santoṣī Mātā's temple. Santoṣī Mātā gave her *darśan* and said to that woman, "Taking on the form of a girl in the Kal Yug, I will destroy the Kal Yug and get rid of inhumanity. Then all the people will live in equality." That woman told this to many people. The people who considered this to be true and, to propagate it, had letters printed and distributed profited greatly. But one man received a letter and let twenty or twenty-five days pass in procrastination. Then his wife died, and he regretted it. In the east, a man kept putting it off for a month. As a result, his two water buffaloes died.
>
> In the east, a farmer had a thousand letters printed and distributed them. He won a lawsuit, and Santoṣī Mātā granted him *darśan* in a dream and said, "There is a lot of money hidden in the western part of your house." Thereupon the farmer dug in his house and found a jar full of gold. He joyfully had a temple built to Santoṣī Mātā and distributed some wealth to the poor. Now he is living happily. A resident of Narayanpur near Aligarh, Man Singh, considered this letter to be false. Then great harm befell him. Whoever reads this letter and at that time has a thousand letters printed and distributed, within only twenty-five days Santoṣī Mātā will perform some miracle for that person. For this reason, all brothers and sisters are requested not to read this letter and throw it away, but to give it to others. Victory to the Mother. Victory to Santoṣī Mātā.

This letter, like the *vrat kathā,* definitely indicates that Santoṣī Mā, while benevolent when pleased, is fierce and destructive when displeased.

References to Santoṣī Mā, and stories about her and her temples have been incorporated into the traditional oral narratives told at *jagrātās*. In one such case the storyteller plays on the meaning of Santoṣī Mā's name to explain her connection with Śerāṅvālī. At the end of "The Story of Queen Tārā," he incorporates the following comment:

> When the king [Harīcand] got Mā's *darśan* all his confusion disappeared. The king attained complete trust. The king attained complete satisfaction [*santoṣ*]. He got satisfaction, so he named the temple "Santoṣī Mātā Temple." We [the storyteller] have also seen this temple. This is the temple which Queen Tārā had the king build. When he got Mā's direct *darśan,* he named the temple "Santoṣī Mātā Temple."[23]

There is in fact such a temple in the town of Haripur, the former capital of Guler State near Kangra, reputed to have been the home of King Harīcand in the story. According to B. N. Goswamy, an expert on the art and temples of the Panjab Hills, it is an old Tantric temple called Dandokṣī Mātā upon which the name Santoṣī Mātā has been recently superimposed.[24]

Another example of the renaming of a temple is at Mani Majra near Chandigarh, about one mile from the larger and more famous Mansā Devī temple. Now called Santoṣī Mātā, the temple was formerly called Annapūrṇā.[25] It was founded at least 140 years ago; a mural on the back wall is dated Samvat 1899 (1842 C.E.). Several years ago the name was changed, a new image was installed, and a semiannual feast was instituted. Packets of jaggery and chick-peas, the standard offerings to Santoṣī Mā, are now sold on the steps to the temple, along with the traditional red scarves and coconuts offered to the original goddess. Loudspeakers blare out songs to Santoṣī Mā and to Śerāṅvālī, set mostly to film tunes. The temple is frequented by pilgrims on the way to nearby Mansā Devī and on Fridays by local people from Chandigarh, Mani Majra, and surrounding villages. When I asked the *pujārī* about the name change, his reply was that Annapūrṇā and Santoṣī Mā are one and the same, because they both fulfill all desires. The name changes, but the deity remains the same. If the priest's approach is functional and experiential, it is also pragmatic. My guess is that the name was changed to attract more patrons to the temple and to give it a needed boost at a time when royal patronage has dried up.[26] This may also have been the case with the Dandokṣī Mātā temple at Haripur. Larger, more established Goddess temples have appropriated Santoṣī Mā by building auxiliary shrines to her within their compounds. The Kāṅgṛevālī Devī temple, for example, has recently installed a Santoṣī Mā statue. At Mansā Devī one can purchase framed "photos" with Mansā Devī on one side and Santoṣī Mā on the other.

Another common indication of Santoṣī Mā's popularity is her inclusion in devotional songs and literature as one of the Seven Sisters. The composition of the Seven Sisters is fluid in any case, drawing from a pool of goddesses to complete the list. A song entitled "The Court of the Seven Sisters" sung by a group of women at the Cāmuṇḍā Devī temple includes Santoṣī Mātā, "who gives everyone satisfaction" (*santoṣ*), appropriately enough, as the seventh and youngest of the Sisters. The other six in this song are Vaiṣṇo Mātā, "who does everyone's work"; Jvālā Mātā, "who lights the sparkling flame"; Durgā Mātā, "who broke Akbar's pride"; Cintpūrṇī, "who eliminates everyone's worry"; Aśāpūrṇī, "who fulfills everyone's hopes [*āśā*]"; and Cāmuṇḍā Mātā, "who killed Caṇḍ and Muṇḍ."

With the increasing popularity of Santoṣī Mā, it is becoming common to hear her named as an *iṣṭ devī,* or personally chosen goddess. A devotee picks an *iṣṭ-devī* on the basis of an affinity with that particular goddess or because he or she has received a favor from that deity. Devotees often express the feeling that the deity has chosen them rather than the other way around. This is particularly true in the case of women who become possessed by Santoṣī Mā as a form of the Goddess Śerāṅvālī. Of the women I have encountered, two have expressly identified their possessing deity as Santoṣī Mā.[27] Both live in Chandigarh, are middleclass Baniyās, and have small followings. One is a young unmarried woman, the other a middle-aged married woman. I met both of them initially when they were performing *caukī* at the Santoṣī Mātā temple in Mani Majra (near Chandigarh) on the occasion of its biannual *bhaṇḍārā* (feast). On that day there were about one thousand devotees at the temple at any given time, standing in line to make offerings and receive *darśan,* eating their meal in an adjacent tent, or joining in one of the several *bhajan* groups that had congregated. Two of these groups featured "living Mātās" who called themselves Santoṣī Mā. The younger of the two was leading her group in devotional singing; the elder was holding her *caukī* while her devotees sang. I was able to meet both of these women later in their homes.

Vīṇā Guptā (a pseudonym), who prefers to be called Santoṣī Mā or Mātājī, was about twenty-two years old and had been living in Chandigarh with her family for about seventeen years when I met her in April 1983. Wearing a pink *salvār-kamīz,* she was seated on a divan in a room of her home; the room had been made into a shrine with a burning *jot* and pictures of Santoṣī Mā, other gods and goddesses, and her guru, whom she identified as Śrī Śrī 1008 Svāmī Bāl Jogījī Arjunpurī Mahārājjī. There was a steady stream of visitors, all of whom washed their hands, took off their shoes before entering the room, and seated themselves beneath her on the floor.

Vīṇā's family is originally from District Gurdaspur, Panjab. Her possession experiences first started after they had moved to Chandigarh when she was about seven years old (1968). At that time she saw a direct vision (*sākṣāt darśan*) of the Goddess's face and played continuously for twenty-four hours. After that it would happen every Tuesday and Friday and during the Navarātras. When the *pavan* (wind) of the Goddess comes, it enters her hair and opens it up, even if her hair has been tied. At first the family thought it was sorcery (*jadū ṭonā*), but after a few years they realized it was Devī. When Vīṇā was eleven or twelve, they tried to lock her up in a room, because it was difficult to control her, but the doors broke down. Vīṇā's mother, listening to this description of events, added that she was afraid when the possession first started happening to her daughter but that now she accepts the fact that the Goddess has chosen to come to her home. Still, she expressed disappointment that her daughter would never marry and have a "normal" life.

Vīṇā has studied up to matric (tenth standard). She was in a government school up to the seventh standard, but the *pavan* would come while she was in class, so she had to drop out and complete her education privately. She speaks an educated style of Hindi well sprinkled with English words as well as her native Panjabi. In 1974 she met the Svāmī, first at Vaiṣṇo Devī and later in Chandigarh, whom she accepted as her guru. He tested her and was convinced of her powers before accepting her as his disciple. She is a strict vegetarian and does *pūjā* and recitation of the *Durgā Saptaśatī (Devī Māhātmya)* every day for several hours, saying that it has helped her control the *pavan,* which now comes usually only on *aṣṭamī.* She attends *jagrātās* when invited; then the *pavan* comes at midnight. The *pavan* also comes at unscheduled times when someone has committed a sin. She does not remember what happens during the *pavan,* what questions people ask, or what answers she gives. She does remember getting the *darśan* and is aware of something very heavy coming on top of her and entering her body.

Santoṣī Mā is Vīṇā's chosen goddess (*iṣṭ-devī*), because she is the first to have appeared in *pavan* form. In deference to her, Vīṇā abstains from sour foods on Thursdays and Fridays. But many other goddesses have appeared as well. She named Nainā Devī, Cintpūrṇī, Vaiṣṇo Devī, Jvālā Mukhī, Kaṅgṛevālī, Kālī, and Caṇḍī, saying that an informed observer can tell the difference by the expression on her face and by her voice. Vīṇā herself can tell, because she receives the *darśan* of the particular goddess just as the *pavan* starts. When Vīṇā told me this, I remarked that I would not be able to tell, since I had only seen some of these Devīs in *piṇḍī* form. She found this amusing and said that she hardly becomes a *piṇḍī* but actually sees the face of the particular Devī and her own face changes accordingly, just like a photograph.

Vīṇā states confidently that she has no intention of getting married; instead she plans to devote her life to the Goddess and to helping her devotees with their problems. She believes that she was chosen to do this because of her faith and a *saṃskāra* (mental predisposition or impression) from a previous life. Although she has heard about both Gumṭivāle Mātā and Ūṣā Bahn, she cannot give a guarantee concerning anyone else's validity, she says, because many are fakes (*pākhaṇḍī*). No one should have faith just from seeing someone shake her head around; it might be due to *jadū ṭonā* or an impure soul. She said that it is *pākhaṇḍī* when girls get up during a *kīrtan* and start shaking and dancing, perhaps referring to an event I had witnessed among her own devotees at the Santoṣī Mā temple.

Her family supports her, albeit with some ambivalence, as evidenced by the fact that they have set aside a room as her shrine in their modest flat. At present her cult is very small, consisting mostly of neighbors and relatives in Chandigarh, but she has hopes for the future. She has had stationery printed in her name in Roman script with a drawing of Śerāṅvālī at the top and the words *jay mātā dī* at the bottom. She told me that "a lot of people come here and give me respect," using the English word "respect." She would like to travel, especially abroad, but said that people need her at home, too. Although she has not yet passed on her power to any disciple, she said that she might do so someday "after building several temples."

Kamlā Devī Aggarwāl (a pseudonym), the elder of the two women, was at the time of our meeting (May 1983) fifty-nine years old. A native of Ambala, Haryana, she had been living in Chandigarh for about twenty-two years. Her husband is a lawyer, and she has six children. She refers to her possessing goddess sometimes as Santoṣī Mā and sometimes as Bālā Sundarī. She also is possessed by Kālī, Vaiṣṇo Devī, and other goddesses, saying that ultimately they are all the same.

Her *caukī* first started on February 24, 1975, when she suddenly started playing. During this state she was able to tell the future, if something was stolen, or if someone had an illness. After the first *caukī* she fell unconscious. A few days later she saw an elderly woman in dirty clothing. The woman disappeared after Kamlā Devī gave her alms. For the next six months she kept seeing different forms of Devī. Her husband, believing she was possessed by Devī, took her to many temples to beg Devī to leave her. Devī did not leave, and gradually the husband was reconciled to the situation. At the end of that six-month period, Kamlā Devī started holding weekly *bhajan* sessions on Friday afternoons during which she becomes possessed and answers questions put forth by her devotees.

It is interesting to note that during the six-month transition period, the film *Jay Santoṣī Mā* was released and that by the end of the six-month period Kamlā Devī had definitely identified her possession deity as Santoṣī Mā and incorporated elements of her ritual into her religious practice. She says that Santoṣī Mā has been her *iṣṭ-devī* since 1975. Before that for many years her *iṣṭ-devī* and *kul-devī* (family goddess) had been the traditional goddess Bālā Sundarī, whose major shrine is in District Nahan, Himachal Pradesh. Bālā Sundarī is the favorite goddess of Haryanavis, particularly of those in the Ambala area. Her name means "beautiful girl," and it is in that form that she appears in legends connected with the shrine. She is often counted as one of the Seven Sisters, especially among Haryanavis.

I was interested to see if there were any differences that could be attributed to the association with the new goddess, Santoṣī Mā, so I attended one of the Friday afternoon sessions. About a dozen women were there, several of whom accompanied the singing with percussion instruments. Kamlā Devī "played" intermittently for about three hours. Women would approach with questions and make small cash offerings in front of the burning flame. The songs sung, mostly in Panjabi, were of the same type as those generally sung to Śerāṅvālī in her various aspects. The only references to

Santoṣī Mā per se were occasional shouted slogans of victory (*jaykārās*) to Santoṣī Mā and the singing of the *ārtī* song from the film *Jay Santoṣī Mā*. The devotees identified Santoṣī Mā so completely with Śerāṅvālī that before the possession, they sang a song with the words "Come, O Śerāṅvālī, your daughters are crying out to you." Once the possession had started, they cried out, "Victory to Santoṣī Mā, victory to the true court, O true flame Mother, your eternal victory" (*jaykārā* Santoṣī Māī *dā, bol sāce darbār kī jay, sacciyāṅ jotāṅ vālī mātā terī sadā hī jay*) and immediately went into a song that said, "Mounted on a golden lion / Look, Śerāṅvālī has come / Proclaim her victory once again / Look, Śerāṅvālī has come."

Kamlā Devī, unlike Vīṇā and the Mātās discussed in chapter 5, has no ambitions to expand her cult. She explained that she calls the congregation for *bhajan* singing only on Fridays. If she did this every day, she would get the *caukī* every day, which would interfere with her family obligations. She has a small shrine for her private use where she performs *pūjā* and recites from the *Durgā Saptasatī* twice a day. Upstairs there is a larger shrine where she holds her Friday sessions. On Fridays she keeps a complete fast, sitting with the *jot* all day and not eating or drinking until evening. She does not go to anyone's house for *jagrātās* but holds her own at home twice a year. One is always on February 23–24, the anniversary of her first *caukī;* the other can be at any time. Only women come to her *jagrātās* and Friday sessions and perform all the rituals, singing, and storytelling. Kamlā Devī said that this is because women have more feeling (*bhāvanā*) than men. She goes on pilgrimages to Devī temples whenever she can, but her only public activity as a living Mātā outside her home is her attendance at the Santoṣī Mātā temple feast in Mani Majra twice a year.

Surely modern media and technology have hastened the spread of Santoṣī Mā's popularity, but these modern means have been used for traditional purposes. There is nothing amiss in the frankly materialistic nature of her worship. Goddesses have always been associated with mundane concerns, with the realities of life and death. One need only remember the description of the Goddess in the *Devī Māhātmya* as *bhuktimuktipradāyinī,* the grantor of material enjoyment as well as liberation. The desires for health, wealth, fertility, and stable family relationships have always been expressed in a religious idiom. Santoṣī Mā is not unique in her functions. Neither is her identification with older goddesses unique. The historical

so they are the same

process of absorbtion and identification of goddesses has gone on for centuries. Other goddesses have retained their specific histories and characteristics while becoming identified as aspects or manifestations of the Great Goddess. Santoṣī Mā is the most recent of such goddesses, her newness acknowledged by all. The case of Santoṣī Mā, who has arisen as it were before our very eyes, provides an excellent opportunity to study processes of deity formation and assimilation in popular Hinduism. These processes may differ in various parts of India. In the greater Panjab, where the worship of the virgin and mother Śerāṅvālī was already a well-established and dominant cult, Santoṣī Mā has become easily absorbed as one of her many aspects. The appearance of Santoṣī Mā on the contemporary scene is testimony to the continued flexibility and vigor of the Hindu tradition.

7

The Goddess as an Enduring Presence

In this study I have approached the cult of the Goddess in northwest India as a regional phenomenon with pan-Indian connections. Śerāṅvālī, identified with the pan-Indian Durgā or Mahādevī, is a goddess of many manifestations, nominal and geographical, such as the Seven Sisters, Nine Goddesses, and various *śakti pīṭhas*. The Goddess also takes on various "forms" (*rūp*) such as the *piṇḍī* (stone), *mūrti* (carved iconic image), *kanyā* (maiden), *jot* (flame), and *pavan* (wind or possession), as well as her "direct form" (*sākṣāt rūp*) with which she sometimes graces her devotees in dreams and visions. In this final chapter I address once more the questions that have guided this study: Who is the Goddess? How do her various forms relate to each other? What is her significance in the lives of her devotees? I offer some comments on the continuing discussion concerning benevolence and malevolence among Hindu female deities, on *bhakti* as an overarching framework for interpreting the Goddess cult, and on the Goddess's multiple manifestations and ambiguity as a key to understanding her enduring popularity.

Benevolence, Malevolence, and the Single Goddess

Vaiṣṇo and Kālī are two different aspects of the Goddess that could roughly be described as gentle (*saumya*) and fierce (*raudra*). Superficially, this distinction resembles one put forth in modern scholarly literature on Hindu goddesses, that of benevolence and malevolence. According to Lawrence Babb, who first introduced this dichotomy, the Hindu pantheon is differentiated on the basis of gender, with male deities being generally benevolent and female deities being generally malevolent unless controlled through marriage.[1] He associates with female deities a whole complex of phenomena—the hot season, disease, heat, possession, pollution through blood sacrifice, and so on. According to Babb, benevolent female deities are those whose power has been tamed and controlled through marriage and subordination to a male deity. Examples of this type of "consort" goddess are Pārvatī, Sītā, and Lakṣmī, who are gentle and are worshiped for general prosperity. Malevolent goddesses, on the other hand, are unmarried or independent goddesses such as Śītalā or Māriammā, who afflict people with diseases and whom people propitiate in order to be left alone.

Babb advanced this theory at a time when little work had been done on Hindu goddesses, so it will be useful to see to what extent it applies in an all-India context and in various regional contexts. It is doubtful to what extent Śerāṅvālī of northwest India, who is neither married nor primarily malevolent, fits this pattern. I suspect there are other examples in other regions of South Asia which will come to light as more research is done. One is the Nepali goddess Swasthānī (Goddess of One's Own Place), whose text and cult have been thoroughly documented by Linda Iltis. In the context of discussing Babb's theory, Iltis writes:

> This view of "married" versus "malevolent" does not fit the Swasthānī context, since the Goddess Swasthānī is neither married nor malevolent. Likewise to refer to Pārvatī as "married" underrates the importance of the highly popular stories concerning her peaceful *unmarried* childhood. Moreover, in South Asia generally and perhaps especially in Newar contexts, the fierce nature of certain deities (both male and female!) is an expression not of malevolence, but of protective potency. It is precisely the fact that such figures represent power in its "controlled" form that makes them gods and goddesses, and hence powerful allies in the struggle against dangerous and demonic counterforces.[2]

fierce doesn't necessarily mean evil

While it is undeniable that the Goddess is ambiguous or ambivalent, the use of the word "malevolent" to describe her power is probably less than accurate. The question arises, malevolent to whom, for what reasons, and under what circumstances? Would devotees of a so-called malevolent goddess consider her to be malevolent? Perhaps it would be more accurate to use the indigenous Indian categories *saumya* (gentle) and *raudra* (fierce) to describe the two aspects of the Goddess. These terms, incidentally, are also used often with respect to male deities. Śiva certainly has fierce forms; indeed, his original name was Rudra, "the Howler," from which the word *raudra* is derived. Furthermore, it makes more sense to see the goddess Pārvatī as the tamer or domesticator of Śiva, rather than the other way around.[3] Similarly, Narasiṃha, the man–lion incarnation of Viṣṇu, is nothing if not fierce. But fierce does not mean malevolent.

Let us consider an example of a goddess Babb considers to be malevolent, the goddess of the Sanskrit *Durgā Saptaśatī* (*Devī Māhātmya*). Babb states, "As she is represented in the [*Durgā*] *Saptasatī*, the only discernable emotion of the goddess is anger—black, implacable, and bloodthirsty. She is something emerging from the highest gods; she is the very essence of their anger."[4] The description of the Goddess as black and bloodthirsty is valid only for Kālī, a *śakti* whom the Goddess produces from her brow during the third episode to drink the blood of the demon Raktabīja. Throughout her battles the Goddess remains beautiful and smiling, exerting a self-controlled energy. She releases *śaktis* and reabsorbs them at will. The anger of the gods has been transformed into the protective power of the Goddess. The two names—besides the generic Devī—by which she is most often called in the text are Caṇḍikā and Ambikā, demonstrating both her fierce destructive and motherly protective qualities. She kills demons in order to protect the gods and restore order to the universe. This is made clear in the text both by her monologues and by the hymns of praise the gods sing to her. As we have seen in chapter 1, the *Devī Māhātmya* presents a complex picture of the Goddess, an integrated theology that embraces all aspects of reality, not just the most pleasant. The Goddess in the *Devī Māhātmya* does not fall into the category of malevolent goddesses. She is invoked to help humankind, not propitiated to leave them alone.

The distinction between consort or domesticated goddesses as benevolent and single or independent goddesses as malevolent is one that many scholars have accepted since it was first suggested by Babb. A. K. Ramanujan, for example, distinguishes between two types of Indian goddesses, Breast Mothers or Consort Goddesses, on one hand, and Tooth Mothers or Virgin Goddesses (Amma<u>n</u>), on the other.[5] The former he associates with the Sanskritic tradition, the latter with villages. He characterizes the Consort Goddesses as married; subordinate to the male consort; benevolent; related to auspicious life-cycle rites; household deities with temples within the village; having well-sculpted faces and images; not born of the earth; pure; chaste; having claims to universality; vegetarian; and with Brahmin or Brahminized priests. He characterizes Virgin Goddesses as basically independent (or, if married, not subordinated to a male consort); associated with crisis rites; causing and removing epidemics and famines; having temples outside the village boundaries; having rough-hewn, faceless images or aniconic representations; being of the earth; lustful; associated with a particular village; ambivalent or malevolent, with possession as part of the ritual; accepting blood sacrifices or substitutes; and having mostly non-Brahmin, often untouchable officiants.

While this dichotomy may hold up in the Karnataka region from which Ramanujan draws his generalizations, it does not hold up when applied to Śerāṅvālī, who straddles the fence on almost every characteristic mentioned (see accompanying table). Going down the list, we see that Śerāṅvālī in her various aspects is unmarried or independent like the Virgin Goddess (VG), benevolent like the Consort Goddess (CG), but with fierce or ambiguous qualities (VG), is related to life-cycle rites (CG), has possession as part of her

Consort	*Virgin*	*Śerāṅvālī*	*Vaiṣṇo*	*Kālī*
Married	Independent	Independent	Independent	Independent
Benevolent	Malevolent	Both	Both	Both
Life-cycle	Crisis rites	Both	Both	Both
In village	Out village	Both	Both	Both
Sculpted	Aniconic	Both	Both	Both
Not of earth	Of earth	Of earth	Of earth	Of earth
Pure	Impure	Pure	Pure	Impure
Chaste	Lustful	Chaste	Chaste	Chaste
Universal	Local	Both	Both	Both
Vegetarian	Sacrifice	Vegetarian	Vegetarian	Sacrifice
Brahmin	Non-Brahmin	Both	Both	Both
No possession	Possession	Possession	Possession	Possession

ritual (VG), is worshiped in villages and households (CG) but also in major pilgrimage sites, has aniconic forms (VG) and well-sculpted images (CG), has both low-caste (VG) and Brahmin (CG) officiants, is universal (CG) but is also of the earth and associated with particular places (VG). Nor is it possible to say that Vaiṣṇo and Kālī as aspects of Śerāṅvālī fit this dichotomy, since both, for example, are unmarried goddesses and have possession as part of their ritual.

More research is necessary to test further the usefulness of the marriage and malevolence theory, but for the time being, I will make the following tentative suggestions. The marriage and malevolence dichotomy as put forth by Babb, Ramanujan, and others may be useful in a limited sense when comparing two specific types of goddesses, the consort goddesses of the Sanskritic tradition and local village disease goddesses. I am sure arguments could be advanced to reject the dichotomy even then, for there are exceptions. And is it appropriate, for example, to lump together such different consort goddesses as Pārvatī and Sītā or Lakṣmī and Rādhā?[6] Leaving these objections aside, however, the marriage and malevolence theory still does not account for all dimensions of the divine feminine in Hinduism, regardless of whether one views individual goddesses as discrete entities or as aspects of one Great Goddess. Taking the former point of view, David Kinsley has written:

> The goddesses . . . often illustrate important ideas of the Hindu tradition, ideas that underlie the great Hindu philosophic visions. Several goddesses, for example, are unambiguously identified with or called *prakṛti,* a central notion in most philosophic systems. . . . Other goddesses [such as Rādhā and Sītā] explore the nature of devotion and the divine–human relationship. . . . Lakṣmī expresses Hindu thinking about kingship and the relationship of the ruler to the fertility of the world. . . . The many goddesses associated with geographical features of the Indian subcontinent suggest Hindu thinking about the relationship between sacred space and spiritual liberation. . . . Several goddesses are cast in untraditional, "masculine" roles that express unconventional, perhaps even experimental, thinking about sexual roles. . . . Other goddesses, in their myths and personalities, express central tensions that characterize the Hindu tradition. The best example is the mythology of Pārvatī, in which the tension between dharma, the human tendency to uphold and refine the social and physical order, and *mokṣa,* the human

> longing to transcend all social and physical limitations, is explored in the relationship between Pārvatī and Śiva. . . . The great variety of goddesses allows one to find in their mythology and worship aspects of almost every important Hindu theme. In short, a study of Hindu goddesses is not so much a study of one aspect of the Hindu tradition as it is a study of the Hindu tradition itself.[7]

In short, many goddesses do not fit either category or only partially fit. It is not always their marital status that is the main issue. I have quoted Kinsley at length because I believe that his point of view is one that has merit, although it is not one that I have emphasized in this study, preferring to view Śerāṅvālī and her various manifestations from the Great Goddess perspective, as her devotees most often do. I do, however, agree with Kinsley that not all goddesses in all contexts and situations throughout the history of Hinduism can be reduced to a single "feminine principle," just as not all gods can be reduced to a single "masculine principle." Furthermore, Kinsley demonstrates quite convincingly that Hindu goddesses cannot be reduced to a single duality but rather express a multiplicity of concerns that are central to Hinduism.

It should be obvious by now that if individual goddesses do not always fit into the benevolent–malevolent dichotomy, the Great Goddess viewed as a supreme being does so even less. Śākta theology describes a Goddess who embraces the totality of reality. In the cult of Śerāṅvālī, *bhakti* is the dominant religious mood. Devotees worship the Goddess out of love and devotion, not simply as a means of flattering her into satisfying their material desires. The Goddess grants her devotees' wishes as a way of showing her grace and gives *darśan* openly. She is accessible, immanent, and worldly. What Babb perceives as malevolence could simply be called realism. Devī is closely connected with the realities and ambiguities of life. She is *prakṛti* (matter), *śakti* (divine power), *māyā* (creative illusion), and *saṃsāra* (the worldly cycle)—which encompass purity and impurity, auspiciousness and inauspiciousness, creation and destruction, life and death.

"This-Worldly" *Bhakti*

Madeline Biardeau has written that the ideology of *bhakti* "englobes" all other values in the Hindu tradition and provides a comprehensive framework through which one can understand Hinduism as "a grandiose edifice, stupefying in its coherence and unity."[8] The major emphasis in the cult of Śerāṅvālī is *bhakti* within a Śākta context. It could be called a kind of "this-worldly" *bhakti* as opposed to an "other-worldly" *bhakti,* one in which the line between the mundane and the spiritual is blurred. That is, love, devotion, and surrender are important themes but are never divorced from the desire for material fulfillment. In the Devī cult, the line between "ulterior devotion" and "disinterested devotion" or between the transcendental and pragmatic[9] aspects of religion is not clearly drawn. The worship of the Goddess has many rewards, ranging from good health and enjoyment of family relationships to peace of mind to ultimate liberation. These goals are all consistent in Śākta theology, as I have discussed in chapter 1.

One way in which *bhakti* to the Goddess differs from, say, *bhakti* to Kṛṣṇa is in the attitude of the worshiper to the deity. In traditional Kṛṣṇa *bhakti,* there are various attitudes or moods (*bhāva*) that the devotee can take vis-à-vis Kṛṣṇa, including *mādhurya* (lover–beloved), *vatsalya* (parent–child), *sakhī* (friend–friend), and *dāsya* (servant–master). Using this typology, the one that applies most to Devī *bhakti* is *dāsya bhāva* and, perhaps secondarily, *vatsalya bhāva,* in the context of worshiping the Goddess in the form of a small girl or *kanyā.* Interestingly enough, in the Kṛṣṇa typology, there is no mood that describes the devotee as child and the deity as parent. Yet this is the mood that most accurately describes the relationship of the devotee to the Goddess. She is the Mother, and all devotees are her children. Perhaps that is why the erotic *mādhurya bhāva* is conspicuously absent from Devī *bhakti;* to see oneself as the lover or consort of the Goddess would violate the incest taboo.

For an example of the overarching ideology of *bhakti,* let us return one more time to the story of Vaiṣṇo Devī that is summarized in chapter 2. The story on one level can be viewed as the tension between two different types of worship of the Goddess, that of the Brahmin Śrīdhar, who engages in vegetarian Vaiṣṇava worship and that of the Nāth Bhairo, who engages in Tantric worship. Śrīdhar is credited with founding and propagating the Vaiṣṇo Devī shrine; the *pujārīs* in service there today trace their descent from him. Bhairo, who was decapitated by the Goddess, is worshiped in a shrine marking the place where his head fell, while his body covers the entrance to the Goddess's cave home.

Bhairo is depicted in the Vaiṣṇo Devī myth and in some popular religious art as a member of the Nāth order of *sādhus*. The Nāths, recognizable by their characteristic bored ears and large earrings, are an unorthodox group of Śaivite mendicants who, as we have seen, have a close connection with the Goddess. As Elizabeth-Chalier Visuvalingam points out, the Nāths long been associated with Bhairava, the fierce form of Śiva, seeing him as the epitome of the ideal of transgressive sacrality.[10] In connection with the Śerāṅvālī cult, at least according to the Vaiṣṇo Devī myth, the Nāths represent a Śaivite or Tantric, as opposed to Vaiṣṇavite, style of religious practice.[11]

It is clear that Vaiṣṇo Devī is identified on several levels with Durgā, the killer of Mahiṣāsura, the buffalo demon. This identification is made explicit in the popular pamphlets that tell the *Devī Māhātmya* myths and then call Vaiṣṇo Devī an *avatār* or incarnation of the same Goddess. Similarly, it is not unreasonable to see Bhairo as a multiform of Mahiṣāsura, particularly when one remembers that Bhairo is a form of Śiva and that Śiva is often identified (particularly, as David Shulman points out,[12] in South Indian sources) with the buffalo demon who is killed by his bride. In some versions of the Mahiṣāsura story, the demon approaches the Goddess sexually, and after being rebuffed and defeated in battle, attains liberation through decapitation at her hands just as Bhairo does at the hands of Vaiṣṇo Devī. The *bhakti* interpretation would be that Bhairo chased her up the mountain out of devotion, however misplaced, and further proved his devotion through decapitation, the ultimate self-sacrifice.

The theme of decapitation, as we have seen, appears again and again in the myths of the Śerāṅvālī cycle. The offering of coconuts at Goddess temples is explained by a charter myth in which the devotee Dhyānū Bhagat cuts off his own head and offers it to the Goddess, who promises that henceforth she will accept coconut offerings instead. In "The Story of Queen Tārā," Queen Tārā, who is accused by her husband of impurity for eating meat at a sweeper's *jagrātā*, forces her husband, King Harīcand, to decapitate and eat his horse and son to satisfy the Goddess. Their heads, like Dhyānū's, are subsequently restored by the Goddess.

The *Rāmāyaṇa* connection adds another rich dimension to the Vaiṣṇo Devī myth, resulting in some rather startling reversals. In the *Rāmāyaṇa* it is Rāma who undergoes tests to win Sītā. In the Vaiṣṇo Devī story it is Vaiṣṇo Devī who performs austerities in order to win Rāma but ultimately loses him for failing to pass a test. In the *Rāmāyaṇa,* it is Sītā's *pativrata* (vow to remain faithful to one husband) that is emphasized. In the Vaiṣṇo Devī story, it is Rāma's *patnīvrata* (vow to remain faithful to one wife) that is emphasized. In the *Rāmāyaṇa,* Rāvana abducts a helpless Sītā. In the Vaiṣṇo Devī story, Bhairo attempts but does not succeed in raping the independent and powerful Vaiṣṇo Devī. In the *Rāmāyaṇa,* Rāma kills Rāvana in order to regain Sītā. In the Vaiṣṇo Devī story, Vaiṣṇo Devī kills Bhairo without any help and makes it clear that she has gone through the whole chase scene as a way of displaying her *līlā* (divine play) as the great Śakti who is the queen of illusion. The scene of Vaiṣṇo Devī "becoming Caṇḍī" and slaying Bhairo is reminiscent not only of Durgā killing the buffalo demon but of Sītā in Tantric versions of the *Rāmāyaṇa* (such as the *Adhyātma Rāmāyaṇa*) taking the form of Kālī and killing Rāvana herself. From this point of view, the events in the Vaiṣo Devī story mirror those in the *Rāmāyaṇa,* and Bhairo can be seen as a multiform of Rāvana, the Vaiṣṇava embodiment of transgressive sacrality par excellence. But Rāvana himself can be seen as a multiform of the buffalo demon, as Alf Hiltebeitel suggests.[13]

At an explicit level, then, in the Vaiṣṇo Devī story, there is an obvious tension between Tantric (or Śaiva–Śākta) values and Vaiṣṇava values. Tantric values are represented by Bhairo, who can be seen as the *vīra* or hero who seeks union with the Goddess through meat, wine, and sex; however, Bhairo ends up worshiping the Goddess not by these methods but by sacrificing his own head. Vaiṣṇava values are represented by Śrīdhar, the Brahmin who performs traditional *pūjās* and makes vegetarian offerings. However, the two are reconciled through the theology of *bhakti.* Bhairo and Śrīdhar can be seen simply as two different types of devotees. Bhairo takes a transgressive approach and attains *mokṣa* at the moment of the most extreme self-sacrifice. But the more moderate Śrīdhar is not neglected either; he receives the full *darśan* of the Goddess and is granted the boon of sons. Bhairo and Śrīdhar are two sides of the same coin. The Goddess graciously accepts both types of devotion.

Conclusion

The cult of the Goddess in northwest India is both ancient and contemporary, reflecting the dynamic quality of the Goddess herself. It is tied in to an all-India conception of the Great Goddess but has unique features of its own. *Śakti* is the concept that ties together all manifestations of the Goddess. The theology, mythology, and cult practice of Goddess worship all contribute to an understanding of the Goddess as the matter–energy that underlies all reality and manifests itself in various forms. Śerāṅvālī and her various aspects in the northwest are identified with the Great Goddess of the *Devī Māhātmya,* who killed the buffalo demon and other demons, and with Satī, who destroyed herself in Dakṣa's sacrifice. Thus, the Goddess is simultaneously the three cosmic forms Mahāsarasvatī, Mahālakṣmī, and Mahākālī—the creator, preserver, and destroyer of the universe—and the innumerable local forms enshrined in the *śakti pīṭhas.* A vivid example of this in the northwest Goddess cult is at Vaiṣṇo Devī, where three *piṇḍīs* are enshrined as Mahāsarasvatī, Mahālakṣmī, and Mahākālī and which is also said to be the spot where Satī's arms fell at the time of her dismemberment. Still further layers are evident in the more local stories of Vaiṣṇo Devī and Bhairo. The scheme of the Seven Sisters, found in many regions of India and probably connected with the Seven Mothers motif of the *Devī Māhātmya* and other texts, serves to highlight popular goddesses within a region and integrate them into a system of pilgrimage.

Through the pilgrimage process, devotees are able to encounter and interact with the Goddess in local, personal, embodied forms. Pilgrims enter the mythic time and space of the pilgrimage place and reexperience the sacred history of the Goddess. Thus, they are able to view the "flame tongue" emerging from the rock at Jvālā Mukhī or crawl through the Ādi Kumārī womb cave at Vaiṣṇo Devī, just as the Goddess herself did while escaping the lusty Bhairo.

The Goddess can be brought into one's home or community in the form of a flame (*jot*), and supplicated and entertained by the Devī *jagrātā* performance. In the *jagrātā,* devotees keep each other and the Goddess awake through the singing of songs and telling of stories that reinforce the mutual interaction of the deity and the devotee so important in *bhakti.*

The most intimate form of contact with the Goddess is divine possession. In the phenomenon of possession, the Goddess enters the body of a human being in her "wind form" (*pavan rūp*). This incursion is considered to be one way in which the Goddess graciously grants *darśan* to her devotees. The people, usually women, so graced become in turn the objects of devotion as manifestations of the Goddess.

Observers have been struck with how quickly and thoroughly Indian religious movements have taken to the use of modern mass media. The Goddess cult of northwest India has become imbued with popular culture, as evidenced by the use of film tunes for devotional songs, calendar art, electronically moving images, and the like. Phenomena such as the spread of the Santoṣī Mā cult almost totally through print and film media have led some scholars to wonder whether Hinduism is undergoing a radical transformation. I have suggested that, on the contrary, such changes do not represent a break with tradition but rather are signs of Hinduism's continued flexibility and adaptability.

Devotees of the Goddess repeatedly told me that it is especially appropriate and auspicious to worship her nowadays, as we are living in the Kali Yuga, the age of confusion, but also the age of redemption in which the Goddess reigns supreme. Perhaps it is equally auspicious to *study* the Goddess, for it is through exploration of her myths, rituals, and symbols that we approach a greater understanding not only of the variety and richness of the Hindu tradition but of human religious expression.

Notes

INTRODUCTION

1. All these areas, including the state of (West) Panjab in present-day Pakistan, were included in the huge administrative area called Panjab before Indian and Pakistani independence in 1947. When the states were reorganized on a quasi-linguistic basis in 1965, the new state of Haryana was formed as a Hindi-speaking area, several hill districts of Panjab were added to Himachal Pradesh, which is also considered Hindi-speaking, and the remainder belonged to Panjab, now a Panjabi-speaking state. Delhi, the national capital, is a union territory, as is Chandigarh, the capital of both Haryana and Panjab. The pilgrimage places that are the focal point of the cult are for the most part located in the hilly areas of the former state of Panjab, now Himachal Pradesh. This area is often referred to as the Panjab Hills. Most of the pilgrims visiting these temples come from the plains.

2. Hindu women are normally expected to keep their hair tied up, that is, "under control." Keeping the hair loose is a sign of impurity, as after the death of a close relative or during menstruation. But it is also a sign of power. This idea is further explored in chapter 5.

3. The concept of Vaiṣṇo as applied to the Goddess has been around for at least a hundred years. Denzil Ibbettson writes, "The other day a Hindu explained that Vaishnavīs do not eat meat: and that Devīs to whom animal sacrifices were not made, were therefore called Vishnu Devīs. This is a probable explanation for the less malignant forms of the goddess being called properly Vaishnavī Devīs" (*Panjab Notes and Queries* 2, no. 24 [September 1885]: 200).

4. Paul Hershman, "Virgin and Mother," in *Symbols and Sentiments: Cross-Cultural Studies in Symbolism,* ed. Ioan Lewis (London: Academic Press, 1977), 269–92.

5. A. K. Ramanujan, "Two Realms of Kannada Folklore," in *Another Harmony: New Essays on the Folklore of India,* ed. Stuart H. Blackburn and A. K. Ramanujan (Delhi: Oxford University Press, 1986), 57.

6. Two recent cross-cultural anthologies on goddesses are Carl Olson, ed., *The Book of the Goddess Past and Present: An Introduction to Her Religion,* (New York: Crossroad, 1983), which takes primarily a history of religions

approach, and James J. Preston, ed., *Mother Worship: Theme and Variations,* (Chapel Hill: University of North Carolina Press, 1982), which takes primarily an anthropological approach.

7. Works in all these areas are being published at a very rapid rate. A few that have become classics are Carol P. Christ and Judith Plaskow, eds., *Womanspirit Rising: A Feminist Reader in Religion* (New York: Harper & Row, 1979); Mary Daly, *Beyond God the Father: Toward a Philosophy of Women's Liberation* (Boston: Beacon Press, 1973); Elizabeth Schüssler Fiorenza, *In Memory of Her: A Feminist Theological Reconstruction of Christian Origins* (New York: Crossroad, 1983); Rosemary Radford Ruether, *Womanguides: Readings toward a Feminist Theology* (Boston: Beacon Press, 1985); and Starhawk, *The Spiral Dance: A Rebirth of the Ancient Religion of the Goddess* (New York: Harper & Row, 1979). An excellent overview of Goddess traditions, ancient and modern, from a feminist perspective is Elinor W. Gadon, *The Once and Future Goddess: A Symbol for Our Time* (San Francisco: Harper & Row, 1989). See also Rita M. Gross, "Hindu Female Deities as a Resource for the Contemporary Rediscovery of the Goddess," *Journal of the American Academy of Religion* 46, no. 3 (September 1978): 269–92.

8. Studies of Hindu goddesses are too numerous to mention. A few of the most notable that have been published in the last ten years are John Stratton Hawley and Donna Marie Wulff, eds., *The Divine Consort: Rādhā and the Goddesses of India* (Berkeley: Religious Studies Series, 1982); Alf Hiltebeitel, *The Cult of Draupadī,* vol. 1, *Mythologies: From Gingee to Kurukṣetra* (Chicago: University of Chicago Press, 1988); David R. Kinsley, *Hindu Goddesses: Visions of the Divine Feminine in the Hindu Religious Tradition* (Berkeley: University of California Press, 1986); Gananath Obeyesekere, *The Cult of the Goddess Pattini* (Chicago: University of Chicago Press, 1984); and James Preston, *Cult of the Goddess: Social and Religious Change in a Hindu Temple,* 2nd ed. (Prospect Heights, Ill.: Waveland Press, 1985).

9. An excellent collection of essays to appear on this theme is Joanne Punzo Waghorne and Norman Cutler, eds., *Gods of Flesh/Gods of Stone: The Embodiment of Divinity in India* (Chambersburg, Penn.: Anima Books, 1985).

10. Ursula M. Sharma, "The Immortal Cowherd and the Saintly Carrier: An Essay in the Study of Cults," *Sociological Bulletin* 23, no. 1 (1974): 137.

11. Prakash Tandon, *Punjabi Century 1857–1947* (London: Chatto and Windus, 1963), 76.

12. Lawrence A. Babb, "Marriage and Malevolence: The Uses of Sexual Opposition in a Hindu Pantheon," *Ethnology* 9, no. 2 (April 1970): 137–48;

Babb, *The Divine Hierarchy: Popular Hinduism in Central India* (New York: Columbia University Press, 1975). See also Ramanujan, "Two Realms of Kannada Folklore," 56–58. I discuss this theory more fully in chapter 7 of this book.

13. Mircea Eliade, "History of Religions and a New Humanism," *History of Religions* 1, no. 1 (1962): 4.

CHAPTER 1

1. *Devī Māhātmya* 11.2, 3, 7, 10, 24, 29, 30. These are selected verses from the "Nārāyaṇī Stuti," which the gods sung to the Goddess after her killing of the demons Śumbha and Niśumbha. The edition I am following in all quotes and references in this chapter is a "vulgate" commonly used for ritual purposes in North India: Śivadatta Miśra, ed., *Śrīdurgā-śaptaśatī* [Sanskrit text and appendices with Hindi translation and ritual instructions] (Vārāṇasī: ṭhākurprasād eṇḍ sans bukselar, 1977).

2. This thesis is accepted by virtually all scholars of Hinduism, both Indian and Western. For a representative discussion of the pre-Vedic elements in Goddess worship, see N. N. Bhattacharyya, *History of the Śākta Religion* (Delhi: Munshiram Manoharlal, 1973), 1–22. While few, if any, deny that Goddess worship is an indigenous religious expression, some are more cautious than others about postulating a continuity between the Indus Valley civilization and later non-Aryan cultures on the subcontinent. For a balanced consideration of the evidence, see Kinsley, *Hindu Goddesses*, 212–20.

3. This hymn has been given particular importance in the later Śākta tradition; it is often chanted as an adjunct to the *Devī Māhātmya*.

4. The *Kena Upaniṣad* (3.12) introduces Umā Haimavatī as the personified knowledge of Brahman, and the *Muṇḍaka Upaniṣad* (1.24) speaks of two of Agni's seven tongues as Kālī and Karālī.

5. This theme is developed in Wendy Doniger O'Flaherty, "The Shifting Balance of Power in the Marriage of Śiva and Pārvatī," in *Divine Consort*, ed. Hawley and Wulff, 129–43.

6. Vasudeva S. Agrawala, *The Glorification of the Great Goddess* (Varanasi: All-India Kashiraj Trust, 1963), xii.

7. David Kinsley, "The Portrait of the Goddess in the *Devī-māhātmya*," *Journal of the American Academy of Religion* 46, no. 4 (December 1978): 498.

8. André Padoux, "Hindu Tantrism," in *The Encyclopedia of Religion*, ed. Mircea Elaide (New York: Macmillan, 1986), 14:274.

9. Sanjukta Gupta, Dirk Jan Hoens, and Teun Goudriaan, *Hindu Tantrism* (Leiden: Brill, 1979), 7–9. Goudriaan may be right that an inactive male partner is an indipensable part of Śākta Tantrism, but as I point out

below, there are also forms of Śāktism in which the male partner plays little or no role.

10. Bhattacharyya, *History of the Śākta Religion,* 73.

11. Pushpendra Kumar, *Śakti Cult in Ancient India* (Varanasi: Bharatiya, 1974), 1.

12. Cf. Thomas B. Coburn, "Consort of None, *Śakti* of All: The Vision of the *Devī–Māhātmya,*" in *Divine Consort,* ed. Hawley and Wulff, 153–65.

13. The most complete study of this text is Thomas B. Coburn, *Devī-Māhātmya: The Crystallization of the Goddess Tradition* (Columbia, Mo.: South Asia Books, 1985), which is particularly valuable for its painstaking tracing of antecedents in the Sanskrit tradition. I am indebted to this work for my interpretation of the *Devī Māhātmya* in this section.

14. Thus, the rationale for including the story of the Goddess in a Purāṇa is that it can be subsumed under *manvantara,* the reigns of the Manus, one of the traditional five characteristics of a Purāṇa.

15. The myth is told in *Mahābhārata* 3.194.8–30.

16. *Mānava Dharma Śāstra* 7.1–11, cited in Coburn, *Devī-Māhātmya,* 229–30.

17. Durgā is called the killer of Mahiṣāsura in the Durgā Stava of the *Mahābhārata,* which is, however, not included in the critical edition. It was interpolated later and is probably post–*Devī Māhātmya.*

18. The earliest representation of the goddess Mahiṣamardinī is in terracotta plaques discovered at Nagar near Uniyara in Tonk District, Rajasthan. One of these has been dated from the first century B.C.E. or first century C.E. These and other iconographic representations are discussed in D. C. Sircar, "Śakti Cult in Western India," in *The Śakti Cult and Tārā,* ed. D. C. Sircar (Calcutta: University of Calcutta, 1967), 87–91.

19. Strictly speaking, this is an etymological impossibility, as I am sure the author of the text was aware. As Kinsley rightly points out, Kālī and Cāmuṇḍā were originally two different goddesses who have been identified ("Portrait of the Goddess," 504, n. 10).

20. *Harivaṃśa* 47.23–37. This episode is translated in Wendy Doniger O'Flaherty, *Hindu Myths* (Baltimore: Penguin, 1975), 206–13.

21. P. V. Kane, *History of Dharmaśāstra,* vol. 5, pt. 1 (Poona: Bhandarkar Oriental Research Institute, 1958), 155n.

22. A full description of such a recitation is found in Babb, *Divine Hierarchy,* 39–47, and Thomas B. Coburn, *Encountering the Goddess: A Translation of the Devī-Māhātmya and a Study of Its Interpretation* (Albany: State University of New York Press, 1991), 159–65. See also Cynthia A. Humes, "The Text and Temple of the Great Goddess" (Ph.D. diss., University of Iowa, 1990), a study that focuses on recitation of the *Devī Māhātmya* at the Vindhyachal temple in Mirzapur District, Uttar Pradesh.

23. Wendell Charles Beane, *Myth, Cult and Symbol in Śākta Hinduism: A Study of the Indian Mother Goddess* (Leiden: Brill, 1977), 41.

24. Some scholars have argued for the pre-Vedic and non-Aryan origins of the Sāṃkhya system, saying that the concept of Prakṛti evolved out of an ancient Mother Earth. For this view, see Bhattacharyya, *History of the Śakta Religion,* 16–17, 87–90. Bhattacharyya further argues that the original Sāṃkhya (as opposed to its systematic formulation by Īśvarakṛṣṇa) stemmed from a matriarchal society.

25. For the ideas in this paragraph, I am indebted to Kinsley, *Hindu Goddesses,* 136–37.

26. This idea is especially prevalent in the *Devī Bhāgavata Purāṇa.* See also Douglas Renfrow Brooks, *The Secret of the Three Cities: An Introduction to Hindu Śākta Tantrism through Bhāskarāya's Commentary on the Tripurā Upaniṣad* (Chicago: University of Chicago Press, 1991).

27. There is also a Tantric Buddhist tradition that the Indian subcontinent is the *vajra* body of the Buddha, divided into twenty-four limbs, or *pīṭhas.* This is discussed in Marilyn Stablein, "Textual and Contextual Patterns of Tibetan Buddhist Pilgrimage in India," *Tibet Society Bulletin* 12 (1978): 7–38.

28. D. C. Sircar, *The Śākta Pīṭhas,* 2d rev. ed. (Delhi: Motilal Banarsidass, 1973), 5–7.

29. This idea was expressed by Diana L. Eck, "Dakṣa's Sacrifice and the Sākta Pīṭhas" (Paper presented at the Meeting of the American Academy of Religion, Atlanta, November 1986).

30. Mircea Eliade, *Yoga: Immortality and Freedom,* trans. Willard R. Trask (Princeton: Princeton University Press, 1969), 347–48.

31. Sircar, *Śākta Pīṭhas,* 7–8.

32. A study devoted to this shrine is Bani Kanta Kakati, *The Mother Goddess Kāmākhyā: Or Studies in the Fusion of Aryan and Primitive Beliefs in Assam* (Gauhati: Lawyer's Book Stall, 1948).

33. India (Republic), Office of the Registrar General, Census of India, 1961, vol. 13, *Punjab,* Pt. 7–B, *Fairs and Festivals,* p. 4.

34. Niharranjan Ray, *The Sikh Gurus and Sikh Society* (Patiala, 1970), 27, quoted in Bhattacharyya, *History of the Śākta Religion,* 139–40.

35. There are other stories explaining the sanctity of Jālandhara Pīṭha. The most well known of these is the *Jālandhara Māhātmya* of the *Padma Purāṇa,* which says that the demon Jalandhara had become very powerful due to the chastity of his wife Vrindā. Śiva cut off the demon's head and buried his body underground to prevent him from being resuscitated. His body is said to have covered a circuit of forty-eight *kos,* or sixty-four miles. According to a local version of the story, Jalandhara's head lay to the north of the Beas River, his mouth at Jvālā Mukhī, his body covering the area between the Beas and Satluj rivers, with his back lying below District

Jalandhar (Panjab) and his feet at Multan. According to some accounts, the Jālandhara Pīṭha is restricted to the area covered by the demon's chest. Cf. Alexander Cunningham, *Archeological Survey of India,* vol. 5, report for the year 1872–73, 145–52.

36. Sircar, *Śātka Pīṭhas,* 24.

CHAPTER 2

1. Often appearing in the list of seven are other local goddess temples such as Bālā Sundarī in District Nahan, Himachal Pradesh, as well as geographically nonspecific goddesses such as Kālī and, more recently, Santoṣī Mā.

2. J. N. Ganhar, *Jammu Shrines and Pilgrimages* (New Delhi: Ganhar, 1973), 9.

3. Frederic Drew, *The Jammoo and Kashmir Territories* (Delhi: Oriental 1971).

4. "Takeover of Vaishno Devi Shrine Hailed," *Times of India,* 5 September 1986, 7. The movement for public accountability of temples is spreading all over India, with the most extensive temple-management laws being found in Tamil Nadu and Andhra Pradesh. In 1984, in the wake of a tragic accident at Nainā Devī, the Himachal Pradesh legislature passed a bill making eleven major temples in the state, including Nainā Devī, Jvālā Mukhī, Kāṅgṛevālī, and Cintpūrṇī accountable to a commissioner. Cf. "Himachal Pradesh: The Temple Take-over," *India Today,* 15 May 1984, 86–87. For a general discussion of the issue, see J. Duncan M. Derrett, "The Reform of Hindu Religious Endowments," in *South Asian Politics and Religion,* ed. Donald Eugene Smith (Princeton: Princeton University Press, 1966), 311–36.

5. "More pilgrims Visit Vaishno Devi." *Times of India,* 6 July 1978.

6. Ibid.

7. The late Prime Minister Indira Gandhi visited Vaiṣṇo Devī several times.

8. *Śrī vaiṣṇo devī darśan aur nau deviyoṅ kī kathā* (Hardvār: harhbajan singh eṇḍ sans, n.d.) is the primary source I am using, mentioning other versions when relevant. The text given here is my own abridged translation, which sticks closely to the colloquial and interpretive tone of the original.

9. These are the Hindi equivalents of the three Sanskrit *guṇas* (qualities), *rajas, tamas,* and *sattva,* which are active, inert, and pure, respectively. Here the three major aspects of the Goddess Mahāśakti (the "Great Energy") are being identified with the three *guṇas* in the same way that the male deities Brahmā, Śiva, and Viṣṇu are. For a discussion of Mahākālī, Mahālakṣmī, and Mahāsarasvatī as Śākta theological concepts, see chapter 1.

10. This last sentence appears to be a non sequitur, as we have just been told that she was produced through the combined powers of the three great Śaktis. The composite nature of the myth is evident here.

11. This is a vernacular allusion to the famous verse in the *Saundāryalaharī,* traditionally attributed to Śaṅkara, which says, "A son may be a bad son, but a mother can never be a bad mother."

12. Recounted in Bālkṛṣṇa Śarmā, *Mātā vaiṣṇo devī kī janm kathā* (Kaṭrā, Vaiṣṇo Devī: bhavānī pustak mahal, n.d.). A similar portrayal of Bhairo is found in a low-budget feature-length film on Vaiṣṇo Devī. The use of the name Bali is suggestive of the antagonist in the story of the Dwarf incarnation of Viṣṇu and may be used in some versions of the Vaiṣṇo Devī story to strengthen Vaiṣṇava associations.

13. Karuna Goswamy, "Vaishnavism in the Punjab Hills and Pahari Painting" (Ph.D. thesis, Punjab University [Chandigarh], 1968), 109.

14. Ibid., 42, 135.

15. Madhu Wangu, "The Sacred Name Rama and the Goddess Khir Bhavani" (Paper presented to the American Academy of Religion, Chicago, 1988).

16. This argument is more fully elaborated in Kathleen Erndl, "Rapist or Bodyguard, Demon or Devotee? Images of Bhairo in the Mythology and Cult of Vaiṣṇo Devī," in *Criminal Gods and Demon Devotees: Essays on the Gods of Popular Hinduism,* ed. Alf Hiltebeitel (Albany: State University of New York Press, 1989).

17. The priests of the temple take pride in the fact that no scientific explanation has been found for the flames. On one trip to Jvālā Mukhī I met some employees of the Indian Geological Survey who were looking for natural gas in the area. They said that they had so far not found any.

18. According to three popular pamphlet sources, the names of the nine flames are (1) Mahākālī (the main flame, encased in a silver frame; it gives both enjoyment and liberation), (2) Annapūrṇā (to the left; it keeps one's pantry full), (3) Caṇḍī or Cāmuṇḍā (next to the previous one; it destroys one's enemies), (4) Hiṅglāj (near the previous two; it destroys suffering), (5) Mahālakṣmī (in the pit; it gives virtue and wealth), (6) Mahāsarasvatī (in the pit; it gives knowledge), (7) Ambikā (in the pit; it gives offspring), (8) Aṅjanā Devī (in the pit; it gives health and happiness), and (9) Vindhyavāsinī (listed in only one source: Darbārā Siṅh, *Pūrā mahātm: nau deviyon kī amar kathā* [Dillī: satkartār pustak bhaṇḍār, n.d.], 10; the other two sources list only eight by name: Cakradhārī "Bezar" Jyotiṣācarya, *Śrī jvālā jī mahātmay* [Jvālā Mukhī: rām svarūp pustakāṅ vālā, 1979], 7–9; Omnāth Śarmā, *Śrī jvālā jī kā mahāttam* [Dillī: sangam ṭreḍing kampanī, 1982], 29–30). According to one of the priests in the temple, the names of the seven flames are Annapūrṇā, Jvālā, Mahākālī, Mahālakṣmī, Mahāsarasvatī, Hiṅglāj, and Vindhyavāsinī.

19. The homologization of flames and tongues is ancient, going back at least as far as the *Muṇḍaka Upaniṣad* I.24, which speaks of the "seven tongues of Agni." For a discussion of the tongues and their relation to the Goddess, see also Beane, *Myth, Cult and Symbol,* 113–14.

20. P. C. Roy, trans., *Mahābhārata* (Calcutta: Datta Bose, n.d.), 2:179, cited in Surinder Mohan Bhardwaj, *Hindu Places of Pilgrimage in India* (Berkeley: University of California Press, 1973), 48.

21. Agehananda Bharati, *The Tantric Tradition* (London: Hillary House, 1965), 353, n. 44.

22. Abul-Fazl-i-'Allami, *'Ain-i-Akbari of Abul-Fazl-i-'Allami,* trans. H. S. Jarrett, revised and further annotated by Sir Jadunath Sarkar (Calcutta: Royal Asiatic Society of Bengal, 1971), 2:314.

23. My telling here is based on Śarmā, *Śrī jvālā jī kā mahāttam,* 19–20. I heard a similar version from a priest at Jvālā Mukhī on March 16, 1983.

24. In reference to animal sacrifice, one pamphleteer writes that many people offer buffaloes and goats but that intelligent devotees have realized that Mātājī cut off the buffalo's head in order to fulfill a promise, so what is the need for slaughtering animals now? He writes that Mātājī wants only love from her devotees and that she will fulfill the wishes of the faithful (Arjun "Amar" Dev, *Jot jvālā kī* [Jālandhar: bhārat pustak bhaṇḍār, n.d.], 8).

25. This story is found in several sources. My summary follows that given in Arjun Dev Amar, *Pūrṇ mahatm: nau deviyoṅ kā itihās* (Jvālā Mukhī: mankoṭiyā pabliśarz, n.d.), 5–6.

26. This story is found in oral tradition and numerous popular pamphlets such as *Śrī vaiṣṇo devī kī kathā* (Hardvār: harhbajan singh eṇḍ sans, n.d.)

27. Śarmā, *Śrī jvālā jī kā mahāttam,* 24. Priests at both the Kāṅgṛevālī Devī temple and the Jvālā Mukhī temple also told me this; however, the head cutting is more popularly believed to have been at Jvālā Mukhī.

28. Quoted in H. A. Elliot and J. Dowson, *History of India as Told by Its Own Historians* (London, 1867–77), 3:318.

29. Cunningham, *Archeological Survey of India* 5:155–168.

30. Sukhdev Singh Charak, *History and Culture of the Himalayan States* (New Delhi: Light and Life, 1978), 1:131.

31. Abul-Fazl-i-'Allami, *'Ain-i-Akbari,* 2:312–13.

32. Personal communication, October 1982.

33. It is quite possible that the *piṇḍī* is not Śiva at all, but that the two *piṇḍīs* are the two breasts of the Goddess, since in all other respects she is worshiped as an independent goddess here, not as the consort of Śiva.

34. According to S. M. Bhardwaj, in 1968 during the Navarātras of Cait, 38 percent of the pilgrims interviewed there were from Uttar Pradesh, as opposed to 12.6 percent at Cintpūrṇī, 13.6 percent at Jvālā Mukhī,

0.4 percent at Nainā Devī, and 0 percent at Mansā Devī ("Some Spatial and Social Aspects of the Mother Goddess Cult in Northwest India" [Paper prepared for discussion at the Third Punjab Studies Conference, Philadelphia, 1971], 21). I would guess that most of those who visited Cintpūrṇī and Jvālā Mukhī did so because they were nearby, but that their main purpose was to visit Kāṅgṛevālī Devī. McKim Marriott writes that the local deity Pattvārī (the Stony One) in his village near Mathura, Uttar Pradesh, "has for at least a generation and probably much longer been identified with a famous manifestation of the great goddess Pārvatī or Satī Devī at Nagarkot in Kangra district" ("Little Communities in an Indigenous Civilization," in *Village India,* ed. McKim Marriott [Chicago: University of Chicago Press, 1955], 216).

35. Hershman states it the other way around, that Cintpūrṇī as the younger sister is bitterly jealous of her elder sister Jvālā Mukhī, "and she allows nothing brought from the temple of the elder to enter into her own domain. There are many stories of the destruction wrought on whole families who were either forgetful enough or presumptious [*sic*] enough, to disregard Cintpūrṇī's injunction. For this reason most Punjabis visit the temple of the younger sister before going on to visit that of the elder" ("Virgin and Mother," 278). I cannot explain this discrepancy, as I met many pilgrims who visited Jvālā Mukhī first for the reason I have stated. As one of the priests of Cintpūrṇī (in an interview on March 3, 1983) told me, "The things which have been offered here cannot go to any other place. For example, the *prasād* from here will not go to Jvālā Mukhī. The things offered there can come here, but the things offered here cannot go there, because she is the youngest sister."

36. Kinsley, *Hindu Goddesses,* 177. My description of Chinnamastā's iconography is paraphrased from the same work, 173.

37. Lack of water is still a problem at Cintpūrṇī today.

38. India (Republic), Office of the Registrar General, Census of India, 1961, vol. 13, *Punjab,* Pt. 7–B, *Fairs and Festivals,* 28. In 1961 Cintpūrṇī was in Tahsil Una, District Hoshiarpur, Panjab.

39. Summarized here from oral accounts at the shrine and a report in India (Republic), Office of the Registrar General, Census of India, 1961, vol. 20, *Himachal Pradesh,* Pt. 7–B, *Fairs and Festivals,* 16–17. The story is similar to that found in the second episode of the *Devī Māhātmya.*

40. This story is found in Omnāth Śarmā, *Nainā devī mahāttm* (Dillī: saṅgam ṭreḍing kampanī, 1981), 15–16, and in India (Republic), Office of the Registrar General, Census of India, 1961, vol. 20, *Himachal Pradesh,* Part 7–B, *Fairs and Festivals,* 15.

41. Śarmā, *Nainā devī mahāttm,* 15–16.

42. Ibid., 16. To what extent Guru Gobind Singh really was a devotee of the Goddess is open to debate. However, that he was intrigued by her

myths and symbolism is undeniable, as evidenced by the fact that he authored several literary translations of the *Devī Māhātmya,* including "*Caṇḍīcarita,*" in *Guru gobind siṁh kā vīr kāvya,* ed. Jaybhagvān Goyal (Patiyālā: Guru gobind siṁh sanstān, 1966).

43. It was during this festival that on August 13, 1983, fifty-seven pilgrims died in a stampede resulting from the collapse of a temporary bamboo shop into the narrow lane leading to the temple. This tragedy was the catalyst for a government investigation into the temple's administration, which resulted in the passage of the Hindu Religious Institutions and Charitable Endowments Bill in April 1984. The bill effectively turned over the administration of the major Goddess temples in Himachal Pradesh to state government control. I was not present at Naiṇā Devī on the day of the tragedy but happened instead to be at Cintpūrṇī, which holds a festival simultaneously. The winding path leading up the mountain to the temple was jammed to capacity with pilgrims in the August heat for over a mile. While no one was seriously injured, many people were trapped in the crowd for hours waiting to get into the temple. Some fainted or became extremely nervous. I was lucky enough to be at the edge of the crowd and was able to climb up into one of the shops that lines the path, where I remained for some time helping the shopkeepers pass cups of water to pilgrims in the crowd and occasionally pulling up a child who was in danger of being crushed.

44. Summarized from Amar, *Pūrṇ mahatm,* 57, and *Śrī vaiṣṇo devī darśan aur nau deviyoṅ kī kathā,* 133.

45. This description, based on my observations and conversations with the *pujārī,* is consistent with the information collected by Bhardwaj on his visits to Mansā Devī in 1967–68 except for Bhardwaj's statement that the *pujārī* is outwardly a Sikh, but wears the sacred thread. He did not appear to me to be a Sikh and identified himself as a Sarasvat Brahmin of the Atri *gotra* (*Hindu Places of Pilgrimage,* 205–6).

46. The story of Manasā Devī, as she is called in Sanskrit, is found in the *Devī Bhāgavata Purāṇa,* 9.47–48.

47. She is probably referring to the snake sacrifice of Parīkṣit (ibid., 9.47) or of Janamejaya (ibid., 9.48).

48. *Devī Māhātmya* 7.27 (third episode). The story is told in more detail in chapter 1 of this study.

49. *Devī ke chah dhāmon kī yātrā* [Hindi text with photos and English captions] (Jammu: Pustak Sansaar, n.d.).

50. E. Alan Morinis, *Pilgrimage in the Hindu Tradition: A Case Study of West Bengal* (Delhi: Oxford University Press, 1984), 26.

51. David Shulman, *Tamil Temple Myths: Sacrifice and Divine Marriage in the South Indian Śaiva Tradition* (Princeton: Princeton University Press, 1980), 40–89.

52. Kees W. Bolle, "Speaking of a Place," in *Myths and Symbols: Studies in Honor of Mircea Eliade*, ed. J. M. Kitagawa and Charles H. Long (Chicago: University of Chicago Press, 1969), 127–39.

CHAPTER 3

1. This is a popular *bheṇṭ* sung by Narendra Chanchal in the Hindi film *Āśā*, also available on recording and in numerous popular pamphlets, including *Cancal bheṇṭān*, [comp.] Bālkṛṣṇ Śarmā (Kaṭrā, Vaiṣṇo Devī: bhavānī pustak mahal, n.d.), 1. It is sung by pilgrims at Vaiṣṇo Devī and other Goddess temples.

2. This song, sung at pilgramage places to the Goddess, is translated here from Panjabi from the pamphlet *Maśhūr bheṇṭān* (Kaṭrā, Vaiṣṇo Devī: bhavānī pustak mahal, n.d.) 33.

3. Georgana Foster suggests that the Dharmarth trust built the road this way in order to downplay the Tantric elements in the cult that Bhairo represents ("A Popular North Indian Pilgrimage Site: The Shrine of Vaishno Devi in Jammu" [Paper prepared for discussion at the Conference on Pilgrimage, Pittsburgh, May 14–17, 1981].

4. Diana L. Eck, *Darśan: Seeing the Divine Image in India* (Chambersburg, Penn.: Anima Books, 1981).

5. Cf. James J. Preston, "Creation of the Sacred Image: Apotheosis and Destruction in Hinduism," in *Gods of Flesh/Gods of Stone*, ed. Waghorne and Cutler, 9–31.

6. Bhardwaj makes this argument in "Spatial and Social Aspects."

7. Bhardwaj, *Hindu Places of Pilgrimage in India*, 160.

8. Bhardwaj suggests this in "Spatial and Social Aspects," 9.

9. Ibid.

10. The *Kālikā Purāṇa* gives the ritual instructions not only for animal sacrifice but also for human sacrifice.

11. I am aware that pilgrimage can also be conducted without actually going anywhere, as in symbolically visiting the *tīrthas* (sacred places, fords) in one's body; still the imagery is spatial.

12. Cf. Victor Turner, *Dramas, Fields, and Metaphors: Symbolic Interaction in Human Society* (Ithaca: Cornell University Press, 1974), 166–230, and Turner, *Process, Performance and Pilgrimage: A Study in Comparative Symbology* (New Delhi: Concept, 1979). Morinis has a point when he says that the goals of the individual Hindu pilgrim are more often individual than communal, and that pilgrimage must be seen within the cultural and religious context of a particular tradition rather than as an expression of a universal human need for "anti-structure" (*Pilgrimage in the Hindu Tradition*, 273–75). However, I believe that Turner's model, while not exhausting the meaning of pilgrimage, is useful as a starting point.

13. Cf. Barbara Nimri Aziz, "Personal Dimensions of the Sacred Journey: What Pilgrims Say," *Religious Studies* 23 (June 1987): 247–61.

CHAPTER 4

1. Part of a *pakkī bheṇṭ* sung by Durgā Bhajan Maṇḍal at a *jagrātā* in Chandigarh on October 27, 1982.

2. A *filmī bheṇṭ* sung by Durgā Bhajan Maṇḍal before the offering of *bhog* during the telling of *Tārārānī kī kathā* at a *jagrātā* in Chandigarh on October 27, 1982.

3. In common usage, unless otherwise specified, *jagrātā* refers to a Devī *jagrātā,* though it is sometimes performed for other deities such as the hermit–saint Bābā Bālak Nāth. This type is patterned after the Devī *jagrātā* and is very recent. The most popular performance for Rām is the *akhaṇḍ Rāmāyaṇ pāṭh,* an uninterrupted recitation of Tulsī Dās's *Rāmcaritmānas.* Among Sikhs the uninterrupted recitation of the *Guru Granth Sāhib* is popular.

4. According to Mahant Omnāth Śarmā of Delhi (personal communication, May 27, 1983), there are two styles of *jagrātā.* One is the *desī* style as it is done in Uttar Pradesh, Rajasthan, and Madhya Pradesh; people who perform this are called Savāyyā. The other is the Panjabi style in which a red turban is given to the *mahant.* In this style there are two *gharānās,* the Kāśī Mātā Gharānā and the smaller Maṇḍī Gharānā. Both of these originated in Lahore, and there are no major differences in style between them. Śarmā was the only informant who told me of this classification, so I have no idea how widely known it is.

5. The most unusual case I came across was a husband and wife who were Christians of the Lohār caste (traditionally blacksmith, a low caste). They have their own *maṇḍali* and have recorded cassettes and printed pamphlets with their own *bheṇṭān.* The wife told me that even though she is a Christian and was married in a church, she worships Devī and plans to go to Jvālā Mukhī, her *iṣṭ-devī,* to offer the first hair of her child.

6. This one, I suspect, was a somewhat unusual case. He was born a Sikh, styled himself "Swami," and said he was of the Gorakhnāth sect but did not have bored ears. He (at the time of our meeting in May 1983) was thirty-one years old. He had received two master's degrees, one in classical music and one in engineering, and had had a career in the Bombay film industry as assistant music director under Soni Komi. He showed me photographs of himself—before and after he became a renunciant—with various film actors, politicians, and celebrities.

7. Despite the prohibition against idol worship in Sikhism and the current trend toward a separate Sikh identity, Sikhs can be observed participat-

ing in all aspects of Goddess worship and other forms of Hindu popular religion.

8. One of the most amusing examples I have come across is the film song "Māmlā gaṛbaṛ hai" ("It's All Messed Up"), which has been turned into a *bheṇṭ* with the words "Jvālā dā parvat hai" ("It's the Mountain of Flame").

9. An Indian-born engineer of Panjabi background has begun leading *jagrātās* once a month at the Hindu Temple of Greater Chicago. He is attempting to revive what he considers to be the more traditional form, eschewing film tunes altogether, as well as incorporating Sanskrit hymns to the Goddess. I was able to attend one of his *jagrātās* in November 1988.

10. This word may be related to the Hindi–Panjabi words *ḍalā* and *ḍāl* (Sanskrit: *ḍalaka;* Prakrit: *ḍallaka*), meaning a wicker basket or a present of fruit or sweets sent by the bridegroom to the bride before the wedding. The word is used here as a technical term; I have not heard it outside of the *jagrātā* context.

11. *Ardās* is also said at Devī temples by the priests on behalf of pilgrims. The word, which probably comes from the Persian *arz-dāśt* (a written supplication), is commonly used in the Sikh religion, from which it has passed into general Panjabi usage.

12. These are for the most part conventional and stress the unity of all castes and religions. At one large Viśāl Bhagavatī Jāgraṇ I attended, a singer took the opportunity to condemn dowry murder, one of the most serious social problems in North India today.

13. According to this scheme, the sixteen *kalās* of Mātā arose in the following order: (1) Nārāyaṇ himself, (2) Sāval Māī (Dark Mother), (3) the three *devatās* (gods), (4) the whole world, (5) the five *prāṇ* (breaths, or, alternatively, the five *tattvas* or elements or the five Pāṇḍavas), (6) the six Nārāyaṇs, (7) the seven *dīp* (lights, probably the seven Ṛṣis or seers, possibly also the seven *dvīp* or continents), (8) Aṣṭabhūjī Mā (eight-armed Mother, i.e., Durgā), (9) the nine Nāths, (10) the ten *avatārs,* (11) the eleven Rudras, (12) the twelve months, (13) the thirteen jewels, (14) the fourteen *bhavans* (mansions), (15) the fifteen *tithis* (lunar dates of each fortnight) and (16) the entire sixteen *kalās*. The four watches (*pahars*) and sixteen *kalās* are often sung as a *bheṇṭ,* the refrain of which is "Mahārānī, we will stay awake your whole night; Śerāṅvālī, we will stay awake your whole night," repeated many times with different epithets of the Goddess.

14. Śambhu is an epithet of Śiva, but I believe the storyteller is alluding to another devotee of the Goddess who figures in the oral tradition.

15. Told by Swami Oṃkarnāth at a *jagrātā* in Panchkula (a Haryana suburb of Chandigarh) on May 7, 1983. I have heard two other versions of this story. A wandering *sādhu* who was camping out at the Bhairo shrine at

Mansā Devī in October 1982 told me that Kālī once took the form of a fly and Guru Gorakhnāth swallowed her; when she came out in the latrine, she was Vaiṣṇo (i.e., vegetarian). When I first heard this story, I wondered if perhaps the *sādhu* was pulling my leg. Later, however, I heard a similar story from the head of the Sādhu Āśram Jagrātā Maṇḍal, who told me that Guru Gorakhnāth had once swallowed Kālī in the form of a fly, which then came out his nose. After this, there was no more *bali* (blood sacrifice), only coconuts, betel nut, betel leaf, and clove offerings. The connection between Gorakhnāth and the Goddess is a fascinating one that deserves further study.

16. Written versions can be found in popular bazaar pamphlets such as *Tārārānī kī kathā* (Hardvār: Randhīr buk sels, n.d.). I have also taped several oral versions in Panjabi at *jagrātās* in Chandigarh. Oral versions tend to be much lengthier, have more episodes, and are interspersed with *bheṇṭāṅ*. Many *maṇḍalis* use a printed text on which they elaborate and improvise. I am particularly indebted to Gopāl Singh Pāl, *pradhān* of the Durgā Bhajan Maṇḍal, Chandigarh, for going over a transcription of his performance with me and elucidating some points of the story.

17. According to some versions, they were daughters of Dakṣa.

18. This is the popular *ekādaśī vrat,* a fast done by women on the eleventh day of the bright half of each lunar month.

19. There is some disagreement in different versions as to whether she actually broke the fast or simply *thought* about it after being tempted by the smell of food on the bazaar. Also, some versions state that she broke the fast by eating rice or some other vegetarian food.

20. This birth plays no further part in the plot of the story and is absent from some versions.

21. Some versions go into great detail about a Goddess temple built by the Pāṇḍavas.

22. In some versions, especially in the printed Hindi texts, he is identified with King Hariścandra of Ayodhyā, the ancestor of Rāma who lived in the Satya Yuga. Other versions clearly identify him as a local king of Kangra whose capital was Harīpur. One informant pointed out that Tārā could not have married Hariścandra of Ayodhyā, because "The Story of Queen Tārā" takes place in the Kali Yuga, after the Pāṇḍavas' sacrifice, which took place in the Dvāpara Yuga. The issue is complicated by the fact that both Harīcand and Hariścandra are forced to sacrifice their sons (though for different reasons) and that in the Panjabi version of the story of King Hariścandra of Ayodhyā, the king's wife's name is Tārā, while in the Sanskrit versions, the wife's name is Śaibyā. Cf. R. C. Temple, *The Legends of the Panjab* (1885; Patiala: Department of Languages, Panjab, 1963), 3:54.

23. Or, according to some versions, Rukko.

24. At this point in the narration of the story, which is called "Rukman's

ardās," the sponsors of the *jagrātā* being performed also come forward and make their own *ardās.*

25. According to some versions, she accepted *ḍal* from Rukman, which is why she was obligated to attend the *jagrātā* in spite of all the obstacles that fell her way. According to other versions, the *maṇḍalī* unwittingly accepted the *ḍal* that Tārā had Rukman send through her messenger, Sain the barber. When they discovered whose *jagrātā* they had agreed to perform, they decided to do only the formalities and not eat or drink anything in Rukman's home unless Tārā would also eat and drink there.

26. It is noteworthy that the king had already unwittingly entered the path of devotion to Devī by staying awake.

27. According to one version, Tārā saw hanging from a window what appeared to be rope but instead turned out to be a snake. This is a clever inversion of the simile used in Vedānta philosophy of the snake that turns out to be a rope, which illustrates the illusory nature of the phenomenal world.

28. At this point in the narration of the story, *bhog* is offered at the *jagrātā* being performed.

29. The implication, since this is a low-caste house, is that the food is meat. Even if it was not meat, cooked food coming from a low-caste person would still be polluting for a high-caste person such as Tārā or Harīcand.

30. According to one version, the king could hardly continue when he bit into the gold ring that his son had worn on one finger.

31. In the printed Hindi version of this story, the king at this point switches to the more respectful *tum* form in addressing Tārā rather than the less respectful *tū.*

32. Bhāī Gurdās, *Vārāṅ bhāī gurdās saṭīk,* [ed.] bhāī sāhib bhāī vīr siṅgh jī (Amritsar: Khālsā samācār, 1977), 168. This is a book written in Panjabi verse about famous devotees. Bhāī Gurdās mentions Tārā and Harīcand in connection with the episode of the slippers, an episode that is not found in all versions of the story. Many informants mistakenly attributed these verses to the *Guru Granth Sāhib,* the sacred book of the Sikhs. This is understandable, since Bhāī Gurdās was the amanuensis of Guru Arjan, the compiler of the *Granth.*

33. Within the story an equation between Vedic sacrifice (*yajña*) and blood sacrifice (*balidān*) is explicitly made when Tārā tells Harīcand, "Make a *yajña* of your son."

34. Simon Digby, "Encounters with Jogis in Indian Sufi Hagiography" (School of Oriental and African Studies, University of London 1970, mimeographed), quoted in Annemarie Schimmel, *Mystical Dimensions of Islam* (Chapel Hill: University of North Carolina Press, 1975), 210–11. I am indebted to James Nye for bringing this story to my attention.

35. From the *Rsi Pancami Vrat Katha,* summarized in Lynn Bennett, *Dangerous Wives and Sacred Sisters: Social and Symbolic Roles of High-Caste Women in Nepal* (New York: Columbia University Press, 1983), 231–32.

36. George L. Hart III, "The Little Devotee: Cēkkilār's Story of Ciruttoṇṭar," in *Sanskrit and Indian Studies,* ed. M. Nagatomi et al. (Dordrecht: Reidel, 1980), 217–36.

37. "Inhuman Ritual Murder of Babe," *Northern Indian Patrika,* 4 April 1972, 1, cited in David M. Wulff, "Prolegomenon to a Psychology of the Goddess," in *Divine Consort,* ed. Hawley and Wulff, 290.

38. A. K. Ramanujan, "On Women Saints," in *Divine Consort,* ed. Stratton and Wulff, 316–24.

39. Ákos Östör, *The Play of the Gods: Locality, Ideology, Structure and Time in the Festivals of a Bengali Town* (Chicago: University of Chicago Press, 1980), 23.

40. Frédérique Apffel Marglin, "Female Sexuality in the Hindu World," in *Immaculate and Powerful: The Female in Sacred Image and Social Reality,* ed. Clarissa W. Atkinson, Constance H. Buchanan, and Margaret R. Miles (Boston: Beacon Press, 1985), 45.

41. In fact, one group of devotees surrounding a charismatic female religious leader make a practice of carrying a flame from Jvālā Mukhī from place to place where they conduct *jagrātās,* only to extinguish it after the end of the Navarātra festival season.

42. Ann Grodzins Gold, *Fruitful Journeys: The Ways of Rajasthani Pilgrims* (Berkeley: University of California Press, 1988), 102.

CHAPTER 5

1. Psychological studies of possession include Sudhir Kakar, *Shamans, Mystics and Doctors: A Psychological Inquiry into India and Its Healing Traditions* (New York: Knopf, 1982); Gananath Obeyesekere, *Medusa's Hair: An Essay on Personal Symbols and Religious Experience* (Chicago: University of Chicago Press, 1981); Vincent Crapanzano and Vivian Garrison, eds., *Case Studies in Spirit Possession* (New York: Wiley, 1977); Stanley A. Freed and Ruth S. Freed, "Spirit Possession as Illness in a North Indian Village," *Ethnology* 3, no. 2 (1964): 152–71. Sociological studies include I. M. Lewis, *Ecstatic Religion: An Anthropological Study of Spirit Possession and Shamanism* (Baltimore: Penguin, 1971); D. F. Pocock, *Mind, Body and Wealth: A Study of Belief and Practice in an Indian Village* (Oxford: Basil Blackwell, 1973), especially chap. 3; and Gerald D. Berreman, "Brahmins and Shamans in Pahari Religion," in *Religion in South Asia,* ed. Edward B. Harper (Seattle: University of Washington Press, 1964), 53–69.

2. Peter J. Claus, "Spirit Possession and Spirit Mediumship from the

Perspective of Tulu Oral Traditions," *Culture, Medicine and Psychiatry* 3 (1979): 49.

3. Recent attempts to view possession within a larger cultural perspective using oral narratives such as myth and legend include Peter Claus, "Mayndala: A Legend and Possession Cult of Tulunad," *Asian Folklore Studies* 38, no. 2 (1979): 94–129; Brenda Beck, *The Three Twins: The Telling of a South Indian Folk Epic* (Bloomington: Indiana University Press, 1982); Stuart Blackburn, "Oral Performance: Narrative and Ritual in a Tamil Tradition," *Journal of American Folklore* 94 (1981): 207–17; and Ann Grodzins Gold, "Spirit Possession Perceived and Performed in Rural Rajasthan," *Contributions to Indian Sociology*, n.s., 22, no. 1 (1988): 35–63. An admirable treatment of possession as a religious expression is John M. Stanley, "Gods, Ghosts, and Possession," in *The Experience of Hinduism: Essays on Religion in Maharashtra*, ed. Eleanor Zelliot and Maxine Berntsen (Albany: State University of New York Press, 1988), 26–59.

4. Susan Wadley, "The Spirit 'Rides' or the Spirit 'Comes': Possession in a North Indian Village," in *The Realm of the Extra-Human: Agents and Audiences*, ed. Agehananda Bharati (The Hague: Mouton, 1976), 233–52.

5. Gananath Obeyesekere, "Psychocultural Exegesis of a Case of Spirit Possession in Sri Lanka," in *Case Studies in Spirit Possession*, ed. Crapanzano and Garrison, 290.

6. Bābā Bālak Nāth is a male "saint–deity" whose cult extends throughout most of Panjab and Himachal Pradesh. Most of those who worship him worship Śerāṅvālī as well. For a discussion of his cult, see Ursula M. Sharma, "The Immortal Cowherd and the Saintly Carrier: An Essay in the Study of Cults," *Sociological Bulletin* 23, no. 1 (1974): 137–52.

7. Gold, "Spirit Possession," 35n. Claus distinguishes between spirit possession and spirit mediumship, defining the former as "an unexpected intrusion of the supernatural into the lives of humans" and the latter as "the legitimate, expected possession of a specialist by a spirit or deity, usually for the purpose of soliciting the aid of the supernatural for human problems" ("Spirit Possession and Spirit Mediumship," 29). I prefer not to make such a hard-and-fast distinction, as there is often considerable overlap and transition from one to the other.

8. Paul Hershman, "Hair, Sex and Dirt," *Man*, n.s., 9, no. 2 (1974): 274–98.

9. Recorded on May 15, 1983, at a *jagrātā* in Chandigarh. The story was told by Bābā Budh Nāth of the Nāth Satsang Sabhā in a mixture of Panjabi prose and verse.

10. In S. P. Dakaur, *Devī kī kathāyeṅ* (Hardvār: harbhajan singh eṇḍ sans, n.d.), 38: "In order to save Tārā's honor, Mā came in wind form / She quickly entered into Tārā and displayed her skill." In Govind Kumār Sak-

senā "Gulśan," *Kālīkā janm kathā evam mahiṣāsur vināś aur tārārānī kī kathā arthāt mātā ke jāgraṇ kā mahātm* (Hardvār: harbhajan singh eṇḍ sans, n.d.), 139: "the Mother came in wind form / She came and entered Tārā's body, the Great Mother said to the king / Offer your son as a sacrifice, who is your own beloved."

11. An example of this kind of song is "Dātī de darbār kanjakāṅ kheḍḍiyā," sung by Narendra Cancal (Polydor Records 2392894), written by Camanlāl Jośī. The words are printed in the pamphlet *Mātā dīyāṅ bheṭān, ghar ghar vic mahimā teri* (Dillī: aśokā prakāśan, n.d.), 7–10.

12. For a full-length study of the concept of play in Hinduism, see David Kinsley, *The Divine Player: A Study of Kṛṣṇa Līlā* (Delhi: Motilal Banarsidass, 1979).

13. See, for example, Richard Lannoy, *The Speaking Tree: A Study of Indian Culture and Society* (New York: Oxford University Press, 1971), who writes "Oracular possession is not accredited by the Great Tradition because it is the attention-getting device of the antipodal society. But it is precisely because it forms an essential part of the cultural expression in India's numerous Little Traditions that it should be regarded as an extremely significant, if archaic and risky, means of social integration. It appears to have spontaneously flared up from time to time in response to a severe crisis in the collective destiny" (198–99). Most studies on the classical or "Great" Tradition of Hinduism do not even mention divine possession as a religious expression.

14. Interview at Cāmuṇḍā Devī temple, June 9, 1983.

15. The Śerāṅvālī cult resembles in several respects the South Indian cults of Murugan and Aiyappan. All three cults are regional rather than local or pan-Indian, all are connected with pilgrimage places, and all are increasing in popularity. They are what William C. McCormack calls external cults in the following statement: "Much has been done to display *internal cults* in popular Hinduism, i.e., particularistic cults surrounding lineage ancestor worship or local deities, while much has yet to be done on the study of external cults, e.g., universalistic cults which link a village with larger socio-political units as through pilgrimages or through symbols generated by the 'teaching' of charismatic sectarian leaders" ("Popular Religion in South India," in *Religion in Modern India,* ed. Giri Raj Gupta [Delhi: Vikas, 1983], 121).

16. Interview, May 13, 1983.

17. This seems to be the case in the ceremony described by Ruth S. Freed and Stanley A. Freed, "Two Mother-Goddess Ceremonies of Delhi State in the Great and Little Traditions," *Southwestern Journal of Anthropology* 18 (1962): 246–77.

18. The same idea is found in the Kumārī cults of Nepal in which specially chosen young girls have a ritual position as goddesses until they have

their first menstruation. See Michael Allen, *The Cult of Kumari: Virgin Worship in Nepal* (Kathmandu: Tribhuvan University, 1975).

19. Interview February 14, 1983. Similar cases of conflict have recorded in the late nineteenth century during the heyday of the Ārya Samāj reform movement. Cf. Kenneth W. Jones, *Arya Dharm: Hindu Consciousness in Nineteenth-Century Punjab* (Berkeley: University of California Press, 1976), 190.

20. Interview, January 12, 1983.

21. The nine Durgās in this temple are the same as those listed in the *Durgā Kavacam,* a Sanskrit prayer often included in editions of the *Devī Māhātmya,* as Śailaputrī, Brahmacāriṇī, Candraghaṇṭā, Kūṣmāṇḍā, Skandamātā, Kātyāyanī, Kālarātrī, Mahāgaurī, and Siddhidatrī. These are the same as those listed in Diana L. Eck, *Banaras: City of Light* (London: Routledge and Kegan Paul, 1983), 360, except that Eck has Citraghaṇṭā for Candraghaṇṭā. In the Gumti temple, there are some slight spelling variations in the names of the goddesses carved on the walls, probably due to the semiliteracy of the artisan.

22. This is interesting in light of the fact that Mātājī is usually possessed by Vaiṣṇo Devī. I have the impression that before her niece started becoming possessed by Kālī, Mātājī herself was alternately possessed by both forms of the Goddess. The fact that the order to build the temple came from the fierce form Kālī made it even more compelling.

23. There is a peculiar story connected with the Bhairo image. When it was being carved into the wall next to the main image, Mātājī told the artisan (*mistrī*) that Bhairo wanted a sacrificial offering (*bali*). After completing the image, the *mistrī* lay down and died.

24. *Satyanarāyaṇ kathā* is a Vaiṣṇavite story and *vrat* that is performed in the various vernaculars in many parts of India. The Sanskrit text is attributed to the *Skanda Purāṇa.*

25. This *jagrātā* took place on the night of October 28–29, 1982. See chapter 4 for a fuller discussion of the *jagrātā.*

26. March 9–10, 1983.

27. The names of her organization and temple demonstrate again the identification of Vaiṣṇo and Kālī as two aspects of the same goddess.

28. The Khattrī is one of the more prominent "middle castes" of the Panjab. While claiming Kṣatriya status, Khattrīs are now primarily merchants and professionals in urban areas.

29. This practice is said to have been common at Cintpūrṇī and Jvālā Mukhī in the past and is not unheard of even today. The same motif is found in the stories of Dhyānū Bhagat, Tārārānī, and others.

30. According to one legend, Bhairo chased Vaiṣṇo Devī up the mountain, attempting to rape her, whereupon she cut off his head with a trident. According to another legend, he appeared at her feast in the guise of a

Gorakhnāth *sādhu* and demanded nonvegetarian food and liquor. See chapter 2.

31. In fact, Ūṣā Bahn, with her conscious use of costuming, staging, and dramatic entrances, reminds me very much of American evangelist Aimee Semple McPherson.

32. The term he used was *visarjan,* the ritual disposal of an icon in a body of water after it has fulfilled its purpose.

33. The poster was given to me by the owner of the tour-booking agency from whom I first heard of Ūṣā Bahn. It has been used as an object of worship, as evidenced by the red *tilak* marks placed on Ūṣā Bahn's and Durgā's foreheads.

34. Listed on either side of this announcement are the names of various officers of the organization: manager (*prabandhak*) of the royal court, *laṅgar* manager, pilgrimage manager, stage manager, makeup manager, treasurer, loudspeaker and sound manager, music parties, servants of the *jot,* pavilion decorators, publicity officer, provincial publicity officers (for Panjab, Delhi, Haryana, Jammu and Kashmir, and Uttar Pradesh), decorators of the temple, various chairmen (*padādhikārī*) and vice-chairmen of the Delhi branch (including the "Ladies' Circle"), followed by a longer list of *sevaks* (servants). At the bottom in large print are three major names, those of the *mahant,* who is also director (*sancālak*), the chief (*pradhān*), and the officer (*mantrī*).

35. This is taken from an oral Panjabi version told by Śrī Śām Raṅgīlā and Party of Ambala, which I tape-recorded at a Viśāl Bhagavatī Jāgraṇ in Chandigarh on November 7–8, 1982. The story of Nandā and Nandlāl is told during the *jagrātā* as an alternative to the story of Dhyānū Bhagat at the point just before the offering of coconuts in order to explain why they are offered. I have heard several oral versions of this story but have encountered no written versions.

36. Manuel Moreno, "God's Forceful Call: Possession as a Divine Strategy," in *Gods of Flesh/Gods of Stone,* ed. Waghorne and Cutler, 103–20.

37. Ibid., 104.

38. Paul Ricoeur, *Freud and Philosophy,* trans. Denis Savage (New Haven: Yale University Press, 1970). See also Ricoeur, *Interpretation Theory: Discourse and the Surplus of Meaning* (Fort Worth: Texas Christian University Press, 1976).

39. While acknowledging the fruitfulness of such an approach, I am unable to follow it any further than I have in the case studies I have presented, due not only to a lack of information about the early childhood and family history of the women but also to a lack of clinical training on my part that would qualify me to make such assessments.

CHAPTER 6

1. This model was first proposed by Robert Redfield, *The Little Community* and *Peasant Society and Culture* (Chicago: University of Chicago Press, 1960), and applied to Indian civilization by Marriott, "Little Communities."

2. Joseph W. Elder, "Mass Culture in Historical and Contemporary India," in *Mass Culture, Language and Arts in India,* ed. Mahadev L. Apte (Bombay: Popular Prakashan, 1979), 23.

3. Milton Singer, *When a Great Tradition Modernizes* (New York: Praeger, 1972), 47–48.

4. Ibid., 149, 187, passim.

5. Stuart H. Blackburn and A. K. Ramanujan, "Introduction," in *Another Harmony,* ed. Blackburn and Ramanujan, 25.

6. This version of the *Rāmāyana* is found in many Tantric and Śākta sources (for example, *Devī Bhāgavata Purāṇa* III.30) and is also quite common in the Bengali vernacular tradition.

7. *Cār yugoṅ meṅ śerāṅvālī* (Haridvār: harbhajan singh eṇḍ sans, n.d.).

8. Apparently the author was unaware of the story in the *Harivaṃśa* (47.23–37) of the Goddess's birth to Yaśodā and Nanda and the reference to it in chap. 12 of the *Devī Māhātmya.*

9. The stories of Vaiṣṇo Devī and Dhyānū Bhagat are found above in chapter 2. The story of Tārārānī is in chapter 4. In the story of King Candradev, the king's daughter (who has been born through the grace of Vaiṣṇo Devī) fasts and prays to the Goddess for nine days in order to revive her dead husband. Thus, it is a *vrat kathā* for the Navarātra.

10. *Śrī vaiṣṇo devī darśan aur nau deviyoṅ kī kathā.*

11. Cf. McKim Marriott, "Changing Channels of Cultural Transmission in Indian Civilization," in *Aspects of Religion in Indian Society,* ed. L. P. Vidyarthi (Meerut, 1961), 13–25, and Susan Snow Wadley, "Popular Hinduism and Mass Literature in North India: A Preliminary Analysis," in *Religion in Modern India,* ed. Giri Raj Gupta (New Delhi: Vikas, 1983), 81–104.

12. Caman Lāl Bhāradvāj "Caman," *Jagrātā* (Amṛtsar: bṛjmohan bhāradvāj pustakālay, 1981), 19–20.

13. May 24, 1983. I also attended one of his performances, a *caukī* at a private home in Delhi a few days later, and had an opportunity to see him perform again with Narendra Chanchal at the Viśāl Bhagavatī Jāgraṇ at Cintpūrṇī during the Sāvan Melā in mid-August of the same year.

14. Śarmā, *Nainā devī mahāttm,* 4–5.

15. Published accounts of Santoṣī Mā include A. L. Basham, "Santoshi Mata: A New Divinity in the Hindu Pantheon?" *28th International Congress of Orientalists, Canberra, 1971 Proceedings* (Wiesbaden: Harrassowitz, 1976),

89–90; Veena Das, "The Mythological Film and Its Framework of Meaning: An Analysis of *Jai Santoshi Ma*," *India International Centre Quarterly* 8, no. 1 (March 1980): 43–56; and Michael Brand, "A New Hindu Goddess," *Hemisphere: An Asian Australian Magazine* 26, no. 6 (May/June 1982): 380–84. Unpublished theses include Michael Brand, "Santoshi Mata: A New Hindu Goddess" (B.A. thesis, Australian National University, Canberra, 1979); Catherine Herbert Howell, "'Discovering' the Goddess: An Analysis of a Vrat Katha" (M.A. thesis, University of Virginia, 1975); and Margaret L. Robinson, "Santoshi Ma: The Development of a Goddess" (University of Wisconsin College Year in India Program, 1978–79). A Ph.D. dissertation by Stanley Kurtz, Department of Anthropology, Harvard University, is forthcoming. A panel, "Santoshi Ma, the Film Goddess," was held at the American Academy of Religion (Chicago, December 1984), with presentations by Michael Brand, Jack Hawley, Stanley Kurtz, and Kathleen Erndl.

16. Two that I have in my possession are *Śrī santoṣī mātā kī kathā arthāt śukravār vrat kathā* (Paṭnā: nārāyaṇ eṇḍ ko, n.d.) and Gurbakhṣ Siṅh "Jnān" eṇḍ sans, *Śukravār vrat kathā: Santoṣī Mātā kī amar kahānī* (Ludhiyānā: satikartār pustak bhaṇḍār, n.d.)

17. Stanley Kurtz (personal communication) has heard reports of a lawsuit filed against the filmmakers by some *paṇḍits,* claiming that the film was a fraud since Santoṣī Mā is not mentioned in any of the Purāṇas. The suit was apparently resolved in the filmmakers' favor, since they were able to find a single reference in one of the Purāṇas to an unnamed mind-born daughter of Gaṇeśa. The film itself was made after two of its stars performed a successful Santoṣī Mā *vrat* based on the instructions given in a popular pamphlet.

18. Tuṣṭi is an abstract feminine noun used as as an epithet of the Goddess in the *Devī Māhātmya* (1.60, 5.30).

19. Brand, "Santoshi Mata." I have made a few changes in wording. The *vrat kathā,* in typical folktale fashion, uses no names for the characters. In the movie the heroine is called Satyavatī and her husband, Bīrju.

20. Brand, "Santoshi Mata"; Das, "Mythological Film and Its Framework of Meaning."

21. Stanley Kurtz, who has done perhaps the most extensive research on Santoṣī Mā, is essentially in agreement with this view (personal communication, April 1984).

22. Personal communication, April 1984.

23. From an oral version told by Gopāl Singh Pāl, Pradhān of the Durgā Bhajan Maṇḍali, Chandigarh, recorded on October 27, 1982.

24. Personal communication, September 1982.

25. The name means "full of grain" or "full of food." Interestingly enough, stories about this goddess frequently appear in the Santoṣī Mā

pamphlets. Her most famous temple is at Varanasi, where she is considered to be the consort of Śiva.

26. The economic motive was suggested to me by the *pujārī* at Jayantī Devī, a small temple in the hills near Chandigarh. Of course, it does not negate the theological statement that all goddesses are one.

27. To my knowledge, the earliest documented case of Santoṣī Mā possession in the Panjab was a five- or six-year-old girl observed by Hershman in 1972 or 1973 ("Virgin and Mother," 278). Unfortunately, he gives neither the location nor any other details.

CHAPTER 7

1. Babb, "Marriage and Malevolence." The same argument is repeated in Babb, *Divine Hierarchy*.

2. Linda Louise Iltis, "The Swasthānī Vrata: Newar Women and Ritual in Nepal" (Ph.D. diss., University of Wisconsin–Madison, 1985), 23–24.

3. Kinsley provides an excellent discussion of Pārvatī's domesticating influence on Śiva in *Hindu Goddesses,* 46–50. Marglin makes the convincing argument that both make and female celibacy are dangerously powerful. ("Female Sexuality in the Hindu World," 39–59).

4. Babb, *Divine Hierarchy*, 221.

5. Ramanujan, "Two Realms of Kannada Folklore," 56–58. My summary of Ramanujan's typology is taken from Table 1.1 on p. 58. Ramanujan has taken the terms "Breast Mother" and "Tooth Mother" from C. G. Jung, "Psychological Aspects of the Mother Archetype," in Jung, *The Archetypes and the Collective Unconscious,* trans. R. F. C. Hull (Princeton: Princeton University Press, 1938), 75–110.

6. An interesting article contrasting Lakṣmī and Rādhā is Carl Olson, "Śrī Lakshmī and Rādhā: The Obsequious Wife and the Lustful Lover," in *Book of the Goddess Past and Present,* ed. Olson, 124–44. See also Frédérique Apffel Marglin, "Types of Sexual Union and Their Implicit Meanings," in *Divine Consort,* ed. Hawley and Wulff, 298–313, for a discussion of three different types of consort goddesses.

7. Kinsley, *Hindu Goddesses,* 3–5.

8. Madeline Biardeau and Charles Malamoud, *Le Sacrifice dans l'inde ancienne* (Paris: Presses Universitaires de France, 1976), 106, quoted in Alf Hiltebeitel, "Toward a Coherent Study of Hinduism," *Religious Studies Review* 9, no. 3 (July 1983): 207.

9. David G. Mandelbaum, "Transcendental and Pragmatic Aspects of Religion," *American Anthropologist* 68 (1966): 1174–91.

10. Elizabeth-Chalier Visuvalingam, "Bhairava's Royal Brahmanicide:

The Problem of the Mahābrāhmaṇa," in *Criminal Gods and Demon Devotees,* ed. Hiltebeitel, 157–230.

11. Paradoxically, however, in other myths of the Śerāṅvālī cycle, Gorakhnāth, the guru of Bhairo, is portrayed as a Vaiṣṇava or vegetarian worshiper. See, for example, the Jvālā Mukhī stories in chapter 2 and the coconut-offering stories in chapter 4.

12. David Shulman, "The Murderous Bride: Tamil Versions of the Myth of Devi and the Buffalo Demon," *History of Religions* 16, no. 2 (November 1976): 120–47.

13. Alf Hiltebeitel, "Rama and Gilgamesh: The Sacrifices of the Water Buffalo and the Bull of Heaven," *History of Religions* 19, no. 3 (February 1980): 187–223.

Bibliography

Abul-Fazl-i-'Allami. *'Ain-i-Akbari of Abul-Fazl-i-'Allami*. Translated by H. S. Jarrett; revised and further annotated by Sir Jadunath Sarkar. Calcutta: Royal Asiatic Society of Bengal, 1971.

Agrawala, Vasudeva S. *The Glorification of the Great Goddess*. Varanasi: All-India Kashiraj Trust, 1963.

Allen, Michael. *The Cult of Kumari: Virgin Worship in Nepal*. Kathmandu: Tribhuvan University, 1975.

Altekar, A. S. *The Position of Women in Hindu Civilization*. Delhi: Motilal Banarsidass, 1959.

Amar, Arjun Dev. *Pūrṇ mahatm: nau deviyoṅ kā itihās*. Jvālā Mukhī: mankoṭiyā pabliśarz, n.d.

Aṅjānā, Subhāṣ Ajnabī Aśok. *Mān kī meṅhadī*. Kaṭrā, Vaiṣṇo Devī: bhavānī pustak mahal, [1981?].

Āp bulāve: māṅ vaiṣṇo devī. Jammū: pustak saṅsār, n.d.

Apte, Mahadev L. *Mass Culture, Language and Arts in India*. Bombay: Popular Prakashan, 1978.

Archer, W. G. *Indian Paintings from the Punjab Hills*. 2 vols. Delhi: Oxford University Press, 1973.

Ashby, Philip H. *Modern Trends in Hinduism*. New York: Columbia University Press, 1974.

Aziz, Barbara Nimri. "Personal Dimensions of the Sacred Journey: What Pilgrims Say." *Religious Studies* 23 (June 1987): 247–61.

Babb, Lawrence A. *The Divine Hierarchy: Popular Hinduism in Central India*. New York: Columbia University Press, 1975.

———. "Marriage and Malevolence: The Uses of Sexual Opposition in a Hindu Pantheon." *Ethnology* 9, no. 2 (April 1970): 137–48.

———. *Redemptive Encounters: Three Modern Styles in the Hindu Tradition*. Berkeley: University of California Press, 1986 [1987].

Banerjea, Jitendra N. *The Development of Hindu Iconography*. Calcutta: University of Calcutta, 1956.

———. *Paurāṇic and Tāntric Religion*. Calcutta: University of Calcutta, 1966.

Basham, A. L. "Santoshi Mata: A New Divinity in the Hindu Pantheon?"

28th International Congress of Orientalists, Canberra, 1971 Proceedings. Weisbaden: Harrassowitz, 1976, 89–90.

———. *The Wonder That Was India.* 3d ed., rev. New York: Taplinger, 1968.

Beane, Wendell Charles. *Myth, Cult and Symbol in Śākta Hinduism: A Study of the Indian Mother Goddess.* Leiden: Brill, 1977.

Beck, Brenda. *The Three Twins: The Telling of a South Indian Folk Epic.* Bloomington: Indiana University Press, 1982.

Bedi, Rajinder Singh. *I Take This Woman.* translated by Khushwant Singh. New Delhi: Oriental, 1967.

Bennett, Lynn. *Dangerous Wives and Sacred Sisters: Social and Symbolic Roles of High-Caste Women in Nepal.* New York: Columbia University Press, 1983.

Berreman, Gerald D. "Brahmins and Shamans in Pahari Religion." In *Religion in South Asia,* edited by Edward B. Harper, 53–69. Seattle: University of Washington Press, 1964.

Bhandarkar, R. G. *Vaiṣṇavism, Śaivism, and Minor Religious Systems.* Strassburg: Trubner, 1913.

Bhāradvāj, Caman Lāl "Caman." *Jagrātā.* Amṛtsar: bṛjmohan bhāradvāj pustakālay, 1981.

———. *Śrī durgā stuti.* Amṛtsar: bṛjmohan bhāradvāj pustakālay, 1977.

Bharati, Agehananda. "Pilgrimage in the Indian Tradition." *History of Religions* 3, no. 1 (1963): 135–67.

———. "Pilgrimage Sites and Indian Civilization." In *Chapters in Indian Civilization,* edited by J. W. Elder, 85–126. Dubuque, Iowa: Kendell/Hunt, 1970.

———. *The Tantric Tradition.* London: Hillary House, 1965.

———. ed. *The Realm of the Extra-Human: Agents and Audiences.* The Hague: Mouton, 1976.

Bhardwaj, Surinder Mohan. *Hindu Places of Pilgrimage in India.* Berkeley: University of California Press, 1973.

———. "Some Spatial and Social Aspects of the Mother Goddess Cult in Northwest India." Paper prepared for discussion at the Third Punjab Studies Conference. Philadelphia, 1971.

Bhattacharji, Sukumari. *The Indian Theogony: A Comparative Study of Indian Mythology from the Vedas to the Purāṇas.* Cambridge: Cambridge University Press, 1970.

Bhattacharyya, Narendra Nath. *History of the Śākta Religion.* Delhi: Munshiram Manoharlal, 1973.

———. *History of the Tantric Religion.* New Delhi: Manohar, 1982.

———. *The Indian Mother Goddess.* New ed. Delhi: Manohar, 1977.

Blackburn, Stuart. "Oral Performance: Narrative and Ritual in a Tamil Tradition." *Journal of American Folklore* 94 (1981): 207–17.

Blackburn, Stuart H., and A. K. Ramanujan, eds. *Another Harmony: New Essays on the Folklore of India*. Delhi: Oxford University Press, 1986.

Bolle, Kees W. "Speaking of a Place." In *Myths and Symbols: Studies in Honor of Mircea Eliade,* edited by J. M. Kitagawa and Charles H. Long, 127–39. Chicago: University of Chicago Press, 1969.

———. "A World of Sacrifice." *History of Religions* 23, no. 1 (August 1983): 37–63.

Brand, Michael. "A New Hindu Goddess." *Hemisphere: An Asian Australian Magazine* 26, no. 6 (May/June 1982): 380–84.

———. "Santoshi Mata: A New Hindu Goddess." B.A. thesis, Australian National University, 1979.

Briggs, George. *Gorakhnāth and Kanphaṭā Yogīs*. Calcutta: YMCA Publishing House, 1937.

Brooks, Douglas Renfrow. *The Secret of the Three Cities: An Introduction to Hindu Śākta Tantrism through Bhāskarāya's Commentary on the Tripurā Upaniṣad*. Chicago: University of Chicago Press, 1991.

Brown, Cheever Mackenzie. *God as Mother: A Feminine Theology in India*. Hartford, Vt.: Stark, 1974.

Brubaker, Richard L. "The Ambivalent Mistress: A Study of South Indian Village Goddesses and Their Religious Meaning." Ph.D. diss., University of Chicago, 1978.

Campbell, J. Gabriel. *Saints and Householders: A Study of Hindu Ritual and Myth among the Kangra Rajputs*. Kathmandu: Ratna Pustak Bhandar, 1976.

Cār yugoṅ meṅ śerāṅvālī. Haridvār: harbhajan singh eṇḍ sans, n.d.

Charak, Sukhdev Singh. *History and Culture of the Himalayan States*. Vol. 1. New Delhi: Light and Life, 1978.

Chaudhury, P. C. Roy. *Temples and Legends of Himachal Pradesh*. Bombay: Bharatiya Vidya Bhavan, 1981.

Christ, Carol P., and Judith Plaskow, eds. *Womanspirit Rising: A Feminist Reader in Religion*. New York: Harper & Row, 1979.

Claus, Peter J. "Mayndala: A Legend and Possession Cult of Tulunad." *Asian Folklore Studies* 38, no. 2 (1979): 94–129.

———. "Spirit Possession and Spirit Mediumship from the Perspective of Tulu Oral Traditions." *Culture, Medicine and Psychiatry* 3 (1979): 29–52.

Coburn, Thomas B. "Consort of None, *Śakti* of All: The Vision of the *Devī Māhātmya*." In *The Divine Consort: Rādhā and the Goddesses of India,* edited by John Stratton Hawley and Donna Marie Wulff, 153–65. Berkeley: Religious Studies Series, 1982.

———. *Devī-Māhātmya: The Crystallization of the Goddess Tradition*. Columbia, Mo.: South Asia Books, 1985.

———. *Encountering the Goddess: A Translation of the Devī-Māhātmya and a*

Study of Its Interpretation. Albany: State University of New York Press, 1991.

Crapanzano, Vincent, and Vivian Garrison, eds. *Case Studies in Spirit Possession*. New York: Wiley, 1977.

Crooke, William. *Religion and Folklore of Northern India*. New ed. 1894. Delhi: Chand, 1925.

Cunningham, Alexander. *Archeological Survey of India*. Vol. 5, report for the year 1872–73.

Dakaur, S. P. *Devī kī kathāyeṅ*. Haridvār: harhbajan singh eṇḍ sans, n.d.

———. *Māṅ kī mahimā*. Haridvār: harhbajan singh eṇḍ sans, n.d.

Daly, Mary. *Beyond God the Father: Toward a Philosophy of Women's Liberation*. Boston: Beacon Press, 1973.

Danielou, Alain. *Hindu Polytheism*. London: Routledge and Kegan Paul, 1963.

Das, Veena. "The Mythological Film and Its Framework of Meaning: An Analysis of *Jai Santoshi Ma*." *India International Centre Quarterly* 8, no.1 (March 1980): 43–56.

Derrett, J. Duncan M. "The Reform of Hindu Religious Endowments." In *South Asian Politics and Religion*, edited by Donald Eugene Smith, 311–36. Princeton: Princeton University Press, 1966.

Dev, Arjun "Amar." *Jot jvālā kī*. Jālandhar: bhārat pustak bhaṇḍār, n.d. [identical pamphlet also available with other titles on cover: *Nayanā devī mahatm*, etc.].

[*Devī Bhāgavata Purāṇa*] *The Srimad Devi Bhagawatam*. Translated by Swami Vijnanananda. New Delhi: Oriental, 1977.

Devī ke chah dhāmoṅ ki yātrā [Hindi text with photos and English captions]. Jammu: pustak sansaar, n.d.

[*Devī Māhātmya*] *The Glorification of the Great Goddess*. edited by and translated by Vasudeva S. Agrawala. Varanasi: All-India Kashiraj Trust, 1963.

———. *Glory of the Divine Mother*. Translated by S. Shankaranarayanan. Pondicherry: Dipti, 1968.

———. *Śrīdurgā-saptaśatī* [Sanskrit text and appendixes with Hindi translation and ritual instructions]. Edited by Śivadatta Miśra. Vārāṇasī: ṭhākurprasād eṇḍ sans bukselar, 1977.

Dhal, U. N. *Goddess Lakshmi: Origin and Development*. New Delhi: Oriental, 1978.

Dhere, Ramchandra. "The Gondhali: Singers for the Devi." Translated by Anne Feldhaus. In *The Experience of Hinduism: Essays on Religion in Maharashtra*, edited by Eleanor Zelliot and Maxine Berntsen, 174–89. Albany: State University of New York Press, 1988.

Diehl, Carl Gustav. *Instrument and Purpose: Studies on Rites and Rituals in South India*. Lund: Gleerup, 1956.

Dikshit, S. K. *The Mother Goddess: (A Study Regarding the Origin of Hinduism)*. New Delhi: Dikshit, [1943].

Drew, Frederic. *The Jummoo and Kashmir Territories*. Delhi: Oriental, 1971.

Eck, Diana L. *Banaras: City of Light*. London: Routledge and Kegan Paul, 1983.

———. "Dakṣa's Sacrifice and the Śākta Pīṭhas." Paper presented at the meeting of the American Academy of Religion, Atlanta, November 1986.

———. *Darśan: Seeing the Divine Image in India*. Chambersburg, Penn.: Anima Books, 1981.

Elder, Joseph W. "Mass Culture in Historical and Contemporary India." In *Mass Culture, Language and Arts in India*, edited by Mahadev L. Apte, 10–29. Bombay: Popular Prakashan, 1979.

Eliade, Mircea. "History of Religions and a New Humanism." *History of Religions* 1, no. 1 (1962): 4.

———. *Patterns in Comparative Religion*. Translated by Rosemary Sheed. New York: Sheed and Ward, 1958.

———. *Yoga: Immortality and Freedom*. Translated by Willard R. Trask. Princeton: Princeton University Press, 1969.

Elliot, H. A., and J. Dowson. *History of India as Told by Its Own Historians*. London, 1867–77.

Erndl, Kathleen M. "The Absorbtion of Santoshi Ma into the Panjabi Goddess Cult." Paper presented at the meeting of the American Academy of Religion, Chicago, 1984.

———. "Fire and Wakefulness: The Devī *Jagrātā* in Contemporary Panjabi Hinduism" *Journal of the American Academy of Religion* 59, no. 2 (1991): 339–60.

———. "Rapist or Bodyguard, Demon or Devotee? Images of Bhairo in the Mythology and Cult of Vaiṣṇo Devī." In *Criminal Gods and Demon Devotees: Essays on the Gods of Popular Hinduism*, edited by Alf Hiltebeitel, 239–50. Albany: State University of New York Press, 1989.

———. "Two Exemplary Devotees of the Goddess: Tārārānī and Dhyānū Bhagat." Paper presented at the Conference on Religion in South India, Research Triangle Park, N.C., 1988.

———. "Worshipping the Goddess: Women's Leadership Roles in the Cult of Śerāṅvālī." In *Women's Rites Women's Desires*, edited by Mary McGee, forthcoming.

Fiorenza, Elizabeth Schüssler. *In Memory of Her: A Feminist Theological Reconstruction of Christian Origins*. New York: Crossroad, 1983.

Foster, Georgana. "A Popular North Indian Pilgrimage Site: The Shrine of Vaishno Devi in Jammu." Paper prepared for discussion at the Conference on Pilgrimage, Pittsburgh, 1981.

Freed, Ruth S., and Stanley A. Freed. "Spirit Possession as Illness in a North Indian Village." *Ethnology* 3, no. 2 (1964): 152–71.

———. "Two Mother-Goddess Ceremonies of Delhi State in the Great and Little Traditions." *Southwestern Journal of Anthropology* 18 (1962): 246–71

Gadon, Elinor W. *The Once and Future Goddess: A Symbol for Our Time*. San Francisco: Harper & Row, 1989.

Ganaute, Ṭīkārām "Rāj." *Bheṇṭoṅ kī jubānī*. Haridvār: harhbajan singh eṇḍ sans, n.d.

Ganhar, J. N. *Jammu Shrines and Pilgrimages*. New Delhi: Ganhar, 1973.

Gatwood, Lynn E. *Devi and the Spouse Goddess: Women, Sexuality, and Marriages in India*. Riverdale, Md.: Riverdale, 1985.

Ghose, Pratapachandra. *Durga Puja*. Calcutta: Hindoo Patriot Press, 1871.

Gold, Ann Grodzins. *Fruitful Journeys: The Ways of Rajasthani Pilgrims*. Berkeley: University of California Press, 1988.

———. "Spirit Possession Perceived and Performed in Rural Rajasthan." *Contributions to Indian Sociology*, n.s., 22, no. 1 (1988): 35–63.

Gonda, Jan. *Change and Continuity in Indian Religion*. The Hague: Mouton, 1965.

Goswamy, B. N. "History at Pilgrim Centers; on Pattas Held by Families of Priests at Centers of Hindu Pilgrimage." In *Sources on Panjab History*, edited by W. Eric Gustafson and Kenneth W. Jones. Delhi: Manohar Book Service, 1975.

Goswamy, Karuna. "Vaishnavism in the Punjab Hills and Pahari Painting." Ph.D. thesis. Punjab University [Chandigarh], 1968.

Goudriaan, Teun, and Sanjukta Gupta. *Hindu Tantric and Śākta Literature*. Wiesbaden: Herrassowitz, 1981.

Gross, Rita M. "Hindu Female Deities as a Resource for the Contemporary Rediscovery of the Goddess." *Journal of the American Academy of Religion* 46, no. 3 (September 1978): 269–92.

Gupt, Dāū Dayāl. *Durgā-mahimā*. Dillī: pustak mahal, 1979.

Gupta, Giri Raj, ed. *Religion in Modern India*. Delhi: Vikas, 1983.

Gupta, Sanjukta, Dirk Jan Hoens, and Teun Goudriaan. *Hindu Tantrism*. Leiden: Brill, 1979.

Gurdās, Bhāī. *Vārāṅ bhāī gurdās saṭīk,* [ed.] bhāī sāhib bhāī vīr singh jī. Amritsar: Khālsā samācār, 1977.

Hart, George L., III, "The Little Devotee: Cēkkilār's Story of Ciṟṟoṇṭar." In *Sanskrit and Indian Studies,* edited by M. Nagatomi et al., 217–36. Dordrecht: Reidel, 1980.

Hawley, John Stratton. *Krishna, The Butter Thief.* Princeton: Princeton University Press, 1983.

Hawley, John Stratton, and Donna Marie Wulff, eds. *The Divine Consort:*

Rādhā and the Goddesses of India. Berkeley: Religious Studies Series, 1982.

Hazra, R. C. *Studies in the Purāṇic Records on Hindu Rites and Customs*. Dacca: University of Dacca, 1940.

———. *Studies in the Upapurāṇas*. Vol. 2, *Śākta and Nonsectarian Upapurāṇas*. Calcutta: Sanskrit College, 1963.

Hershman, Paul. "Hair, Sex and Dirt." *Man*, n.s., 9, no. 2 (1974): 274–98.

———. "Virgin and Mother." In *Symbols and Sentiments: Cross-Cultural Studies in Symbolism*, edited by Ioan Lewis, 269–92 London: Academic Press, 1977.

Hiltebeitel, Alf. *The Cult of Draupadī*. Vol. 1. *Mythologies: From Gingee to Kurukṣetra*. Chicago: University of Chicago Press, 1988.

———. "Rama and Gilgamesh: The Sacrifices of the Water Buffalo and the Bull of Heaven." *History of Religions* 19, no. 3 (February 1980): 187–223.

———. "Toward a Coherent Study of Hinduism." *Religious Studies Review* 9, no. 3 (July 1983): 206–12.

———. ed. *Criminal Gods and Demon Devotees: Essays on the Guardians of Popular Hinduism*. Albany: State University of New York Press, 1989.

"Himachal Pradesh: The Temple Take-over." *India Today*, 15 May 1984, 86–87.

Holland, Barron. *Popular Hinduism and Hindu Mythology: An Annotated Bibliography*. Westport, Conn.: Greenwood Press, 1979.

Howell, Catherine Herbert. "'Discovering' the Goddess: An Analysis of a Vrat Katha." M.A. thesis, University of Virginia, 1975.

Humes, Cynthia A. "The Text and Temple of the Great Goddess." Ph.D. diss., University of Iowa, 1990.

Ibbetson, Denzil. *Panjab Castes, Being a Reprint of the Chapter on "The Races, Castes, and Tribes of the People" in a Report on the Census of the Punjab, Published in 1883 by the Late Sir Denzil Ibbetson*. Lahore, 1916.

———. ed. *Panjab Notes and Queries*, 1883–87.

Iltis, Linda Louise. "The Swasthānī Vrata: Newar Women and Ritual in Nepal." Ph.D. diss., University of Wisconsin–Madison, 1985.

India (Republic). Office of the Registrar General. Census of India, 1961. Vol. 13, *Punjab*, Pt. 7–B, *Fairs and Festivals*. Vol. 20, *Himachal Pradesh*, Pt. 7–B, *Fairs and Festivals*.

Jones, Kenneth W. *Arya Dharm: Hindu Consciousness in Nineteenth-Century Punjab*. Berkeley: University of California Press, 1976.

Jvālā jī kā itihās kathā aur bheṇṭeṅ. Jvālā Mukhī: pujārī rām praśād, n.d.

Jyotiṣācarya, Cakradhārī "Bezar." *Śrī jvālā jī mahātmay*. Jvālā Mukhī: rām svarūp pustakān vālā, 1979.

Kakar, Sudhir. *Shamans, Mystics and Doctors: A Psychological Inquiry into India and Its Healing Traditions*. New York: Knopf, 1982.

Kakati, Bani Kanta. *The Mother Goddess Kāmākhyā: Or Studies in the Fusion of Aryan and Primitive Beliefs in Assam*. Gauhati: Lawyer's Book Stall, 1948.

Kālikāpurāṇa, (Worship of the Goddess According to the). Translated, with an introduction and notes of chaps. 54–69, by K. R. Van Kooij. Leiden: Brill, 1972.

Kalyāṇ-sakti-aṅk. Chandigarh: Sri Gita Press, 1981. [Reprint of *Śaktyaṅk*. *Kalyāṇ*. Gorakhpur: Gita Press, 1934.]

Kane, P. V. *History of Dharmaśāstra*. Vol. 5, pt. 1. Poona: Bhandarkar Oriental Research Institute, 1958.

Kapera, Constance. *The Worship of Kali in Banaras: An Inquiry*. Delhi: Motilal Banarsidass, n.d.

Kinsley, David R. *The Divine Player: A Study of Kṛṣṇa Līlā*. Delhi: Motilal Banarsidass, 1979.

———. *Hindu Goddesses: Visions of the Divine Feminine in the Hindu Religious Tradition*. Berkeley: University of California Press, 1986.

———. "The Portrait of the Goddess in the *Devī-māhātmya*." *Journal of the American Academy of Religion* 46, no. 4 (December 1978): 489–506.

———. *The Sword and the Flute: Kālī and Kṛṣṇa: Dark Visions of the Terrible and the Sublime in Hindu Mythology*. Berkeley: University of California Press, 1975.

Kramrisch, Stella. "The Indian Great Goddess." *History of Religions* 14, no. 4 (May 1975): 235–65.

Kumar, Pushpendra. *Śakti Cult in Ancient India*. Varanasi: Bharatiya, 1974.

Lalye, P. G. *Studies in Devī Bhāgavata*. Bombay: Popular Prakashan, 1973.

Lannoy, Richard. *The Speaking Tree: A Study of Indian Culture and Society*. New York: Oxford University Press, 1971.

Larson, Gerald James, Pratapaditya Pal, and Rebecca P. Gowen. *In Her Image: The Great Goddess in Indian Asia and the Madonna in Christian Culture*. Santa Barbara: UCSB Art Museum, 1980.

Lewis, I. M. *Ecstatic Religion: An Anthropological Study of Spirit Possession and Shamanism*. Baltimore: Penguin, 1971.

McCormack, William C. "Popular Religion in South India." In *Religion in Modern India*, edited by Giri Raj Gupta, 105–27. Delhi: Vikas, 1983.

McDaniel, June. *The Madness of the Saints: Ecstatic Religion in Bengal*. Chicago: University of Chicago Press, 1989.

Maity, Pradyot Kumar. *Historical Studies in the Cult of the Goddess Manasā*. Calcutta: Punthi Pustak, 1966.

Mānak Hindī Koś. Edited by Rāmcandra Varmmā. Prayāg: Hindī Sāhitya Sammelan, 1966.

Mandelbaum, David G. "Transcendental and Pragmatic Aspects of Religion." *American Anthropologist* 68 (1966): 1174–91.

Marglin, Frédérique Apffel. "Female Sexuality in the Hindu World." In *Immaculate and Powerful: The Female in Sacred Image and Social Reality*, edited by Clarissa W. Atkinson, Constance H. Buchanan, and Margaret R. Miles, 39–60. Boston: Beacon Press, 1985.

———. "Types of Sexual Union and Their Implicit Meanings." In *The Divine Consort: Rādhā and the Goddesses of India*, edited by John Stratton Hawley and Donna Marie Wulff, 298–315. Berkeley: Religious Studies Series, 1982.

Marriott, McKim. "Changing Channels of Cultural Transmission in Indian Civilization." In *Aspects of Religion in Indian Society*, edited by L. P. Vidyarthi. Meerut, 1961.

———. "Little Communities in an Indigenous Civilization." In *Village India*, edited by McKim Marriott, 171–222. Chicago: University of Chicago Press, 1955.

Maśhūr bheṇṭāṅ. Kaṭrā, Vaiṣṇo Devī: bhavānī pustak mahal, n.d. [also available in Gurmukhi script].

Mātā dīyāṅ bheṭāṅ, ghar ghar vic mahimāterī. Dillī: aśokā prakāsan, n.d.

Mātā kā sampūrṇ jagrātā. Haridvār: harhbajan singh enḍ sans, n.d.

"More Pilgrims Visit Vaishno Devi," *Times of India*, 6 July 1978.

Moreno, Manuel. "God's Forceful Call: Possession as a Divine Strategy." In *Gods of Flesh/Gods of Stone: The Embodiment of Divinity in India*, edited by Joanne Punzo Waghorne and Norman Cutler, 103–20. Chambersburg, Penn.: Anima Books, 1985.

Morinis, E. Alan. *Pilgrimage in the Hindu Tradition: A Case Study of West Bengal*. Delhi: Oxford University Press, 1984.

Obeyesekere, Gananath. *The Cult of the Goddess Pattini*. Chicago: University of Chicago Press, 1984.

———. *Medusa's Hair: An Essay on Personal Symbols and Religious Experience*. Chicago: University of Chicago Press, 1981.

———. "Psychocultural Exegesis of a Case of Spirit Possession in Sri Lanka." In *Case Studies in Spirit Possession*, edited by Vincent Crapanzano and Vivian Garrison. New York: Wiley, 1977.

O'Flaherty, Wendy Doniger. *Hindu Myths*. Baltimore: Penguin, 1975.

———. *The Origins of Evil in Hindu Mythology*. Berkeley: University of California Press, 1976.

———. "The Shifting Balance of Power in the Marriage of Śiva and Pārvatī." In *The Divine Consort: Rādhā and the Goddesses of India*, ed. John Stratton Hawley and Donna Marie Wulff, 129–43 Berkeley: Religious Studies Series, 1982.

———. *Women, Androgynes, and Other Mythical Beasts*. Chicago: University of Chicago Press, 1980.

Olson, Carl. "Śrī Lakshmī and Rādhā: The Obsequious Wife and the Lustful Lover." In *The Book of the Goddess Past and Present: An Introduction to Her Religion,* edited by Carl Olson, 124–44. New York: Crossroad, 1983.

———. ed. *The Book of the Goddess Past and Present: An Introduction to Her Religion.* New York: Crossroad, 1983.

Östör, Ákos. *The Play of the Gods: Locality, Ideology, Structure and Time in the Festivals of a Bengali Town.* Chicago: University of Chicago Press, 1980.

Padoux, André. "Hindu Tantrism." In *The Encyclopedia of Religion,* edited by Mircea Elaide. Vol. 14, s.v. New York: Macmillan, 1986.

Payne, Ernest A. *The Śāktas: An Introductory and Comparative Study.* Calcutta: YMCA Publications, 1933.

Pictorial: Call of Goddess Vaishno. Hardwar: Harbhajan Singh & Sons, for and on behalf of Pustak Sansaar, Jammu, n.d.

Pocock, D. F. *Mind, Body and Wealth: A Study of Belief and Practice in an Indian Village.* Oxford: Basil Blackwell, 1973.

Preston, James J. "Creation of the Sacred Image: Apotheosis and Destruction in Hinduism." In *Gods of Flesh/Gods of Stone: The Embodiment of Divinity in India,* edited by Joanne Punzo Waghorne and Norman Cutler, 9–31. Chambersburg, Penn.: Anima Books, 1985.

———. *Cult of the Goddess: Social and Religious Change in a Hindu Temple.* 2d ed. Prospect Heights, Ill.: Waveland Press, 1985.

———. ed. *Mother Worship: Theme and Variations.* Chapel Hill: University of North Carolina Press, 1982.

Raghavan, V. "Methods of Popular Religious Instruction in South India." In *Traditional India: Structure and Change,* edited by Milton Singer. Philadelphia: American Folklore Society, 1959.

Ramanujan, A. K. "Two Realms of Kannada Folklore." In *Another Harmony: New Essays on the Folklore of India,* edited by Stuart H. Blackburn and A. K. Ramanujan, 41–75. Delhi: Oxford University Press. 1986.

Ranchan, Som P., and H. R. Justa. *Folk Tales of Himachal Pradesh.* Bombay: Bharatiya Vidya Bhavan, 1981.

Randhawa, M. S. *Travels in Western Himalaya.* Delhi: Thompson Press, 1974.

Ray, Niharranjan. *The Sikh Gurus and Sikh Society.* Patiala, 1970.

Redfield, Robert. *The Little Community* and *Peasant Society and Culture.* Chicago: University of Chicago Press, 1960.

Ricoeur, Paul. *Freud and Philosophy.* Translated by Denis Savage. New Haven: Yale University Press, 1970.

———. *Interpretation Theory: Discourse and the Surplus of Meaning.* Fort Worth: Texas Christian University Press, 1976.

Robinson, Margaret L. "Santoshi Ma: The Development of a Goddess." University of Wisconsin College Year in India Program, 1978–79.

Ruether, Rosemary Radford. *Womanguides: Readings toward a Feminist Theology*. Boston: Beacon Press, 1985.

Saksenā, Govind Kumār "Gulśan." *Kālīkā janm kathā evam mahiṣāsur vināś aur tārārānī kī kathā arthāt mātā ke jāgraṇ kā mahātm*. Haridvār: harhbajan singh eṇḍ sans, n.d.

Śarmā, Bālkṛṣṇa [comp.]. *Cancal bheṇṭāṅ*. Kaṭrā, Vaiṣṇo Devī: bhavānī pustak mahal, n.d.

———. *Mātā vaiṣṇo devī kī janm kathā*. Kaṭrā, Vaiṣṇo Devī: bhavānī pustak mahal, n.d.

Śarmā, Haṅsrāj. *Śrī jvālāmukhī devī-māhātmya*. Jvālā Mukhī: prabandhak kāriṇī kameṭī mandir, n.d.

Śarmā, Omnāth. *Nainā devī mahāttm*. Dillī: sangam ṭreḍing kampanī, 1981.

———. *Pāṅc deviyoṅ kī kathā*. Dillī: sangam ṭreḍing kampanī, 1982.

———. *Śrī jvālā jī kā mahāttam*. Dillī: sangam ṭreḍing kampanī, 1982.

Schimmel, Annemarie. *Mystical Dimensions of Islam*. Chapel Hill: University of North Carolina Press, 1975.

Sharma, Ursula M. "The Immortal Cowherd and the Saintly Carrier: An Essay in the Study of Cults." *Sociological Bulletin* 23, no. 1 (1974): 137–52.

Shulman, David Dean. "The Murderous Bride: Tamil Versions of the Myth of Devi and the Buffalo Demon." *History of Religions* 16, no. 2 (November 1976): 120–47.

———. *Tamil Temple Myths: Sacrifice and Divine Marriage in the South Indian Śaiva Tradition*. Princeton: Princeton University Press, 1980.

Singer, Milton. "The Great Tradition in a Metropolitan Center: Madras." In *Traditional India: Structure and Change*, edited by Milton Singer. Philadelphia: American Folklore Society, 1959.

———. *When a Great Tradition Modernizes*. New York: Praeger, 1972.

Singh, Guru Gobind. "*Caṇḍīcarita*." In *Guru gobind siṅh kā vīr kāvya*, edited by Jaybhagvān Goyal. Patiyālā: guru gobind siṅh sanstān, 1966.

Siṅh, Darbārā. *Bābe dīyāṅ bheṇṭāṅ*. Dillī: satkartār pustak bhaṇḍār, n.d.

———. *Pūrā mahātm: nau deviyoṅ kī amar kathā. Dillī: satkartār pustak bhaṇḍār*, n.d.

Siṅh, Durgā "Pyās" eṇḍ Sans. *Durgā avatar nau deviyoṅ kā pūrā itihās*. Ludhiyānā: durgā pustak bhaṇḍār, n.d.

Siṅh, Gurbakhṣ "Jñan" eṇḍ sans. *Śukravār vrat kathā: santoṣī mātā kī amar kahānī*. Ludhiyānā: satikartār pustak bhaṇḍār, n.d.

Sircar, D. C. *The Śākta Pīṭhas*. 2d rev. ed. Delhi: Motilal Banarsidass, 1973.

———. *Studies in the Religious Life of Ancient and Medieval India*. Delhi: Motilal Banarsidass, 1971.

———. ed. *The Śakti Cult and Tārā*. Calcutta: University of Calcutta, 1967.

Smith, W. L. *The Myth of Manasā: A Study in the Popular Hinduism of Medieval Bengal*. Stockholm, 1976.

Śrī santoṣī mātā kī kathā arthāt śukravār vrat kathā. Paṭnā: Nārāyaṇ eṇ ko, n.d.

Śrī siddh bābā bālak nāthe. Jālandhar: śarmā pustak bhaṇḍār, n.d.

Śrī vaiṣṇo devī darśan aur nau deviyoṅ kī kathā. Hardvār: harbhajan singh eṇḍ sans, n.d.

Śrī vaiṣṇo devī kī kathā. Haridvār: harhbajan singh eṇḍ sans, n.d.

Śrī vaiṣṇo devī kī sampūrṇ kahānī. Haridvār: raṇdhīr buk sels, n.d.

Srivastava, M. C. P. *Mother Goddess in Indian Art, Archeology and Literature*. Delhi: Agam Kala Prakashan, 1979.

Stablein, Marilyn. "Textual and Contextual Patterns of Tibetan Buddhist Pilgrimage in India." *Tibet Society Bulletin* 12 (1978): 7–38.

Stanley, John M. "Gods, Ghosts, and Possession." In *The Experience of Hinduism: Essays on Religion in Maharashtra*, edited by Eleanor Zelliot and Maxine Berntsen, 26–59. Albany: State University of New York Press, 1988.

Starhawk. *The Spiral Dance: A Rebirth of the Ancient Religion of the Goddess*. New York: Harper & Row, 1979.

Stein, Burton. "Devi Shrines and Folk Hinduism in Medieval Tamilnad." In *Studies in the Language and Culture of South Asia*, edited by Edwin Gerow and Margery D. Lang, 75–90. Seattle: University of Washington Press, 1973.

"Takeover of Vaishno Devi Shrine Hailed," *Times of India*, 5 September 1986, 7.

Tandon, Prakash. *Punjabi Century 1857–1947*. London: Chatto and Windus, 1963.

Tārā rānī kī kathā. Haridvār: raṇdhīr buk sels, n.d.

Temple, R. C., ed. *Panjab Notes and Queries*. Allahabad, 1883–87.

———. *The Legends of the Panjab*. 3 vols. 1885. Patiala: Department of Languages, Panjab, 1963.

Turner, Victor. *Dramas, Fields, and Metaphors: Symbolic Interaction in Human Society*. Ithaca: Cornell University Press, 1974.

———. *Process, Performance and Pilgrimage: A Study in Comparative Symbology*. New Delhi: Concept, 1979.

———. *The Ritual Process: Structure and Anti-Structure*. London: Routledge and Kegan Paul, 1969.

Visuvalingam, Elizabeth-Chalier. "Bhairava's Royal Brahmanicide: The Problem of the Mahābrāhmaṇa." In *Criminal Gods and Demon Devotees: Essays on the Guardians of Popular Hinduism*, edited by Alf Hiltebeitel, 157–230. Albany: State University of New York Press, 1989.

Hiltebeitel, 157–230. Albany: State University of New York Press, 1989.

Vogel, J. P. "The Head-offering to the Goddess in Pallava Sculpture." *Bulletin of the School of Oriental and African Studies* 6 (1932): 539–43.

Wadley, Susan Snow. "Popular Hinduism and Mass Literature in North India: A Preliminary Analysis." In *Religion in Modern India,* edited by Giri Raj Gupta, 81–104. New Delhi: Vikas, 1983.

———. *Shakti: Power in the Conceptual Structure of Karimpur Religion*. Chicago: University of Chicago Press, 1975.

———. "The Spirit 'Rides' or the Spirit 'Comes': Possession in a North Indian Village." In *The Realm of the Extra-Human: Agents and Audiences,* edited by Agehananda Bharati, 233–52. The Hague: Mouton, 1976.

Waghorne, Joanne Punzo, and Norman Cutler, eds. *Gods of Flesh/Gods of Stone: The Embodiment of Divinity in India*. Chambersburg, Penn: Anima Books, 1985.

Wangu, Madhu Bazaz. "The Sacred Name Rama and the Goddess Khir Bhavani." Paper presented at the meeting of the American Academy of Religion, Chicago, 1988.

Whitehead, Henry. *The Village Gods of South India*. 1921. Reprint. New Delhi: Cosmo, 1983.

Woodroffe, John (Arthur Avalon), *Śakti and Śākta: Essays and Addresses*. Madras: Ganesh, 1918.

———. *The World as Power*. Madras: Ganesh, 1966.

———, ed. *Hymns to the Goddess and Hymn to Kali*. 3d ed. Madras: Ganesh, 1982.

Wulff, David M. "Prolegomenon to a Psychology of the Goddess." In *The Divine Consort: Rādhā and the Goddesses of India,* edited by John Stratton Hawley and Donna Marie Wulff, 283–97. Berkeley: Religious Studies Series, 1982.

Index

CPSIA information can be obtained
at www.ICGtesting.com
Printed in the USA
BVOW08s2222200717
489881BV00001B/14/P

9 780195 070156